The Reagan Revolution and the Rise of the New Right

Recent Titles in the Guides to Historic Events in America
Randall M. Miller, Series Editor

The Underground Railroad: A Reference Guide
Kerry Walters

Lincoln, the Rise of the Republicans, and the Coming of the Civil War: A Reference Guide
Kerry Walters

America in the Cold War: A Reference Guide
William T. Walker

Andrew Jackson and the Rise of the Democrats: A Reference Guide
Mark R. Cheathem

The Progressive Era: A Reference Guide
Francis J. Sicius

Reconstruction: A Reference Guide
Paul E. Teed and Melissa Ladd Teed

The War for American Independence: A Reference Guide
Mark Edward Lender

The Constitutional Convention of 1787: A Reference Guide
Stuart Leibiger

The Civil Rights Movement: A Reference Guide
Peter B. Levy

The Immigration and Nationality Act of 1965: A Reference Guide
Michael C. LeMay

The Watergate Crisis: A Reference Guide
Michael A. Genovese

Votes for Women! The American Woman Suffrage Movement and the Nineteenth Amendment: A Reference Guide
Marion W. Roydhouse

The 1960s Cultural Revolution: A Reference Guide
John C. McWilliams

THE REAGAN REVOLUTION AND THE RISE OF THE NEW RIGHT

A REFERENCE GUIDE

Kenneth J. Heineman

Guides to Historic Events in America
Randall M. Miller, Series Editor

BLOOMSBURY ACADEMIC
NEW YORK · LONDON · OXFORD · NEW DELHI · SYDNEY

BLOOMSBURY ACADEMIC

Bloomsbury Publishing Inc, 1359 Broadway, 12th Floor, New York, NY 10018, USA
Bloomsbury Publishing Plc, 50 Bedford Square, London, WC1B 3DP, UK
Bloomsbury Publishing Ireland, 29 Earlsfort Terrace, Dublin 2, D02 AY28, Ireland

BLOOMSBURY, BLOOMSBURY ACADEMIC and the Diana logo
are trademarks of Bloomsbury Publishing Plc

First published in the United States of America by ABC-CLIO 2021
Paperback edition published by Bloomsbury Academic 2025

Copyright © Bloomsbury Publishing Inc, 2026

For legal purposes the Acknowledgments on p. xi constitute
an extension of this copyright page.

COVER PHOTO: President Ronald Reagan, 1982.
(World History Archive/Alamy Stock Photo)

All rights reserved. No part of this publication may be: i) reproduced or transmitted in any form, electronic or mechanical, including photocopying, recording or by means of any information storage or retrieval system without prior permission in writing from the publishers; or ii) used or reproduced in any way for the training, development or operation of artificial intelligence (AI) technologies, including generative AI technologies. The rights holders expressly reserve this publication from the text and data mining exception as per Article 4(3) of the Digital Single Market Directive (EU) 2019/790.

Bloomsbury Publishing Inc does not have any control over, or responsibility for, any third-party websites referred to or in this book. All internet addresses given in this book were correct at the time of going to press. The author and publisher regret any inconvenience caused if addresses have changed or sites have ceased to exist, but can accept no responsibility for any such changes.

Library of Congress Cataloging-in-Publication Data
Names: Heineman, Kenneth J., 1962- author.
Title: The Reagan revolution and the rise of the New Right : a reference
guide / Kenneth J. Heineman.
Description: Santa Barbara, California : ABC-CLIO, an imprint of ABC-CLIO,
LLC, [2021] | Series: Guides to historic events in America |
Includes bibliographical references and index.
Identifiers: LCCN 2020053971 (print) | LCCN 2020053972 (ebook) |
ISBN 9781440871849 (hardcover) | ISBN 9781440871856 (ebook)
Subjects: LCSH: Reagan, Ronald—Influence. | Conservatism—United
States—History—20th century. | United States—Politics and
government—1981-1989.
Classification: LCC E877.2 .H445 2021 (print) | LCC E877.2 (ebook) |
DDC 973.927092—dc23
LC record available at https://lccn.loc.gov/2020053971
LC ebook record available at https://lccn.loc.gov/2020053972

ISBN: HB: 978-1-4408-7184-9
PB: 979-8-2163-9246-0
ePDF: 978-1-4408-7185-6
eBook: 979-8-2161-3655-2

Series: Guides to Historic Events in America

For product safety related questions contact productsafety@bloomsbury.com.

To find out more about our authors and books visit www.bloomsbury.com
and sign up for our newsletters.

Contents

Series Foreword ix
Preface and Acknowledgments xi
Historical Overview: The Evolution of the U.S. Presidency xiii
Chronology xxvii

Chapter 1. Ronald Reagan's Political Odyssey: From New Deal Democrat to Conservative Republican, 1911–1980 1

Chapter 2. "Tear Down This Wall!": Foreign Policy in the Time of Reagan 39

Chapter 3. Trickle-Down Prosperity: Economic Policy during the Reagan Revolution 73

Chapter 4. "Just Say No": Social Policy in Reagan's America 107

Chapter 5. "Do We Get to Win this Time?": Popular Culture and Presidential Public Relations in the Eighties 139

Epilogue: Legacies of the Reagan Revolution 175

Biographical Essays

Menachem W. Begin (1913–1992)	195
Leonid I. Brezhnev (1906–1982)	195
Edmund "Pat" Brown (1905–1996)	196
William F. Buckley Jr. (1925–2008)	196
William J. Casey (1913–1987)	197
John Terrence "Terry" Dolan (1950–1986)	197
Barry M. Goldwater (1909–1998)	197
Mikhail S. Gorbachev (1931–)	198
William Philip "Phil" Gramm (1942–)	198
Jeane Jordan Kirkpatrick (1926–2006)	199
David H. Koch (1940–2019)	199
Arthur B. Laffer (1940–)	200
Andrew W. Mellon (1855–1937)	200
Walter F. Mondale (1928–)	201
Oliver L. North (1943–)	201
Sandra Day O'Connor (1930–)	202
Thomas "Tip" O'Neill (1912–1994)	202
Phyllis Stewart Schlafly (1924–2016)	202
Arnold A. Schwarzenegger (1947–)	203
Alan K. Simpson (1931–)	203
David A. Stockman (1946–)	204
Margaret H. Thatcher (1925–2013)	204

Primary Documents

1. "A Time for Choosing." Ronald Reagan Delivers His First National Political Speech, Championing Republican Presidential Candidate Barry Goldwater, 1964 — 205

2. Ronald Reagan's First California Gubernatorial Inaugural Address, January 5, 1967 — 207

3. Ronald Reagan's First Presidential Inaugural Address, January 20, 1981 — 208

4. Ronald Reagan Address before a Joint Session of the Congress on the Program for Economic Recovery, February 18, 1981 — 210

5. Ronald Reagan Oval Office Address to the Nation on Federal Tax Reduction Legislation, July 27, 1981 — 212

6. Ronald Reagan Remarks at the Annual Meeting of the International Association of Chiefs of Police in New Orleans, Louisiana, September 28, 1981 — 213

7. National Security Decision Directive Number 17: National Security Directive on Cuba and Central America, January 4, 1982 — 215

8. Ronald Reagan Remarks at the Conservative Political Action Conference Dinner, Washington, DC, February 18, 1983 — 216

9. Ronald Reagan Remarks at the Annual Convention of the National Association of Evangelicals, Orlando, Florida, March 8, 1983 — 218

10. Ronald Reagan Proclamation 5147: National Sanctity of Human Life Day, January 13, 1984 — 220

11. Ronald Reagan Address to the Nation on United States Policy in Central America, May 9, 1984   221

12. Ronald Reagan Remarks Accepting the Presidential Nomination at the Republican National Convention in Dallas, Texas, August 23, 1984   223

13. Ronald Reagan Remarks at an Ecumenical Prayer Breakfast in Dallas, Texas, August 23, 1984   225

14. Ronald Reagan Foreword Written for a Report on the Strategic Defense Initiative, January 3, 1985   226

15. Ronald Reagan Remarks at the Opening Ceremonies of the Statue of Liberty Centennial Celebration in New York, New York, July 3, 1986   228

16. Ronald Reagan Remarks on East-West Relations at the Brandenburg Gate in West Berlin, June 12, 1987   230

17. Remarks and a Question-and-Answer Session with the Students and Faculty at Moscow State University, May 31, 1988   232

18. Ronald Reagan Remarks at the Veterans' Day Ceremony at the Vietnam Veterans Memorial, Washington, DC, November 11, 1988   233

19. Ronald Reagan Farewell Address to the Nation, January 11, 1989   235

Annotated Bibliography   237

Index   247

Series Foreword

Perhaps no people have been more difficult to comprehend than the Americans. As J. Hector St. Jean de Crèvecoeur asked during the American Revolution, countless others have echoed ever after—"What then is this American, this new man?" What, indeed? Americans then and after have been, and remain, a people in the process of becoming. They have been, and are, a people in motion, whether coming from a distant shore, crossing the mighty Mississippi, or packing off to the suburbs, and all the while following the promise of an American dream of realizing life, liberty, and happiness. The directions of such movement have changed, and sometimes the trajectory has taken a downward arc in terms of civil war and economic depression, but always the process has continued.

Making sense of that American experience demands attention to critical moments—events—that reflected and affected American ideas and identities. Although Americans have constructed an almost linear narrative of progress from the days of George Washington to today in relating their common history, they also have marked that history by recognizing particular events as pivotal in explaining who and why they believed and acted as they did at particular times and over time. Such events have forced Americans to consider closely their true interests. They also have challenged their commitment to professed beliefs of freedom and liberty, equality and opportunity, tolerance and generosity. Whether fighting for independence or empire, drafting and implementing a frame of government, reconstructing a nation divided by civil war, struggling for basic rights and the franchise, creating a mass-mediated culture, standing up for capitalism and democracy and against communism, to name several critical developments, Americans have understood that historic events are more than just moments. They are processes of change made clear through particular events but not bound to a single moment or instance. Such thinking about the character and consequence of American history informs this new series of *Guides to Historic Events in America*.

Drawing on the latest and best literature, and bringing together narrative overviews and critical chapters of important historic events, the books in the series function as both reference guides and informed analyses to critical events that have shaped American life, culture, society, economy, and politics and fixed America's place in the world. The books do not promise a comprehensive reading and rendering of American history. Such is not yet, if ever, possible for any single work or series. Nor do they chart a single interpretive line, though they share common concerns and methods of inquiry. Each book stands alone, resting on the expertise of the author and the strength of the evidence. At the same time, taken together the books in this new series will provide a dynamic portrait of that on-going work-in-progress, America itself.

Each book follows a common format, with a chronology, historical overview, topical chapters on aspects of the historical event under examination, a set of biographies of key figures, selected essential primary documents, and an annotated bibliography. As such, each book holds many uses for students, teachers, and the general public wanting and needing to know the principal issues and the pertinent arguments and evidence on significant events in American history. The combination of historical description and analysis, biographies, and primary documents also moves readers to approach each critical event from multiple perspectives and with a critical eye. Each book in its structure and content invites students and teachers, in and out of the classroom, to consider and debate the character and consequence(s) of the historic event in question. Such debate invariably will bring readers back to that most critical and never-ending question of what was/is "the American" and what does, and must, "America" mean.

Randall M. Miller
Saint Joseph's University, Philadelphia

Preface and Acknowledgments

The American system of governance has endured for over two hundred years. At least twice in that span of time has the United States experienced crises that threatened its very existence: the Civil War and the Great Depression/World War II. On both those occasions, a president emerged to lead the nation forward. Whether in times of prosperity or economic peril, peace or war, on balance, Americans have had political leaders who faced the challenges of their day and overcame most obstacles.

None of this is to say, however, that the United States has not had disastrous presidents, dysfunctional legislators, and judges who overreached their constitutional powers to make law from the bench. Americans have elected their fair share of incompetents as well as those who were overwhelmed by the tide of events. But it is to say that, in comparison, other nations have done worse. The French, after all, are on their fifth republic since the 1790s, not to mention two failed empires and a Nazi-collaborationist regime.

In spite of their democratic sensibilities, Americans often conjure up the idea of political dynasties: Adams, Taft, Roosevelt, Kennedy, and Bush. French political thinker Alexis de Tocqueville had been amused back in the early nineteenth century as to how Americans who opposed monarchy still clung to royal trappings. He had a point. The vey term "dynasty" reeks of undemocratic, imperial ambition. On the other hand, the nice thing about American dynasties (whether political or economic) is that they have a habit of self-destructing or disappearing after three generations or less.

How we access our political leaders, most especially our presidents, requires an understanding of historical context and evolutionary change. Most of all, it requires the kind of perspective that can only come with the passage of time. The temptation to pronounce snap judgments is only human. Moreover, in a democracy, where elections are held on a regular basis, there is a bias toward rendering conclusions fairly quickly. We refer to presidential "terms," not "eons." Some might deploy "epoch" to describe a presidential administration, but in a nation without medieval castles and shrines, that is a stretch.

In this book, we are studying what the news media, and many scholars, have called the "Reagan Revolution." As with all revolutions, real or overblown, there is often as much continuity as there is change. Ronald Reagan was a product of early twentieth-century America, coming from the financially insecure ranks of the small-town lower-middle class. He came of age during the Great Depression, revered President Franklin Delano Roosevelt, and watched with alarm as World War II gave way to the Cold War and an age of atomic weapons.

Reagan responded to the economic, political, and foreign challenges of his day, moving along a peculiar path that led him from sports broadcaster to Hollywood celebrity, speaker at corporate-sponsored events, television host, California governor, and then U.S. president. Among his presidential peers, Reagan had an exceptional background. Reagan's experiences shaped his view of what government should and should not do. He also believed in an America that defended freedom at home and abroad—an America where anything was possible if one worked hard and maintained a positive outlook.

* * *

In the past two decades, more Reagan-related archival works have become available to scholars and journalists. From those works has emerged a Reagan who was an accomplished, pragmatic, results-oriented politician. Presidential libraries, including Reagan's, have placed more primary documents online, providing greater access to the public.

As with any work of historical synthesis, authors stand on the shoulders of those who have preceded them. I cite them in the endnotes and bibliography. Additionally, I am enormously indebted to Randall Miller, the series editor of the ABC-CLIO Guides to Historic Events in America series and a well-respected historian at St. Joseph's University, in Philadelphia. His careful editing and suggestions have strengthened this book and enhanced its readability.

Kenneth J. Heineman
Angelo State University
December 2019

HISTORICAL OVERVIEW: THE EVOLUTION OF THE U.S. PRESIDENCY

In the early evening hours of November 4, 1980, Democratic Party leaders and news media commentators were stunned when Republican presidential candidate Ronald Reagan (1911–2004), not only won the White House but also helped elect twelve senators—giving the Republicans control of that legislative chamber for the first time since 1954. Democrats had predicted a close contest but expected to keep control of the Senate and see President Jimmy Carter (1924–) win reelection. Instead, Carter received just 49 electoral votes to Reagan's 489. Meanwhile, such liberal Democratic icons as Senators Gaylord Nelson (Wisconsin) and George McGovern (South Dakota) went down in defeat. The oldest candidate up to that time to ever win the presidency, and an actor to boot, had triumphed. Conservatives proclaimed that the "Reagan Revolution" had begun.

Nearly two centuries earlier, the framers of the U.S. Constitution had gathered in Philadelphia to create "a new order of the ages." Their challenge was to create a federal government that could defend the nation from its enemies, promote economic growth, and preserve private property while not trampling on the rights of states and individuals. Their solution was to establish three coequal branches of the federal government: executive, legislative, and judicial. Each branch would check the others, promoting a balance of power at the federal level and allowing the states latitude in how they governed themselves.

The executive branch, the Office of the President, was the only office elected by all citizens and states and, therefore, served as the symbolic embodiment of the nation. On the other hand, the president was to be no dictator or monarch. Whether they were advocates of enhanced federal power or champions of states' rights, all the supporters and critics of the Constitution had studied history. Pure democracy, the direct vote of the people, had failed in ancient Greece and spawned demagogues and endless war. The Roman Republic, with a representative senate, had given way to a dictatorial Julius Caesar and an expansionist empire.

Against the backdrop of Greek and Roman history, and their own experiences and experiments in forming state governments during the Revolution, Americans forged a new form of government. The founders created a federal republic with powers divided within the government and with the states. Each state would be guaranteed two members in the U.S. Senate, chosen (until the Seventeenth Amendment to the Constitution was ratified) by the state legislatures. The size of the state's population would determine how many members it would have in the U.S. House of Representatives, with every state guaranteed at least one representative. House members were elected by popular vote. Every state would have a set number of electoral votes determined by the size of its congressional delegation.

The constitutional framers feared that if the popular vote for president was close, then some might not accept the legitimacy of whoever was elected. Additionally, they were concerned that presidential candidates would be tempted to rack up decisive leads in a handful of states to collect popular votes and ignore citizens in other states. The Electoral College was established to award presidential candidates decisive tallies, given its winner-take-all format, in the states. Constitutional framers hoped that the Electoral College would force candidates to campaign in all parts of the nation—not just in a handful of states and cities.

At the founding of the American republic, no one was sure of the extent of presidential power. Successive occupants of the White House developed their own view of presidential power. Some interpreted their powers broadly. Others regarded the presidency as a ceremonial office and vowed to do as little as possible. Nearly half of America's presidents have been placeholders, though that may not have necessarily been their intention when they ran for office. Some presidents aspired to irrelevance; others had it thrust upon them.

Historical Overview: The Evolution of the U.S. Presidency

As the first president, George Washington (1732–1799) set many of the parameters of the office that are still in place. If others insisted on giving him a title, he preferred "chief executive." He saw himself as an administrator, not a monarch. Administrators, Washington believed, should serve no more than two terms, lest they evolve into monarchs. Washington asserted his authority as commander in chief when called upon to quell violent civil uprisings. He had pledged to protect the United States from both domestic and foreign enemies and would do so with vigor. Additionally, Washington regarded Congress as a partner in building a sound national financial system.

Washington warned Americans of the dangers of forming partisan political organizations that would poison public discourse. He also argued that the United States should not establish permanent alliances with other nations. Americans, Washington argued, had permanent interests, not permanent allies. His successors did not heed his warnings on either point.

Thomas Jefferson (1743–1826) believed that the federal government, including the executive branch, should have limited power. Still, he asserted his authority as chief executive (1801–1809) to buy half a continent from the French (the Louisiana Purchase) at a bargain-basement price. It was revealing that Jefferson did not include his service in the White House among the accomplishments listed on his grave marker. To Jefferson, being president did not rank among the most important things he had done in his life.

Andrew Jackson (1767–1845) showed that the executive branch had more political leverage than his predecessors had realized (or had sought to assert). Throughout his presidency (1829–1837), Jackson feuded with the press, using the White House as a platform to stir up public revulsion against journalists. (Jackson was convinced that media attacks on his wife Rachel's moral character had caused her to die before they were able to move into the White House.) When an unemployed house painter attempted to assassinate Jackson, his supporters blamed journalists and rival politicians for creating a climate of violence. "Jacksonians," as Jackson's followers called themselves, had little use for constitutional guarantees of free speech if such guarantees protected their political opponents.

Beyond smearing foes, Jackson politicized the U.S. Supreme Court. The constitutional framers had envisioned Supreme Court justices as objective arbiters of the law. Jackson, however, fumed when the Supreme Court handed down two decisions in 1831 and 1832 that challenged the constitutionality of the federal government relocating Native Americans to the west of the Mississippi River. Southern slave owners wanted Native American lands and were behind the 1830 Indian Removal Act, which Jackson had championed.

Jackson defied the U.S. Supreme Court and proceeded with the removal of the Native American tribes. His next action was even more damaging to the rule of law. In 1836, the Democratic Senate had approved Jackson's nomination of Roger Taney (1777–1864) to be chief justice of the Supreme Court. Taney had been Jackson's attorney general and political enforcer. In 1857, twelve years after Jackson's death, the Taney Court ruled in *Dred Scott v. Sandford* that no territory could prohibit slavery and thereby interfere with individuals' property rights. Taney was a southern slave owner. Many people in northern states, which had prohibited slavery and sought to prevent its expansion to the West, were outraged.

In 1860, Abraham Lincoln (1809–1865) won the presidency with less than a majority of the popular vote. Although his predecessor, James Buchanan (1791–1868) had also failed to win a popular-vote majority, his total in a three-person contest in 1856 had been 45 percent. Lincoln, as one of four candidates, received 40 percent of the popular vote. His electoral vote tally of 180, however, gave him a decisive victory over his next closest rival, who had received 72. As if that were not bad enough, Lincoln was not on the ballot in many southern states, and he performed poorly among northern urban Catholics. Southerners mistakenly believed that Lincoln wanted to abolish slavery outright, while Catholics accurately regarded many of his supporters as religiously intolerant evangelical Protestants. Eleven southern states left the Union in the months after the 1860 election.

To win the Civil War (1861–1865), Lincoln asserted his authority as commander in chief of the armed forces. In the process, Lincoln expanded his power in areas outside military mobilization and operations. Scores of Democratic newspapers, along with numerous politicians, criticized the war and military conscription. Chief Justice Taney supported legal challenges to the Lincoln administration's vigorous prosecution of the war, especially Lincoln's suspension of the *writ of habeas corpus*, contained in Article I of the Constitution. The writ of habeas corpus protected citizens

Historical Overview: The Evolution of the U.S. Presidency   xvii

from being arrested by the federal government without ever being charged with a crime or brought to trial. Over the course of the war, the Lincoln administration and the military detained fifteen thousand persons, many of them northern Democrats.[1]

Before the Civil War, the federal government had largely financed its limited operations with land sales and tariffs on imports. Given that the costs of financing the war exceeded the assets of the federal treasury, the Lincoln administration came up with two remedies. First, Republicans levied the nation's first federal income tax. Though it was abolished in 1871, the federal income tax would be resurrected decades later—though this time by constitutional amendment (the Sixteenth) rather than by congressional and presidential action.

Second, the Lincoln administration created a "paper" currency. Before the Civil War, the federal government minted gold and silver coins, and state and private banks issued "paper" banknotes, which circulated as money though they were not legal tender. Once the U.S. government began printing greenbacks (so called because of the color of the ink used), a sea change occurred in federal finance. While gold theoretically backed up paper currency, the reality was that the federal printing press could make as much money as it wanted—regardless of the size of gold reserves. Thanks to Lincoln, the federal government opened up its printing presses, contributing to significant inflation and raising the cost of living for all citizens.

In January 1863, Lincoln issued the Emancipation Proclamation, freeing slaves in states and places still in rebellion but not freeing those in slaveholding states that had remained in the Union (Delaware, Kentucky, Maryland, and Missouri), or in southern territory already occupied by federal troops. Presidents always had the power to issue proclamations (or, in contemporary times, executive orders), but Lincoln was the first to take such a sweeping legal action and bypass Congress. Given that such proclamations could be revoked at any time, the Constitution would have to be amended (the Thirteenth Amendment) to prohibit slavery altogether.

Republicans recognized that the departure of southern Democrats in 1861 had given them the opportunity to change the role of the federal government in broad areas of American life. In 1862, Lincoln's party embraced three initiatives. The first, the Pacific Railway Act, provided federal subsidies to companies to construct a transcontinental railroad to the West Coast. Second, the Homestead Act authorized federally subsidized land in the West to settlers. Third, the Morrill Act gave federal land grants to states to assist in the establishment of agricultural and mechanical colleges—which became state universities. Democrats, who were then the opposition party and had limited federal power, had opposed such ideas for years. Lincoln and the Republicans were not about to let the political opportunities opened up by the Civil War go to waste—even if the initiatives seemingly had nothing to do with directly defeating the rebellion.

Lincoln's final contribution to the transformation of the presidency was not one of his choosing. In April 1865, Lincoln became the first president to be assassinated. Republicans seized on the fact that a rebel sympathizer had killed Lincoln on Good Friday. Like Christ, Lincoln became a martyr for a holy cause. For years, Republicans preserved his bloodstained clothes and referred to them when attacking Democrats as traitors.

It would be more than thirty years before Lincoln's successors resumed the broadening of presidential power. William McKinley (1843–1901) and especially Theodore Roosevelt (1858–1919) understood the potential of the press to elevate the president's public image and power. The media's influence had grown after newspapers in the late nineteenth century acquired the ability to publish photographs. A carefully posed, mass-produced photo image, McKinley and Roosevelt understood, could sway peoples' emotions and perceptions more than the written word could.

Asserting his role as the embodiment of "the public," Roosevelt intervened in a 1902 coal strike as a mediator between labor and management. No previous president had ever taken such a course of action. Moreover, he forced congressional action by making such issues as forest conservation, meat inspection, and various social matters public causes.

Roosevelt also accepted the invitation of the Japanese government to negotiate a peace settlement between Russia and Japan. He became the first president to win the Nobel Peace Prize. But what Roosevelt did not understand was that the Japanese Army had suffered great losses and its government wanted to end the war but not appear weak at home or abroad. After Roosevelt secured peace, the Japanese government blamed the United States for depriving their nation of total victory over Russia. Roosevelt would not be the last president to be played for a fool on the international stage.[2]

Historical Overview: The Evolution of the U.S. Presidency

Whereas Roosevelt's domestic and foreign policy initiatives were often undertaken on an ad hoc basis, President Woodrow Wilson (1856–1924) had a fixed agenda. Wilson believed that as president (1913–1921), he had the duty to set the nation's cultural tone. Subsequently, he racially segregated federal facilities and arranged for a White House screening of a landmark 1915 film: *The Birth of a Nation*. D. W. Griffith's film celebrated the founding of the first Ku Klux Klan after the Civil War as the savior from Republican Reconstruction and supposed Black barbarism. Wilson praised the film as "writing history with lightning." The film inspired the founding of a second Ku Klux Klan, which was predominantly northern as well as anti-Catholic, anti-Semitic, and nativist.

Wilson, an admirer of the British government, championed the creation of a powerful administrative state that could resolve social conflict at home and international tensions abroad. His opportunity to change American domestic and foreign policy came with the outbreak of World War I, in 1914. Citing the threat posed to U.S. security interests by German submarines that fired on American ships carrying military supplies to Great Britain, Wilson found his pretext for armed intervention in 1917. He proclaimed that the United States was going to make "the world safe for democracy."

At home, the federal government enhanced its power. Citing the need for wartime mobilization, Wilson authorized the seizure of the nation's railroads and telegraph communications network for the war effort and the rationing of sugar and fuel sold in the United States. Wilson also created the first federal propaganda agency in U.S. history (the Committee on Public Information) to "sell" American military intervention to voters and to demonize war critics. A Democratic Congress passed the 1917 Espionage Act and the 1918 Sedition Act to make it a crime to criticize the war, the U.S. military, and the president. Federal agents placed antiwar leaders under surveillance, infiltrated peace organizations, and arrested hundreds.

In Europe, Wilson championed the idea of "collective security" though a proposed postwar League of Nations. An attack on one member of the League would be considered an attack on all and met with military action. He also advocated the dismemberment of the central European empires in order to provide national "self-determination" to ethnic minorities.

The United States' British and French allies had no intention of embracing self-determination since, in theory, it would mean that they would have to give up their overseas colonies. As for creating a framework for peace in postwar Europe, the British and French governments were not going to welcome a defeated Germany into the family of nations as an equal; they thirsted for revenge. Wilson did not understand that whatever influence he had with his allies diminished as U.S. troops went home with the end of the war in 1918.

Wilson further failed to take seriously the fact that the U.S. Senate had the constitutional power to approve treaties, including American membership in the proposed League of Nations. As a college professor, Wilson had shown contempt for the legislative process, believing in an all-powerful chief executive who stood above Congress. Unwilling to accept a compromise with Republican senators, Wilson ensured that the United States did not join the League of Nations. Meanwhile, Americans began to question why they had sacrificed over one hundred thousand men in Europe and expressed resentment of federal wartime rationing and surveillance.

As had happened after the Civil War, presidential power receded with the conclusion of World War I. While a crisis could enhance executive authority, once the perceived threat—whether internal or external—passed, the president lost leverage over the nation. Presidential power could only increase on a permanent basis if the crisis facing the nation was long term and threatened the United States simultaneously on both the domestic and international fronts.

In 1929, a global depression spawned massive economic hardship and the rise and consolidation of expansionist dictatorships in Europe and Asia. By 1932, one-quarter of the American workforce was unemployed, and nearly half of industry was idled or shuttered. Germans, who were impoverished and embittered by losing World War I, increasingly turned to Nazi leader Adolf Hitler for salvation. In the Soviet Union, communist strongman Joseph Stalin starved, enslaved, or exterminated millions of his people. Across the Pacific, the Empire of Japan plotted territorial expansion through military conquest. Everywhere, it seemed, democracies were collapsing in the 1930s.

Franklin D. Roosevelt (1882–1945) grasped the gravity of the situation when he became president in 1933. Normally, Congress wrote legislation, printed and distributed proposed bills to senators and representatives, debated bills' merits, and then voted on whether to send legislation

Historical Overview: The Evolution of the U.S. Presidency

forward to the president for approval. In the first one hundred days of the Roosevelt administration, however, the executive branch drafted bills on legal pads written in longhand and sent them to a cooperative Congress for action. Much legislation was neither printed nor circulated, and few members of Congress read the bills before voting.

Over the 1930s, federal agencies and entitlement programs arose in response to the Great Depression: from Social Security and unemployment compensation, to public works projects and protection of workers' right to join labor unions and bargain collectively with employers. Federal jobs' programs, agricultural subsidies, and work-relief programs to encourage youths to stay in high school or college blossomed across the nation in what became known as the "New Deal." One such New Deal program, the Works Progress Administration, provided a job to Jack Reagan, an alcoholic shoe salesman from small-town Illinois. Jack Reagan's younger son, Ronald, remained forever grateful to Roosevelt for saving his family from starvation.[3]

Roosevelt's political skills were considerable; it was not for nothing that he was elected to an unprecedented four terms. (The Twenty-Second Amendment subsequently limited presidents to two terms.) Although paralyzed below the waist as a result of contracting polio in 1921, Roosevelt found ways to draw attention away from his affliction. He was careful not to be photographed in a wheelchair or wearing leg braces. He was always pre-positioned at a podium and used vigorous hand gestures to give the illusion of motion.

Newly developed radio communication technology was the perfect tool for Roosevelt's warm, vigorous speaking style. Radio allowed Roosevelt to seem as if he was standing in every voter's living room, speaking to them in pleasant conversation about policy matters and public concerns. Most importantly, radio allowed Roosevelt to bypass hostile newspaper publishers and congressional critics and speak directly to the public.

His distant cousin, Theodore Roosevelt, while a practitioner of media manipulation, nonetheless had had to contend with newspapers and magazines that "filtered" his words. Worse, whenever Theodore Roosevelt wanted to put political pressure on a member of Congress, he had had to travel in person to that representative's district and speak. Radio freed Franklin Roosevelt from media "filters" and from going to the district or state of every uncooperative member of Congress.

In trying to mitigate the effects of the Great Depression and revive the national economy, the federal government and the presidency garnered immense power; fighting a world war in Europe and Asia consolidated that power. World War II required an unprecedented level of American economic and military mobilization. Roosevelt had two goals: first, win the war; second, win the peace so there would not be World War III.

Winning the war against Imperial Japan and Nazi Germany required improved weapons technology, from the development of long-range bomber planes to the atomic bomb. For the first time in U.S. history, a president had the ability to kill hundreds of thousands of people. Bringing down Hitler required an alliance with the Soviet Union—which in the end led to the Soviet Union occupying half of Europe. Defeating the Japanese Empire would lead to the removal of a major impediment to the growth of Chinese communism. If the Chinese communists won their civil war with their nationalist enemies, they could potentially take the place of the Japanese in Asia.

Winning the peace, Roosevelt believed, required the United States to take the lead in reconstructing the world economy. He was convinced that the Great Depression had undermined democracy; if the world fell into another depression, then the nationalist dictators would return and launch another world war. Roosevelt hoped that a revised League of Nations—a United Nations (UN)—would ensure global stability. The UN would have a multinational military force to ensure the peace. Its governing body would be a Security Council, which would have five permanent members—the World War II allies: China, France, Great Britain, the Soviet Union, and the United States. Roosevelt assumed that wartime collaboration among wildly different powers would continue into peacetime.

Although Roosevelt did not live to see the defeat of Germany and Japan, he left an enormous inheritance, and burden, to his successors. World War II had unleashed American production while destroying or crippling its potential competitors. Americans came to regard a rising standard of living and expanding federal aid programs as fundamental rights. Voters also expected presidents to have served in the military during the war. Eight presidents did serve in the military during World War II—nearly twice the number who had been in the Civil War. Indeed, every president between 1953 to 1993 had been in the military during World War II.

Historical Overview: The Evolution of the U.S. Presidency xxiii

Roosevelt's heirs had to deal with the expansion of Soviet power in Europe and the victory of Chinese communists in Asia. Neither the Soviet Union nor communist China accepted postwar American economic and military leadership. It seemed that as soon as World War II ended, a "Cold War" commenced in Europe. President Harry Truman (1882–1972), who had been Roosevelt's vice president, provided economic and diplomatic aid to European nations resisting Soviet expansion. He also forged a military alliance, the North American Treaty Organization (NATO), committing the United States to defend Western Europe from Soviet aggression.

Truman extended "communist containment" from Europe to Asia following the communist invasion of South Korea in 1950. Rather than initially going to Congress for a declaration of war, Truman went to the UN for authorization to rescue South Korea. Fearful that the Soviet Union, which had acquired the atomic bomb in 1949, would annihilate the capitals of Western Europe, Truman fought a conventional war against a vast communist Chinese army. Americans were frustrated by the Korean War, but it ended with Stalin's death (in 1953) before the domestic political fallout became too great.

President Dwight Eisenhower (1890–1969) insisted that Republicans embrace Roosevelt's domestic programs and continue Truman's expansion of the Cold War. Subsequently, Eisenhower undertook the largest infrastructure project in U.S. history, the construction of forty-one thousand miles of interstate highway, and expanded Social Security eligibility to cover ten million Americans. In 1954, he created an Asian version of NATO with the South East Asian Treaty Organization (SEATO). Eisenhower also improved the U.S. atomic arsenal and laid the groundwork for a defense strategy known as "mutual assured destruction" (MAD). The assumption of MAD was that the Soviet Union would not attack the United States if it knew the United States would respond with enough nuclear warheads to annihilate the Soviet population.

The system of collective security arrangements that evolved in the 1940s and 1950s gave a president the authority to go to war without first consulting Congress. Presidential war-making power also increased due to ever-improving weapons delivery systems. If the Soviet Union launched a missile strike against the United States or its allies, the president would have only hours, or, more likely, minutes, to respond—not enough time to consult Congress. It seemed as if every year of the Cold War enhanced the executive branch at the expense of the legislative branch. By the 1960s, scholars and journalists would refer to an "imperial presidency" that appeared to be more Roman than American.

Television transformed presidential power just as radio and newspaper photographs had done earlier. President John Kennedy (1917–1963) demonstrated that attractive politicians with a smooth performance style on camera could shape the news and set the political agenda. Looks and style could also divert the public's attention away from a president's potentially controversial words and actions. Conversely, television could amplify presidential weakness, especially if that president snapped at critics (Richard Nixon), repeatedly tripped or bumped his head (Gerald Ford), vomited on a foreign leader during dinner (George H. W. Bush), or mispronounced basic words (George W. Bush).

Eisenhower's presidency had seemingly spawned an era of ideological congruence, or "liberal consensus," between Democrats and Republicans. At the heart of the liberal consensus was an embrace of New Deal domestic programs and a bipartisan, anticommunist foreign policy. The liberal consensus fell apart during Lyndon Johnson's (1908–1973) presidency. Johnson's escalation of the Vietnam War, and the United States' inability to win it, gave rise to an antiwar movement that mainly grew inside the Democratic Party. Johnson also added new social welfare programs, including Medicare and Medicaid, which placed greater demands on the federal budget and, consequently, on taxpayers.

Johnson's support for civil rights legislation went toward correcting the historical injustices of state-mandated racial segregation and Black disfranchisement, but the Civil Rights Act of 1964 and the Voting Rights Act of 1965 did not address endemic racial discrimination. Frustrated Blacks responded with angry criticism of a mission yet unaccomplished and even with violence against "the system." Such criticism and violence alienated many whites who thought they had already done enough to redress wrongs.

Unfortunately for Johnson, large numbers of southern white and northern urban ethnic and Catholic Democrats believed that Johnson was indifferent to their needs, especially with regard to rising violent crime rates. Inner-city and campus riots dominated the television news, while inflation began to outpace wage growth—particularly among working-class Americans, who were already bearing the brunt of the fighting in Vietnam and seeing their urban neighborhoods become more dangerous.

Meanwhile, U.S. industry, buckling under the pressure of revived foreign competition, started to lay off workers or shut down.

At the same time, Johnson's Great Society initiatives that centered on a "War against Poverty" dramatically expanded federal power and responsibilities, even in areas previously the province of the states or the private sector, such as health care and education. And with the civil rights legislation and Great Society programs, executive power grew, as enforcement often rested with federal bureaucrats and the executive branch.

While Johnson's grandiose vision and bullying political style helped undermine his presidency, there was more to the story. By the time Richard Nixon (1913–1994) became president in 1969, the United States had spent a generation asserting its military power overseas while spending, and taxing, billions of dollars to create an ever-expanding host of entitlement programs. The resolutions to the "permanent crisis" that began in the 1930s proved difficult to sustain by the 1970s. Nixon, in his desire to surveil foes in the news media and Democratic Party, became the first president to resign in disgrace once his illegal activities came to light and impeachment loomed.

Arab nations, who were members of the Oil Petroleum Exporting Countries (OPEC), embargoed oil to the United States in retaliation for American support of the Jewish state of Israel. The oil embargoes caused a great deal of social disruption while fueling rising inflation. Meanwhile, the Soviet Union, watching as the United States staggered in South Vietnam, became more aggressive in supporting communist insurgencies in Africa, Asia, and Latin America. The Soviet Union also increased its nuclear arsenal in the belief that American fear of annihilation would (as had happened in Korea) force the United States into conventional wars and counterinsurgencies that the public would not support.

Democrat Jimmy Carter entered the White House in 1977, having promised to scale back the Cold War; withhold support from authoritarian, anticommunist allies; and restore "trust" in the federal government. Carter also pledged to increase employment and reduce inflation while further expanding federal aid programs and fixing rising tax rates that hammered the struggling middle class. He even appeared on television, dressed in soft, fuzzy sweaters, smiling as he told Americans that they expected too much from government and were wasting precious fuel by turning their home thermostats up too high.

Domestically, more industries faltered, while unemployment and inflation rose in tandem. Overseas, the Soviet Union gained a foothold in the oil-rich Middle East and, for the first time since World War II, invaded a country that was not one of its satellites (Afghanistan). Meanwhile, fundamentalists overthrew the Shah of Iran, an American ally, and proclaimed an "Islamic Republic." Iranian extremists subsequently seized the U.S. Embassy in Tehran, holding scores of Americans hostage for more than a year.

Carter and his supporters insisted at the end of the 1970s that the presidency was simply too big a job for any man or woman. The United States' economic and foreign challenges were more complex and intractable than what Roosevelt, Truman, or Eisenhower had faced. Looking at the floundering, defensive Carter, Ronald Reagan retorted that the presidency was not too big for any one person to command. Rather, Reagan argued, Carter was too small a man to be president.

NOTES

1. For an excellent discussion of Abraham Lincoln, Roger Taney, and the suspension of the writ of habeas corpus, see Brian McGinty, *Lincoln and the Court* (Cambridge, MA: Harvard University Press, 2009).

2. George C. Herring, *From Colony to Superpower: U.S. Foreign Relations since 1776* (New York: Oxford University Press, 2011), 360–62.

3. William E. Leuchtenburg, *In the Shadow of FDR: From Harry Truman to Ronald Reagan* (Ithaca, NY: Cornell University Press, 1987), 214.

Chronology

1911	Ronald Wilson Reagan is born above a Tampico, Illinois, tavern.
1921	U.S. Treasury secretary Andrew Mellon formulates a tax plan that later will inspire "supply-side" economics.
1928	Reagan enrolls in Eureka College, in Eureka, Illinois, majoring in economics.
1929	The Great Depression disrupts economies and societies around the world.
1932	Democratic presidential candidate Franklin D. Roosevelt pledges to give Americans a "new deal."
	Reagan graduates from Eureka College and obtains a job with radio station WOC, in Davenport, Iowa. He casts his first presidential ballot, for Roosevelt.
1936	Reagan, while working as a radio announcer at WHO, in Des Moines, Iowa, thrills at the sight of President Franklin Roosevelt, who is making campaign stops across the Farm Belt.
	Roosevelt wins a historic landslide victory in reelection.
1937	Reagan signs a film contract with Warner Brothers in Hollywood.
	Massive labor union strikes sweep across the American Midwest and East.
	Reagan joins the Screen Actors Guild (SAG).
	Imperial Japan invades China, launching World War II in Asia.
	Reagan enlists in the U.S. Army Reserve.

1938	In reaction to labor unrest and a stalled economic recovery, voters elect more conservative Democrats and Republicans to Congress. An alliance between southern Democrats and northern Republicans bottles up most social reform legislation for a generation.
1939	Nazi Germany and the Soviet Union forge an alliance, and both invade Poland, launching World War II in Europe.
1940	Reagan marries actress Jane Wyman. They will have one child, a daughter, Maureen (1941), and adopt a son, Michael (1945). *Knute Rockne, All American*, gives Reagan a strong supporting film role and a nickname that he will carry into his subsequent political career: "The Gipper."
1941	Hitler invades the Soviet Union. Roosevelt extends lend-lease military aid to Great Britain and the Soviet Union. Reagan joins the SAG board of directors. Imperial Japan attacks the U.S. Pacific Fleet at Pearl Harbor, bringing the United States into World War II. Nazi Germany declares war on the United States.
1942	Due to poor eyesight, Reagan receives an assignment to make military training films.
1945	Roosevelt dies; Vice President Harry Truman ascends to the White House. Allies (United States, Great Britain, and the Soviet Union) defeat Nazi Germany and Imperial Japan, and the Soviet Union occupies Eastern Europe.
1947	President Truman commits the United States to containing Soviet expansion in Europe. Reagan becomes the SAG president. The House Committee on Un-American Activities launches the Hollywood Hearings; Reagan assures the congressmen that the federal government did not need to intervene in the film industry. Reagan participates in the founding of the Americans for Democratic Action (ADA), an organization

1948	committed to continuing the New Deal's domestic programs and supporting Truman's policy of communist containment. He serves as the California ADA leader. The national Democratic Party is divided, as some southern Democrats reject Truman's civil rights policies and champion the independent candidacy of South Carolina governor Strom Thurmond. Meanwhile, those Democrats who oppose Truman's Cold War foreign policy support the independent candidacy of former U.S. vice president Henry Wallace. Reagan campaigns for Truman, while New York graduate student Jeane Jordan (Kirkpatrick) enthusiastically casts her first presidential ballot for Truman. Oscar winner Jane Wyman files for divorce from Reagan, whose own film career is fading. Truman wins a stunning reelection in spite of Democratic Party divisions.
1949	Mao Tse-Tung defeats the nationalists and seizes power in China. The Soviet Union successfully tests an atomic bomb, ending the U.S. monopoly and placing Western Europe in peril.
1950	Soviet-backed North Korea invades South Korea, drawing the United States into the conflict and leading to the extension of "communist containment" from Europe to Asia. The threat of an atomic third world war prevents Truman from invading China after it intervenes in the Korean War against the U.S.-led United Nations forces.
1952	Reagan marries Nancy Davis; they will have a daughter, Patti (1952), and a son, Ron Jr. (1958). Former General Dwight Eisenhower defeats isolationist and anti–New Deal factions in the Republican Party to become its presidential nominee. He proclaims the birth of "Modern Republicanism," which he defines as continuing many of the domestic and foreign policies of Roosevelt and Truman.

	Phoenix, Arizona, department store heir Barry Goldwater wins election to the U.S. Senate as a conservative Republican critic of the New Deal.
1953	Soviet leader Joseph Stalin dies.
	The Korean War ends in a stalemate, with a communist North Korea and an authoritarian, U.S.-allied South Korea left in ruins.
1954	Vietnamese communists defeat French colonialists, leading to the establishment of an independent North Vietnam (communist), South Vietnam (authoritarian and U.S. allied), Laos (neutral), and Cambodia (neutral).
	The U.S. Supreme Court, in *Brown v. Board of Education*, unanimously strikes down the "separate but equal doctrine" that permitted the racial segregation of public schools.
	Reagan begins working for General Electric (GE), first by touring plants and speaking to workers and then by hosting a regular television series.
1955	Oil heir William F. Buckley Jr., establishes the *National Review* magazine in the hope of revitalizing conservative opposition to Modern Republicanism.
1956	All but three southern Democrats in Congress sign the "Southern Manifesto" pledging "massive resistance" to racial integration.
1957	Eisenhower sends federal troops to Little Rock, Arkansas, after the Democratic governor attempted to use the National Guard to prevent the racial integration of Central High School. Many southern Democrats are outraged.
1960	Democratic Party presidential nominee John F. Kennedy narrowly defeats the Republican nominee, Vice President Richard Nixon. Kennedy, a Roman Catholic, is the first U.S. president to not be a Protestant.
1961	The Soviet Union erects the Berlin Wall to prevent people in occupied Eastern Europe from fleeing to the West and freedom.

Chronology

1962 The United States and the Soviet Union nearly begin World War III over the communists' deployment of nuclear missiles to their Cuban ally.

Convinced that the Democrats were growing government and raising taxes at a rate that Roosevelt would have found objectionable, and fearful of Soviet aggression, Reagan changes his voter registration to Republican.

1963 Civil rights protestors and police clash in Birmingham, Alabama.

South Vietnamese president Ngo Diem dies in a military coup, depriving the United States of the only national leader capable of effectively fighting a North Vietnamese–backed insurgency.

Vice President Johnson becomes president following John F. Kennedy's assassination.

1964 Congress passes the 1964 Civil Rights Act with a coalition of northern Democrats and Republicans. The 1964 Civil Rights Act is intended to end discrimination in employment and segregation in lodging and restaurants, among other things.

Three civil rights workers are found dead outside Philadelphia, Mississippi.

Arizona senator Barry Goldwater wins the Republican presidential nomination, pledging to repeal the New Deal and to promote a more anticommunist foreign policy.

Conservative activist Phyllis Schlafly acquires national stature by self-publishing a best seller, *A Choice Not an Echo*, promoting Goldwater's campaign.

Student activists at the Berkeley campus of the University of California stage a much-publicized free speech demonstration that escalates into a confrontation with police.

Desperate national Republicans, facing empty campaign coffers, ask Reagan to host a televised fundraising appeal. Reagan's talk subsequently becomes known as "A Time for Choosing," which raises millions of dollars for the Republican Party but does little to prevent Goldwater's historic electoral defeat.

1965 The Watts neighborhood of Los Angeles erupts following rumors that white police officers had beaten an African American during a traffic stop.

President Johnson commences bombing North Vietnam and sending the first U.S. combat troops to South Vietnam.

Congress, in the face of southern Democratic opposition, passes the Voting Rights Act in an effort to end electoral disenfranchisement.

Civil rights protestors and police clash in Selma, Alabama.

1966 California Republican leaders, watching as the public turn against disruptive students, mounting violent crime, and urban unrest, persuade Reagan to run for governor against incumbent Democrat Edmund "Pat" Brown. Reagan's convincing victory launches his political career and sends electoral shockwaves all the way to Washington.

1967 Johnson sends federal troops to Detroit to quell rioting.

Campus protests against the escalating Vietnam war become more confrontational and disruptive.

1968 North Vietnam launches the Tet Offensive, inflicting high casualties on the United States and undermining Johnson's will to continue fighting and run for reelection.

Rioting erupts in over one hundred cities following the assassination of civil rights leader Martin Luther King Jr.

Antiwar protestors and Chicago police engage in street battles during the Democratic National Convention.

Soviet leader Leonid Brezhnev crushes Czechoslovakian democracy protests, announcing that no nation, once a part of the Soviet Empire, will be allowed to leave (Brezhnev Doctrine).

Chronology

Segregationist and former Alabama governor George Wallace breaks with the Democratic Party and runs as an independent candidate for president. He vows to restore law and order to U.S. cities and college campuses. Wallace siphons sufficient votes from Democratic presidential nominee Hubert Humphrey to ensure the election of the Republican candidate, former vice president Richard Nixon.

1969 Nixon replaces the military draft with a Selective Service lottery while withdrawing U.S. troops from South Vietnam. Nixon guesses correctly that once the fear of the draft subsides, most college unrest will end.

1970 Reagan wins a convincing reelection as California governor.
Nixon creates the Environmental Protection Agency (EPA).

1971 Nixon creates the Occupational Safety and Health Administration (OSHA).

1972 Nixon wins a landslide victory in reelection as many Democrats, disaffected with their party's liberal presidential nominee, George McGovern, vote Republican or sit out the election.

1973 OPEC oil embargo sparks shortages in the United States and accelerates inflation.
In *Roe v. Wade*, the U.S. Supreme Court recognizes abortion (at least in the first trimester) as a constitutional right.

1974 Nixon resigns rather than face impeachment, making his appointed vice president, Gerald Ford, president.

1975 North Vietnam conquers South Vietnam; communism triumphs in Cambodia and Laos as well.
Reagan leaves the California governorship and begins national political broadcasts.
The U.S. Supreme Court, in *O'Connor v. Donaldson*, orders that mentally ill patients could not be confined against their will—though the decision presumes that family members will take care of newly released

patients. Instead, hundreds of thousands of former mental patients will end up living homeless on the streets.

1976 Reagan challenges incumbent president Gerald Ford in the Republican primaries. Although Reagan narrowly loses the nomination, he establishes himself as a national political contender and attracts the votes of hundreds of thousands of working-class white Democrats.

Ford loses presidential election to Democrat Jimmy Carter.

Anti-communist Democrats and Republicans establish the Committee on the Present Danger. Many of its members will end up in the Reagan administration and will become known as "neoconservatives."

1977 At the University of Notre Dame commencement, President Jimmy Carter repudiates the Truman Doctrine and celebrates that the days of an "inordinate fear of communism" are over.

1978 *Wall Street Journal* editor Jude Wanniski publishes the best seller, *How the World Works*, helping to simplify economist Arthur Laffer's ideas for the general public.

The Deer Hunter proves to be the most controversial Vietnam War film made to that date, as some Americans call the movie racist while others stand up in the theater at the end to sing *God Bless America*.

The debut of the television series *Dallas* creates a popular sensation. Some denounce the series as a celebration of Sunbelt greed, while others embrace the show as free-market capitalism at its soap-opera best.

1979 The American economy experiences a wave of shocks as inflation and unemployment rise in tandem, creating "stagflation." The prime interest rate also increases, further slowing down business expansion and making home ownership more expensive. Pennsylvania and Ohio steel mills close, and Michigan automobile plants begin the elimination of 250,000 jobs.

Polish-born Pope John Paul II goes to Poland to encourage Catholics to stand up nonviolently for their beliefs and to resist Soviet oppression.

Jerry Falwell founds the Moral Majority to promote a socially conservative national political agenda and defeat Jimmy Carter for reelection.

Communists seize power in Nicaragua.

Islamic revolutionaries overthrow a U.S. ally, the Shah of Iran.

Iranian Islamic revolutionaries seize the U.S. Embassy in Tehran and take American hostages.

In part fearing the spread of Iran's Islamic revolution, the Soviet Union invades Afghanistan. Afghani tribes, in response, launch a Holy War against Soviet troops.

1980 Inspired by Pope John Paul II, Polish activists, among them Lech Walesa, organize an illegal, independent trade union, Solidarity.

Reagan wins the Republican Party presidential nomination in spite of intraparty opposition to his proposed economic and foreign policies. He tries to mute internal party dissension by offering critic George H. W. Bush the vice presidential slot on the ticket. The Reagan-Bush ticket subsequently defeats Jimmy Carter in the general election, and the Republicans capture control of the U.S. Senate for the first time since 1954.

The Iran-Iraq War begins as Iraq struggles to contain the Islamic Revolution.

1981 Democratic House Speaker Thomas "Tip" O'Neill warns Reagan that he will get no legislation passed, while former Democratic and Carter White House officials mock Reagan's intelligence and dismiss his political skills.

An assassin nearly kills Reagan.

Without informing the United States, Israeli leader Menachem Begins bombs a nuclear reactor in Iraq, contending that it will produce weapons that will be used against his country.

Texas representative Phil Gramm organizes fellow southern Democrats behind Ronald Reagan's tax and budget proposals, prompting Tip O'Neill to denounce Gramm and his allies as parasitical "Boll Weevils."

Congress passes Reagan's Omnibus Budget Reconciliation Act of 1981, establishing funding priorities—including increasing defense expenditures—and trimming the rate of growth in social welfare programs.

Congress passes Reagan's Economy Recovery Tax Act of 1981, reducing the top marginal tax rate and capital gains taxes while cutting overall taxes by 25 percent.

Reagan, in a move to protect U.S. industry and jobs, threatens West German and Japanese automakers with tariffs unless they stop flooding the American market with government-subsidized, lower-priced cars. Taking Reagan's threats seriously, foreign automakers locate new plants in the United States, generating some industrial job recovery in the American economy.

Reagan, using the power of the executive order, begins to review federal regulations to determine if they are too burdensome to the U.S. economy.

The Professional Air Traffic Controllers' Union (PATCO) conducts an illegal strike. Reagan does not hesitate to attack a government employee union, firing all except for those few members who had returned to work. The majority of Americans support Reagan's action.

Music Television (MTV) debuts, changing the recording industry, popularizing alternative music, and influencing television series and films.

Office of Management and Budget director David Stockman leaks attacks on Reagan's economic policy and advisers to the press, in an effort to force the president to eliminate New Deal legacy programs.

1982 Soviet leader Leonid Brezhnev dies, elevating Yuri Andropov to the leadership.

Israel intervenes in the Lebanese civil war in an effort to destroy the Palestinian Liberation Organization (PLO), which had set up operations in that nation.

Iranian agents found the terror group *Hezbollah* (Party of God) in Lebanon in response to the Israeli invasion.

House Democrats pass the Boland Amendment to the 1982 defense appropriations bill, which prohibits Reagan from arming and funding the anticommunist Contra fighters in Nicaragua. The Republican Senate, eager to increase overall defense appropriations, concurs with the House.

The television series *Family Ties* debuts, introducing a character, Alex P. Keaton, who will become the popular, fictional face of youthful conservatism.

The U.S. economy heads into another recession, with congressional Democrats blaming Reagan's economic policy. Reagan urges Americans to stay the course, but the 1982 midterm elections result in a number of House Republicans losing their seats. Tip O'Neill believes that 1982 midterm elections will be a precursor to Democratic victory in the 1984 presidential election.

1983 Reagan addresses the nation on his vision of a Strategic Defense Initiative (SDI) to protect Americans from nuclear missiles. Hostile Democrats and news media personnel derisively call SDI "Star Wars."

Reagan invades the Caribbean island of Grenada to prevent communist Cubans and Soviets from building an air base there.

Hezbollah launches a terrorist attack on U.S. peacekeepers in Lebanon, killing 241 American military personnel. Reagan withdraws the remaining U.S. troops.

Reagan refers to the Soviet Union as an "evil empire" in a speech to the National Association of Evangelicals. No president had talked that way publicly about the Soviet Union since Harry Truman.

	Reagan maneuvers House Democrats into working with the White House and the Republican Senate to save Social Security from financial collapse. Reagan believes Tip O'Neill wanted Social Security to collapse in order to give Democrats a major political issue going into the 1984 election.
1984	Soviet leader Yuri Andropov dies, elevating Konstantin Chernenko to the leadership.
	The 1984 Summer Olympics, located in Los Angeles, generates an enormous amount of patriotic sentiment and pride in the United States.
	Reagan becomes the first incumbent president to visit (and speak at) the Normandy D-Day site during the fortieth anniversary commemoration.
	Congress passes the Reagan-supported Comprehensive Crime Control Act. This legislation imposes federal mandatory prison sentences on repeat offenders and compels asset forfeiture to the government by criminals—among other penalties.
	The anticommunist film *Red Dawn* depicting the United States in the aftermath of a Soviet invasion generates millions in profits and becomes a cult classic.
	Walter Mondale, Jimmy Carter's vice president, wins the Democratic presidential nomination. He vows to undo all of Reagan's domestic and foreign policies and to raise taxes.
	Reagan wins a landslide victory in reelection, winning all the states but Walter Mondale's native Minnesota.
1985	Soviet leader Konstantin Chernenko dies, elevating Mikhail Gorbachev to the leadership.
	Oliver North and Robert McFarlane launch an illegal arms deal with Iran, with proceeds from the sale going to fund the Contras in Nicaragua.
	Reagan authorizes the CIA to provide advanced Stinger missiles to the Mujahedeen (Holy Warriors) fighting against the Soviet occupiers of Afghanistan.

1986

The anticommunist film *Rambo II* generates tens of millions of dollars in profits as its hero returns to Vietnam to win the war the second time around.

A catastrophic nuclear reactor accident at Chernobyl in the Soviet Union poisons tens of thousands. Even as a massive radioactive cloud moves across Eastern Europe, Soviet leader Mikhail Gorbachev denies that there is a problem. Chernobyl weakens Gorbachev's image in the West as a reformer.

Congress passes the Reagan-supported Anti-Drug Abuse Act which mandates minimum prison sentences for narcotics possession and places greater penalties on crack users than on cocaine users.

Congress passes the Reagan-supported Immigration Reform Control Act, giving amnesty to three million people who came into the United States before 1982. To Reagan's dismay, Congress refuses to impose significant penalties on employers who exploit illegal immigrant labor.

The soundtrack of the film *Top Gun*, when paired with its scene outtakes, becomes a popular MTV video and inspires a host of recruits to the U.S. Navy.

Reagan hosts a nationally televised celebration of the renovation of Ellis Island and the Statue of Liberty.

1987

Reagan and Mikhail Gorbachev negotiate the Intermediate-Range Nuclear Forces Treaty, leading to the reduction of Soviet and American missiles in Europe.

Reagan goes to West Berlin, where, standing in front of the Brandenburg Gate, he demands that Gorbachev tear down the wall dividing the city.

Congress launches an investigation into what became known as the Iran-Contra Scandal. Ironically, Congress had withdrawn the Boland Amendment's prohibition of providing military aid to the Contras even as Oliver North and Robert McFarlane were completing their scheme.

1988	Reagan speaks freely with students at Moscow State University.
	Republican vice president George H. W. Bush wins the presidential election, pledging to continue Reagan's policies.
1989	Jerry Falwell, claiming that religious conservatives had achieved their goals, disbands the Moral Majority.
	Pat Robertson founds the Christian Coalition to focus on electing religious conservatives at the state and congressional levels.
	The Berlin Wall comes down, marking the beginning of the end of the Soviet Union.
1990	Iraq leader Saddam Hussein, after receiving assurances from the United States that it would not intervene if he invaded Kuwait, is stunned when President George H. W. Bush goes to war. The Persian Gulf War destabilizes Iraq and opens the door to greater Iranian political and military influence in the region. The war also arouses anger across the Middle East and inspires Holy Warrior Osama Bin Laden, who had fought the Soviets in Afghanistan, to seek vengeance against the United States.
1992	Democratic Party presidential nominee Bill Clinton defeats President George H. W. Bush. Clinton promises to govern as a moderate.
1994	Republican House strategist Newt Gingrich of Georgia announces a Contract with America, pledging a continuation of Reagan's reform agenda if the Democrats lose control of Congress. Republicans capture both the House and the Senate. Working with Democratic president Bill Clinton, who has rejected the liberalism of Walter Mondale and Tip O'Neill, Gingrich initiates major welfare reform.
	Reagan reveals that he has Alzheimer's.
2001	Terrorists financed by Osama Bin Laden launch successful attacks on the Pentagon and the twin towers of the World Trade Center, killing close to three thousand (confirmed) people.

	President George W. Bush, the son of President George H. W. Bush, launches a War on Terror that will add trillions of dollars to the national debt.
	Congress passes the Bush-supported Providing Appropriate Tools Required to Intercept and Obstruct Terrorism (PATRIOT) Act, which gives the federal government the ability to surveil Americans, wiretap their phones, and open their mail.
2003	President Bush, claiming (incorrectly) that Saddam Hussein possesses weapons of mass destruction, receives authorization from Congress to invade Iraq. An anti-American insurgency breaks out in Iraq, leading to a state of permanent war and further elevating Iran's political and military position.
2004	Reagan dies, his domestic and foreign policy legacy largely voided.
2015	The U.S. Supreme Court, in *Obergefell v. Hodges*, rules that all states have to recognize the validity of gay marriage. Reagan-appointed judge Anthony Kennedy cast the deciding affirmative vote.
2016	Nancy Reagan dies.

CHAPTER 1

RONALD REAGAN'S POLITICAL ODYSSEY: FROM NEW DEAL DEMOCRAT TO CONSERVATIVE REPUBLICAN, 1911–1980

In the early twentieth century, industrial centers dominated the American landscape. Native-born midwesterners left failing family farms and stagnate towns for the promise of a steady paycheck in Chicago, Cleveland, and Detroit. At the same time, millions of impoverished Roman Catholic, Jewish, and Russian Orthodox immigrants settled in those same cities. Industrial communities might choke on fouled air, but they generated jobs. Although few workers ever achieved great wealth, most were content with not starving to death and the promise of a better life.

While Chicago's meatpacking plants and steel mills earned international renown, a host of obscure towns dotted the Illinois landscape. Immigrants and migrants in search of work did not flock to Tampico or Dixon. While one's chance of being robbed in Dixon was far less than if one resided a hundred miles east, in Chicago, making a living was not easy. If not a farmer, then one made a precarious living in the lower rungs of white-collar employment. Those who lacked accounting skills often went into sales. A smile and a gift for gab could mask the fear that if the commissions were not high enough, the family would be without shelter and food. When you sold shoes, you were not just unloading footwear; you were selling a piece of yourself to seal the deal.

Everyone liked Jack Reagan (1883–1941), a descendant of such immigrant Irish clans as O'Regan, Murphy, and Mulcahey. (Though the name was anglicized from O'Regan to Reagan, the family maintained something approximating an Irish pronunciation—"Reegen.") Jack Reagan, as the saying went, "never met a stranger," just friends he did not yet know. That did not mean, however, that he was blind to human failings. He once stomped out of a hotel when the manager assured him that they did not allow Jews. Jack angrily replied, "I'm a Catholic. If it's come to the point where you won't take Jews, then some day you won't take *me* either."[1]

In 1904, Jack married Nelle Wilson (1883–1962), a fervent member of the Christian Disciples Church. Nelle Reagan believed in the power of prayer to heal the afflicted and so despised alcohol that she became a local Woman's Christian Temperance Union leader. Although Jack remained Catholic, it was less because of faith and more due to the fact that he was Irish—which many of his tribe believed was indistinguishable from being Catholic. Jack was also an alcoholic, but of the buoyant, rather than abusive, variety.

The Reagans moved from town to town, with Nelle giving birth to Neil in 1908 and Ronald in 1911. As a struggling salesman, Jack Reagan could not afford to rent a good house, let alone buy one. Consequently, Ronald was born above a Tampico tavern. They finally moved on to Dixon, where the family continued to experience life on the financial margins.

Due to his father's money and drinking problems, Ronald, though the younger brother, set out to help his family. Ronald did not complain when he found his father passed out in a snowdrift; he simply dragged Jack into the house before he froze to death. He understood, as did Nelle, that Jack had a disease, not a sinful nature. Ronald became a lifeguard at the Rock River swimming hole. The Rock River flowed with a fast undercurrent that made it dangerous to swim in, but Dixon residents had few other sources of recreation. He saved seventy-seven people from drowning.

The Reagan family: (from left) Jack Reagan, Neil Reagan, Ronald Reagan, and Nelle Reagan, 1916 or 1917. Born into the struggling ranks of the lower-middle class, Ronald Reagan later achieved a level of upward social mobility and national political influence that would have astounded him in his youthful days. (Ronald Reagan Presidential Library and Museum)

Young Reagan was a popular figure in high school, where he served as student council president. He was also a well-rounded athlete. Graduating from Dixon High School in 1928, Reagan attended Eureka College, a Christian Disciples institution of higher education located in Eureka, Illinois, eighty-eight miles south of Dixon. Reagan majored in economics. He was drawn to theater but knew he had to select a practical major that would lead to employment. While Reagan may have been an academically average student, he was a campus leader and athlete. Reagan worked to pay his tuition, room, and board. There was no federal financial aid for college students.

Reagan was in junior high school when Pittsburgh billionaire and U.S. secretary of the treasury Andrew Mellon (1855–1937) had devised an income tax reform that prefigured "supply-side economics" in the 1980s. Mellon, and the three Republican presidents he served, believed that if the federal government reduced the tax burden on corporations and their leaders, they could use their cash to expand their operations—thus increasing employment and incomes for all. Mellon proved partially correct; businesses did invest in new plants and did hire more workers. America's victory in World War II rested on the expanded industrial infrastructure built in the 1920s.

While Mellon's tax policies were successful on the "supply" side of the economic equation, they were a failure on the "demand" (or consumer) side. In the 1920s, 60 percent of Americans lived at or below the level of subsistence. That meant they had sufficient money to purchase clothing and food and to rent (not buy) shelter. Anything other than the basic necessities was beyond their financial reach. Industry recognized this reality, settling on the extension of credit, the "installment plan," to enable consumers to acquire automobiles and other higher-priced goods. Seventy percent of automobiles were bought on credit in the 1920s.

Eventually, consumer debt, together with overproduction and underconsumption, resulted in a stock market crash. The United States had had economic crashes before, and they had always passed. No one in 1929 anticipated that this crash would be different. To be sure, the stock market crash did not cause the Great Depression. Fundamental imbalances in the economy did, especially the inability of consumers to buy all the products and goods flooding the markets. But the crash did signal a loss of confidence in big business and point to the need for government action. The Great Depression was global and seemingly permanent. It shaped an entire generation's outlook on life, including that of Reagan, who had just begun college.

Between 1929 and 1932, unemployment rose from four million to twelve million—one-quarter of the workforce. U.S. industry operated at 55 percent of capacity, meaning that the other 45 percent was idle. Due to job cuts and the expansion of part-time labor, blue-collar income fell 40 percent in just three years. Meanwhile, as workers' incomes declined and households reduced their food purchases, farmers confronted a shrinking market. Between the 1929 crash and 1932, farm income declined 50 percent.[2]

To struggling Americans such as the Reagan family, the economic crisis had revealed the hollowness of the Republican establishment. Jack

Reagan, like many Democrats, had always given Republicans the benefit of the doubt—though they might be wrong, Republicans were not necessarily evil. President Herbert Hoover (1874–1964) and congressional Republicans changed the public perception of the party. For Jack Reagan, disgust with Republican businessmen and politicians came to a head on Christmas Eve when, opening what he thought was a holiday greeting card from his employer, was, instead, a notice of termination. Stunned, Jack Reagan said in a soft voice, "That's quite a Christmas present."[3]

Faced with collapsing consumer demand, Hoover responded by giving federal funds to banks, which were then to be loaned to businesses so that they could produce more unsellable goods. When that policy inevitably failed, Hoover warned that Democrats were plotting to undermine the Eighteenth Amendment, adopted after World War I, which had outlawed the sale and production of alcohol (Prohibition). He contended that alcohol, not unemployment and low wages, led to crime and poverty. Congressional Republicans echoed Hoover's rhetoric, holding hearings on the illegal trade in alcohol, narcotics, and pornography—all of which, they insisted, were Americans' true sources of misery.

As the 1932 Democratic presidential nominee, New York governor Franklin Delano Roosevelt promised Americans a "new deal." He was not specific about what changes he would make in domestic policy because he had no plan or policy, just the promise to do something. A "Gentleman C" graduate of Harvard, no one ever called Roosevelt an intellectual. U.S. Supreme Court justice Oliver Wendell Holmes described Roosevelt as having "a second-rate intellect, but a first-rate temperament." By that, Holmes meant that though Roosevelt might not be a scholar, he knew how to read people. Decades later, academics would call this ability "social intelligence." Reagan did not realize it in 1932, but he and Roosevelt had a lot in common.[4]

Reagan cast his first presidential ballot in 1932 for Roosevelt. He would vote three more times for Roosevelt over the next twelve years. His hope that Roosevelt would usher in fundamental change proved justified. Given that most cities and states were fiscally insolvent by the time Roosevelt took office in 1933, the federal government became the go-to source for financial aid.

Nearly every group got something out of the New Deal. Urban workers, who were mainly Catholics, Jews, and Black Protestants, got public works jobs, unemployment compensation, and Social Security. Farmers received crop subsidies, rural electrification, and water projects—including reservoirs to control flooding, generate hydroelectric power, and provide water to irrigate fields. The only group not receiving government assistance belonged to the 3 percent of the population that had a high enough income to be required to pay federal taxes. Taxing the few to benefit the many had an enormous political upside; it helped make the Democratic Party nationally dominant for decades.

Reagan was among the millions of citizens who hung onto every word Roosevelt spoke over the radio. Roosevelt never hid his upper-class accent, but he also never talked down to people. The president delivered evocative phrases that Reagan recited until they became a part of his own vocabulary: "rendezvous with destiny" and the "forgotten man," among others. Reagan took to heart Roosevelt's warning that federal relief programs had to require recipients to work, otherwise welfare would become "a narcotic, a subtle destroyer of the human spirit." It was just such a relief program, the Works Progress Administration (WPA), that gave Jack Reagan a job as well as a sense of self-respect.[5]

Having graduated from college during the lowest point of the Great Depression (1932), Reagan was fortunate to secure a job as a sports announcer on radio station WOC, in Davenport, Iowa. He then moved on to WHO, in Des Moines. Although Des Moines, with a population of 142,000, was no Chicago, the city had enough voters to place it on Roosevelt's 1936 reelection campaign schedule. Reagan fondly recalled seeing Roosevelt:

> What a wave of affection and pride swept through that crowd as he passed by in an open car—which we haven't seen a president able to do for a long time—a familiar smile on his lips, jaunty and confident, drawing from us reservoirs of confidence and enthusiasm some of us had forgotten we had during those hard years. Maybe that was [Roosevelt's] greatest gift to us. He really did convince us that the only thing we had to fear was fear itself.[6]

Since Iowa did not have a Major League baseball franchise, Des Moines residents were avid followers of the Chicago Cubs. In 1937, WHO sent Reagan to California to watch the Cubs in spring training. Friends had

Ronald Reagan as sports announcer at WHO-Des Moines, Iowa, mid-1930s. His "voice talent" gained Reagan employment during the depths of the Great Depression. While in Des Moines, during the 1936 presidential election, he saw his political hero, Franklin Roosevelt—an experience he fondly recalled for decades. (Ronald Reagan Presidential Library and Museum)

told him that in addition to a great voice, he had the looks of a movie star. Reagan took a screen test, which led Warner Brothers Studios to offer him a two-hundred-dollar-a-week contract. The Warner contract gave Reagan an annual salary four times higher than what a unionized steelworker earned in 1937. His income enabled him to relocate his parents to Los Angeles and buy them a home of their own.

Reagan's move to Los Angeles proved life changing. Concerned with the increased aggression of Germany, Italy, and Japan, he enlisted in the U.S. Army Reserve as a cavalry soldier. Reagan enjoyed riding horses and performing military drills. His severe nearsightedness, however, and wariness of wearing glasses that might mar his looks on film, made him a more of a threat—and to friends rather than foes—than if he did take up a gun.

His second major life change was to join the Screen Actors Guild (SAG). Founded in 1933, SAG had just won the right to negotiate with the film studios. Organized labor had been rejuvenated in the 1930s thanks to federal collective-bargaining legislation, the founding of the Congress of Industrial Organizations (CIO), and the dynamic leadership of John L. Lewis and Philip Murray. By 1937, when the CIO launched a national strike wave, organized labor was a major player in the Democratic Party. Lewis had earlier told workers that Roosevelt wanted them to join a union. Reagan seemed to believe Lewis; not only did Reagan join SAG but he also became a member of the union's board of directors in 1941.

Although Reagan never made it onto the A-list of actors who earned princely salaries, he was successful in Hollywood. He was adept at playing comedic and dramatic roles, which opened up a number of film opportunities. Within a few years, Reagan was among the top B-list actors, either playing leads in low-budget films or supporting characters in A-list productions. He averaged $42,000 for each film (or $810,000, when adjusted for inflation). In the 1942 film *Desperate Journey*, Reagan successfully went toe-to-toe with A-list actor Errol Flynn, who was notorious for stealing scenes. While Reagan knew his place in the Hollywood pecking order, no one upstaged him. In his personal life, Reagan married an actress, Jane Wyman, with whom he had one daughter and adopted a son. Reagan led a charmed existence; it seemingly came to end all too soon.

The Japanese attack on the U.S. Pacific Fleet at Pearl Harbor in the Hawaiian Islands, followed by Germany's declaration of war against the United States, brought America into World War II. Reagan expected to be mobilized for combat, but the U.S. Army had little need for horse soldiers, let alone nearsighted ones. Reagan settled for an officer's commission in the U.S. Army Signal Corps, remaining in Hollywood to make military training films. It upset Reagan that other actors, notably Jimmy Stewart, were flying bombing missions over Germany.

Reagan's career suffered during World War II. He devoted a great deal of time to the war effort—leaving less time to make commercial films. There was an additional reason Reagan made fewer films. To pay for the war, the U.S. government had raised the marginal tax rate. For every dollar earned above two hundred thousand dollars annually, the federal government took ninety-four cents. Reagan realized that it made no financial

Ronald Reagan, in his U.S. Army uniform, with Nelle Reagan, early 1940s. Unfit for combat duty because of poor eyesight, Reagan was determined to serve his country—even if it meant making military training films. (Ronald Reagan Presidential Library and Museum)

sense to make more than three or four films a year. He largely removed himself from the movie screen while in his prime years as an actor. In a Hollywood that worshipped youth, most actors and actresses "aged out" of roles quickly.

While Reagan's film career slackened, his interest in labor and national politics grew. To the bewilderment of his wife, he read debates in the *Congressional Record* more closely than the gossip in the film-trade magazine *Variety*. Reagan, like many in Hollywood, regarded the Soviet Union as a valuable ally against Hitler. But he wondered, What would the Soviets do once they liberated half of Europe from Adolf Hitler? Would they leave on their own accord?

Closer to home, Reagan had become disenchanted with Hollywood communists who sought to dominate the SAG and other film-related unions. In the 1930s, Hollywood leftists called for a "popular front" between the democracies and the Soviet Union, in order to fight Hitler. Then in 1939, Hitler and Joseph Stalin forged an alliance, and the Soviet Union subsequently invaded Poland, Estonia, Latvia, Lithuania, and Finland. Hollywood radicals endorsed Soviet aggression. As soon as Hitler invaded the Soviet Union in 1941, Hollywood communists demanded that the United States aid Stalin in the fight against Hitler. Reagan concluded that the Hollywood Left would defend the indefensible.

Roosevelt's death in 1945 elevated Vice President Harry Truman (1884–1972) to the presidency. Roosevelt's loyalists had kept Truman, a product of the corrupt Kansas City, Missouri, Democratic political machine, in the dark about a number of important military and foreign policy developments, including the invention of the atomic bomb. If ever there was a president who was not prepared for the job but ended up (mostly) excelling in the position, it was Truman.

Truman recognized that the Soviet Union was not going to give up its territorial gains in Eastern Europe. Stalin would impose a military occupation, as well as a communist economic and political system, on Eastern Europe. Further Soviet expansion in Europe, Truman believed, had to be contained. Truman also, belatedly, realized that Chinese nationalists, crippled by the war against Japan, would lose their struggle against communist insurgents. And then there were the Republicans, who had swept Congress in the 1946 midterm elections in a backlash against labor strikes. Many, especially conservative Ohio senator Robert A. Taft, the son of President William Howard Taft (1857–1930), wanted to repeal the New Deal by any means necessary—including red-baiting Democrats as treasonous communists.

John Parnell Thomas, the chair of the House Committee on Un-American Activities, decided in 1947 to investigate communism in Hollywood. He calculated that the "Hollywood Hearings" would generate favorable publicity and boost Republican electoral prospects. Anticommunist Republicans relished the opportunity to show up the Hollywood Left as hypocrites who preached a workers' revolution from their positions of privilege.

Reagan, who had been elected SAG president in 1947, regarded Thomas's hearings as an assault on the New Deal. Along with such Hollywood friends as Bill Holden and Olivia de Havilland, Reagan had been quietly moving communists out of positions of influence in Hollywood's unions. He and Holden also attended cocktail parties to argue with communists

As president of the Screen Actors Guild (SAG), Ronald Reagan testified before the House Committee on Un-American Activities in 1947, at the "Hollywood Hearings." Reagan assured the Republican-controlled committee that Hollywood had communists at bay and did not need federal interference. (Ronald Reagan Presidential Library and Museum)

and peel some of their supporters away. Meanwhile, Reagan secretly fed the FBI information on Hollywood communists and organized crime figures. Like CIO president Phil Murray, Reagan feared that if their efforts to isolate communists became public knowledge, conservatives would try to discredit all social reformers.

Appearing before the Un-American Activities Committee, Reagan noted forcefully, but politely, that Hollywood was taking care of its own affairs and did not need congressional oversight. He also told Thomas that if Congress wished to outlaw the Communist Party, then the federal government needed to prove that its members were agents of a foreign power. Reagan further argued, "As a citizen, I would hesitate to see any political party outlawed on the basis of its political ideology. We have spent a hundred and seventy years in this country on the basis that democracy is strong enough to stand up and fight against the inroads of any ideology."[7]

Although anticommunist Republicans such as Thomas were a concern, Roosevelt's heirs were more alarmed by the brewing civil war inside Democratic Party ranks. On the Left, Henry Wallace, whom the urban political machine bosses had thrown off the ticket as vice president in 1944, denounced Truman's anticommunist foreign policy. He vigorously opposed the U.S.-led economic reconstruction of Western Europe. Wallace received support from college faculty and other white-collar professionals outside the business sector.

On the Right, South Carolina governor Strom Thurmond complained that Truman wanted to end racial segregation in the armed forces. World War II had inspired hundreds of thousands of southern Blacks and whites to move away in search of jobs. With the ability to vote in the North and West, Blacks were placing increased pressure on the national Democratic Party to embrace civil rights.

In 1947, a group of political activists founded an organization to save the party of the New Deal. The Americans for Democratic Action (ADA) championed civil rights and communist containment while supporting the New Deal's labor and social welfare legislation. ADA founders included labor leader Phil Murray and Minneapolis, Minnesota, mayor Hubert Humphrey. Reagan served as leader of the California ADA chapter.

The Democratic Party splintered at its 1948 national convention. Thurmond ran as the presidential candidate of the States' Rights Party, or "Dixiecrats," warning that "there is not enough troops in the army to force the southern people to break down segregation and admit the n— race into our theaters, into our swimming pools, into our homes, and into our churches." Wallace ran as the presidential candidate of the Progressive Party. He accused Truman of orchestrating a "reactionary war policy which is dividing the world into two armed camps and making inevitable the day when American soldiers will be dying in their Arctic suits in the Russian snow."[8]

Reagan appeared at Truman presidential campaign events, injecting them with a little Hollywood glamour. He also recorded radio spots for Minnesota senatorial candidate Hubert Humphrey. Reagan warned that Humphrey's Republican rival was a "banner carrier for Wall Street." Humphrey, in contrast, was "fighting for all the principles advocated by President Truman: for adequate low-cost housing; for civil rights; for prices people can afford to pay." Defying conventional political wisdom, Truman won. Humphrey also claimed victory.[9]

Anyone who watched Reagan either campaign for Truman or lead SAG discussions recognized how much he enjoyed politics. He was an effective, likeable warm-up speaker. There were also good reasons why the acting community elected him to six terms as SAG president. Reagan knew that most actors and actresses would never earn even the (relatively) modest sums he had made on the B-list, and he wanted to help the rank and file.

As SAG president, Reagan had two objectives. First, newly emerging television networks were broadcasting movies, but the performers received no "residual" (or royalty) payments. Reagan argued that the men and women he represented deserved to be paid residuals when their work went on the television screen. (They were already receiving residuals for television show and commercial reruns, thanks to earlier SAG negotiations.) Second, Reagan believed that the studios should contribute toward medical insurance and pensions for performers. The studio and television network heads scorned Reagan, dismissing him as the washed-up actor who had once costarred with a chimpanzee (*Bedtime for Bonzo*, 1951; the chimp liked Reagan; the studio heads, not so much).

In 1960, Reagan led a disruptive SAG strike. He secured residuals for films made after 1960 and shown on television. For films made between 1948 and 1959, Reagan got the studios to pay $2.25 million to SAG (or $19 million when adjusted for inflation). He used that money to fund a union health insurance and pension plan.

Reagan's personal life came apart as his union and political activism increased. Wyman's star had been rising even as Reagan's had been fading. She secured her place on the A-list with *Johnny Belinda* in 1948, which netted her the Academy Award for Best Actress. She filed for divorce that year, officially dissolving the marriage in 1949. Wyman had always been dismissive of Reagan's labor and political activism. The divorce was not amicable. Whenever Reagan was due to see their children (she had won custody), Wyman placed them out on the curb so he would not go up to her door.

The divorce shattered Reagan. Bill Holden took him out for nightclub adventures in an effort to cheer him up. Unlike Holden, Reagan usually drank little. He was mindful of his father's alcohol addiction, though when he did imbibe, he was just as congenial as Jack Reagan on a bender.

Being what was once called "a ladies' man," however, was something Reagan fully embraced. Reagan had numerous affairs but was careful not to be like some of the predatory studio heads whom he detested.

In the fall of 1949, a young actress, Nancy Davis (1921–2016), went to see Reagan, hoping that he could help her. Due to a case of mistaken identity, she had been labeled a communist sympathizer, which resulted in her losing roles. Fearing adverse publicity and congressional scrutiny, the studios had imposed a blacklist on Hollywood. Leftist screenwriters could always earn money writing scripts under an alias, but blacklisted performers could not hide their identities on the movie or television screen. Davis became "smitten" by Reagan, even though he was hoping to reconcile with Wyman.[10]

Nancy Davis's mother had been a New York City stage actress; her biological father abandoned his family shortly after her birth. Her mother subsequently married a wealthy Chicago surgeon, who financed Nancy's education at elite Smith College, in Massachusetts. After getting some Broadway theatrical experience, and with her mother's influence, Nancy obtained a Hollywood film contract. While her film career was solid, though not stellar, once she set a goal for herself, Nancy was an unstoppable force of nature. She wanted to become Mrs. Ronald Reagan—and achieved that goal in 1952. Holden was Reagan's best man. Reagan expressed his appreciation for Nancy having brought him in "from the cold." He was, however, embarrassed that she had to scrounge for film work because he was barely paying the bills. It was as if the ghost of Jack Reagan had come for a visit.[11]

In 1954, the management of General Electric (GE) invited Reagan to play host to a proposed television show: *General Electric Theater*. The $125,000 salary GE offered to Reagan had nothing to do with altruism and everything to do with public relations. (Adjusting for inflation, Reagan's GE salary was the equivalent of nearly $1.2 million.) GE wanted a television presence—and a congenial host who would tour plants and chat with workers. Reagan may have been near the end of his film career, but many people out in the heartland loved celebrities who appeared to be down-to-earth. He was a perfect commercial spokesman. GE's public relations strategy represented a far-reaching update of its corporate strategy born in the 1930s.

During the Great Depression, GE leader Gerard Swope had made peace with the New Deal. Swope had calculated that GE could absorb

Ronald and Nancy Reagan wedding, 1952. After a demoralizing divorce from actress Jane Wyman, Reagan rebounded with Nancy Davis, who would become his confidant and morale booster. (Ronald Reagan Presidential Library and Museum)

the greater production costs associated with a unionized workforce and higher corporate taxes mainly by passing on expenses to customers spread across a large number of electrical appliances. Smaller appliance manufacturers, however, could ill afford to follow GE's example, since producing fewer units meant raising prices much higher. If they raised prices, they would likely go bankrupt; if they did not raise prices, they would likely go bankrupt. Swope saw this as a win-win scenario for GE.

By the 1950s, GE's management had become alarmed by expanding federal social welfare programs, escalating taxes, and the ability of organized labor to shut down production. Lemuel Boulware, GE vice president for public and community relations, was convinced that the company had to explain to its employees that there was a relationship between corporate profits and their wages and job security. GE workers should also be made aware that growing federal regulations cut into profits—and, therefore, their wages. Boulware thought workers should be instructed in the "free market." He was smart enough to understand that the message had to come from someone other than a corporate manager. Boulware needed Reagan.

Nancy Reagan and GE have been credited with turning Reagan into a conservative in the 1950s. There was some truth in that analysis but also some misunderstanding. Although Wyman disdained politics, she had grown to dislike Roosevelt (and taxes). However, Wyman did not convert Reagan into a Roosevelt hater, and she was as forceful a personality as Nancy was. Certainly, Nancy had absorbed conservative views from her anti–New Deal stepfather and was very conscious of social status.

Accepting a position with General Electric (GE) in 1954, Ronald Reagan gave speeches at GE plants and hosted a television program. The GE experience not only saved Reagan's finances but also honed his public speaking skills and gave him a great familiarity with television. (Ronald Reagan Presidential Library and Museum)

She led Reagan into the Presbyterian Church, which had a higher-class profile than the Christian Disciples. Both of their children were raised as Presbyterians. Nancy also got her husband to change the pronunciation of his surname from the Irish "Reegen" to what she thought was a more high-toned Scottish inflection: "Ray-gun."

Still, as Nancy observed, Reagan was no pushover; he took his time to study an issue and weigh the value of others' viewpoints. Moreover, Nancy had little interest in politics—conservative or liberal—before her marriage. If anything, Reagan converted his wife from political apathy—something he had never accomplished with Wyman.

As for GE luring Reagan away from the New Deal, there is an implicit assumption that Reagan was an empty vessel that the corporation filled with right-wing views. Anyone in Hollywood who had ever sat across from Reagan at a negotiating table knew he was beyond manipulation. Once Reagan concluded that his position was correct, he might compromise, but he did not surrender. No one ever manipulated Reagan, though he sometimes encouraged others—whether friends or foes—to believe that they had done so. This tactic hid the fact that Reagan was the one doing the manipulation.

Most importantly, Reagan's ideological evolution in the 1950s was less than it seemed to be. During World War II the federal government had not only imposed an enormous marginal tax rate but also adopted payroll tax withholding. Before the war, Americans paid their federal income tax at the end of the year. Wartime fiscal realities, however, required the government to collect cash as soon as possible rather than wait a year.

After the war, the federal government kept the high marginal rates and payroll withholding. While high marginal rates took money away from the private sector for investment and job creation, the downside of payroll withholding was subtler. Reagan believed that Americans were losing sight of how much they paid in taxes, because the amounts withheld from paychecks appeared to be so small. Paying once at the end of the year had given Americans a more accurate view of the cost of government. In effect, Americans had mentally forfeited oversight of the federal budget—even as a rising standard of living meant that the majority of working people were paying taxes, which had not been true in the 1930s.

Both Truman and Eisenhower, along with Congress, added more people to Social Security rolls and launched new domestic spending projects.

Politicians placed ever more weight on the New Deal's social welfare foundation. Reagan never repudiated Roosevelt. Rather, he complained that Roosevelt's successors did not understand that government expansion and rising taxes threatened to destroy the New Deal's legacy. Consequently, he had no problem with criticizing taxes and pointing to the virtues of the free market.

Reagan, who was simultaneously sincere, self-serving, and defensive, concluded that he "did not leave the Democratic Party; it left me." It hurt when the national leadership of organized labor in 1961 branded him an "extremist" for working with GE. That attack occurred just a year after Reagan had led a successful SAG strike. Despite this insult, Reagan was not prepared to become a registered Republican until 1962. Like many of his generation, the memory of Hoover haunted him.[12]

The decade of the 1960s transformed Reagan from an actor who dabbled in politics to a seasoned politician who used his acting skills to sway voters. He observed John Kennedy, Lyndon Johnson, and Richard Nixon—and found them lacking.

Kennedy waffled on civil rights legislation, not wishing to aggravate southern Democrats, and was largely uninterested in domestic policy beyond a tax cut—which Reagan believed was his best idea. It was foreign policy that animated Kennedy, but his performance was, to Reagan, alarming. Kennedy stood by while the Soviet Union walled off the American zone of occupation in West Berlin, nearly stumbled into a nuclear war with the Soviets over the placement of missiles in Cuba, and increased the U.S. military commitment to South Vietnam—a nation that appeared to be on the verge of conquest by communist North Vietnam.

After Kennedy's assassination in 1963, Vice President Johnson took command. Johnson aspired to be a transformative president. He believed the federal government could abolish poverty, end racial discrimination, and, in what was an afterthought, defeat communism in Vietnam. At the University of Michigan spring graduation commencement in 1964, Johnson announced that he was going to build a "Great Society." He would push civil rights legislation through Congress and launch an array of antipoverty programs. Although the military situation in South Vietnam was deteriorating, Johnson did not want to get bogged down in an Asian war. He feared that Congress would choose to fight a war in Vietnam rather than fund a "War on Poverty."

Since the Great Depression, Republicans had been divided over how to respond to the New Deal. The United States' postwar foreign policy had also exposed differences between Republican internationalists and isolationists. Eisenhower's victory in 1952 seemingly turned the Republicans into a pro–New Deal, internationalist party. President Eisenhower's loyalists included Vice President Nixon, Connecticut senator Prescott Bush, New York governor Nelson Rockefeller, and Pennsylvania governor William Scranton. Like their northern Democratic counterparts, such Republicans embraced civil rights and hoped to draw African Americans back to "the Party of Lincoln."

Dissenters complained that Eisenhower had turned the Republicans into the "me too" party. Among the critics was Arizona senator Barry Goldwater (1909–1998), a Phoenix department store heir. Goldwater argued that the New Deal had created "dependency" on the government. He also contended that the CIO stood for "chaos," "riots," and "bloodshed." Truman, he said, was an "architect of socialism," and Eisenhower was not much better.[13]

Goldwater embodied the restless conservative faction within the Republican Party. The conservatives rejected Senator Taft's isolationist foreign policy while asserting that Eisenhower had to "roll back," not contain, international communism. Conservatives also believed it was pointless to lure Blacks away from the Democratic Party; they were lost for good. Instead, Republicans should oppose civil rights legislation and appeal to southern white Democrats. Academics and journalists, as well as some conservative intellectuals, referred to this idea as the "Southern Strategy."

Conservatives wanted Goldwater for president in 1960, but most Republicans believed it was Nixon's turn, following his eight years as vice president. Nixon lost a close election to Kennedy. Deciding that he needed to hold a political office from which to run for president in 1964, Nixon ran for governor of California against incumbent Democrat Edmund "Pat" Brown (1905–1996) in 1962. Nixon suffered a humiliating loss that appeared to end his political prospects. He lashed out at the news media, accusing journalists of being biased against him. His problem, however, was not a hostile press. Nixon found it difficult to connect with voters and never appeared at ease in front of television cameras.

In 1964, well-organized and well-financed conservatives captured control of the Republican Party and nominated Goldwater. The Arizona senator proved to be the most self-destructive presidential candidate in American history. He ridiculed Social Security as a welfare program that should be abolished. He vowed to eliminate federal subsidies for crops, electricity, and water. He denounced labor unions. Goldwater also attacked the 1964 Civil Rights Act, arguing that business owners had the right to refuse service to anyone, regardless of race. Collectively, Goldwater alienated senior citizens, farmers, working-class whites, and African Americans.

On the foreign policy front, Goldwater called for a tougher stance against the Soviet Union and China. Jokingly, he suggested lobbing bombs into the men's room of the Soviet Kremlin. Johnson easily depicted Goldwater as unhinged. The Johnson campaign released a television spot showing a small girl being killed by an atomic bomb as she plucked the petals off a daisy. Goldwater denounced the "Daisy Girl ad" at every campaign stop. Ironically, the paid ad had only run once, but every time Goldwater mentioned it, the television networks showed the ad for free to let viewers know what Goldwater was attacking.

Anti-Goldwater Republicans understood that the senator was going to lose in a landslide. Worse, many voters were afraid that if they voted for Johnson but then chose Republicans down ticket, they would end up invalidating their ballots. They were scared of Goldwater—so scared that millions of voters, including independents and Republicans, cast a straight-line Democratic ballot. Goldwater unintentionally ended the careers of dozens of Republican House and Senate members.

Desperate Republicans asked Reagan to make a fundraising appeal. A week before the election, far too late to influence the outcome but timely enough to inject cash into the debt-ridden Republican Party, Reagan delivered a nationally televised speech. Reagan's address, which would become known as "A Time for Choosing," electrified viewers. Over eight million dollars flowed into campaign coffers (or nearly sixty-three million dollars, when adjusted for inflation). Reagan became a national political star.

There were a number of notable points in Reagan's speech. In the 29 minutes it took Reagan to speak 4,621 words, he mentioned Goldwater 7 times. Reagan told an anecdote about what a nice person Goldwater was and waved away Democrats' charges that Goldwater was going to destroy farmers. Rather than go into detail defending Goldwater, Reagan criticized Johnson, warning that the United States was drifting toward war in

Ronald Reagan's Political Odyssey: From New Deal Democrat to Conservative Republican

Arizona senator and Republican presidential nominee Barry Goldwater, 1964. Desperate Republican Party leaders turned to Ronald Reagan, asking him to do a televised fundraiser for Goldwater right before the election. While Reagan raised a great deal of money and gave himself a national political profile, he could not save Goldwater from a landslide electoral defeat. (Library of Congress)

Vietnam without a coherent strategy and that the Great Society would waste even more of the taxpayers' dollars on ineffective programs.

Unlike Goldwater, Reagan did not speak ill of Roosevelt. Indeed, Reagan concluded by deploying a stirring Roosevelt phrase—which he meshed with Lincoln: "You and I have a rendezvous with destiny. We will preserve for our children this, the last best hope of man on Earth, or we will sentence them to take the last step into a thousand years of darkness." Watching from home, viewers might have forgotten that Goldwater, not Reagan, was the Republican presidential nominee.[14]

Not only did Goldwater lose by sixteen million popular votes, he carried just six of the fifty states in the Electoral College. He did, however, win five southern, traditionally Democratic, states: Alabama, Georgia,

Louisiana, Mississippi, and South Carolina. There was reason to suspect that Goldwater's performance in those states had more than a little to do with his opposition to the 1964 Civil Rights Act. While some national Democrats were concerned with the defection of those southern states, most were confident that the Republican Party had been severely damaged—with its conservative faction wiped out.

Johnson wasted no time pushing Congress to enact his domestic agenda. As with the 1964 Civil Rights Act, the 1965 Voting Rights Act only passed thanks to the fact that more Republicans than Democrats voted for it. The 1965 Voting Rights Act provided federal enforcement to the Fifteenth Amendment, which was ratified nearly a century earlier. Once African Americans in the South could vote, segregationist Democrats either went down in defeat or adapted to a changing electorate and embraced civil rights. Others seethed, their attachment to the national Democratic Party weakening.

Beyond civil rights, the Great Society waged the War on Poverty. New federal programs emerged, including the provision of federally subsidized legal aid to the poor. Northern Democratic mayors and police chiefs resented legal aid attorneys, who filed lawsuits against them for abusive law enforcement and poor trash collection.

Meanwhile, violent crime, which disproportionately affected working-class whites and minorities, increased 100 percent in the 1960s. Urban rioting, from Los Angeles to Detroit, claimed 225 lives and caused $112 billion in property damage (or $808 billion, when adjusted for inflation). Northern working-class white voters blamed Johnson for the social disorder that filled the television airwaves.[15]

The War on Poverty included three initiatives that would haunt the federal budget balance sheet. In 1966, Congress adopted a floor, or minimum benefit, for Social Security. It was possible to work at a minimum-wage job for decades and then, upon retirement, receive a poverty-level pension based on meager payroll contributions. Creating the pension floor immediately lifted two million senior citizens out of poverty. On the other hand, the reform eliminated whatever relationship had existed between what people paid into Social Security and what they later received. In the (not so) long term, Johnson had placed Social Security on a fiscally unsustainable path. This situation would become increasingly dire as more Americans were living longer and collecting Social Security longer.

In an effort to create the framework of a national health insurance program, Johnson pushed for the enactment of Medicare and Medicaid. Medicare would provide some measure of health insurance to the elderly, while Medicaid was meant to aid the poor. The Johnson administration predicted that Medicaid would be a two-billion-dollar-a-year program by 1990. In fact, the 1990 cost was ninety billion dollars. (Adjusted for inflation, two billion dollars in 1965 would have been fifteen billion dollars in 1990.) The states, which contributed to Medicaid financing, would share in the nation's future budget dilemma. They would have to consider some combination of tax increases and reduction in spending on education, policing, and other programs to help finance Medicaid.

Johnson left future politicians to deal with the domestic problems he had helped create; the fallout from his foreign policy was more immediate. In 1964, Johnson insisted that he was the peace candidate and Goldwater was a warmonger. When North Vietnamese patrol boats attacked a U.S. destroyer in the Gulf of Tonkin, Johnson asked the Senate to pass the Gulf of Tonkin Resolution, authorizing him to respond to North Vietnamese aggression. A few senators expressed reservations, given that the wording of the resolution was open ended. Johnson assured them that he just wanted to launch a few carrier-based planes to bomb a handful of North Vietnamese naval targets at the port of Haiphong. All but two senators voted for the resolution.

After Johnson's election and as South Vietnam teetered on collapse, he used the Gulf of Tonkin Resolution as his congressional mandate to commence bombing North Vietnam in February 1965. When that failed to stop communist infiltration, Johnson deployed the first official U.S. combat troops to South Vietnam in March. Within three months, Johnson had sent 125,000 troops to South Vietnam. That number grew to over 500,000 by 1967.

Johnson did not want it to appear that the United States was at war. He feared that Congress would throw the War on Poverty overboard in order to fight a war in Vietnam. Consequently, Johnson insisted that he had no intention of escalating the war and that he wanted peace. His assurances rang hollow in the United States as he sent more troops to South Vietnam. Meanwhile, North Vietnam realized that Johnson's resolve was weak—which meant that the United States could be defeated politically, if not militarily.

As the costs of the Vietnam conflict and Great Society social welfare programs mounted, Johnson tried to avoid raising taxes or cutting spending. Doing either would have sent a message to his congressional critics that the United States was at war and had to make Vietnam its priority. Instead, Johnson oversaw rising federal budget deficits and an overheated, stressed economy that generated inflation. The post–World War II era of rising wages, as adjusted for inflation, was seemingly coming to an end.

The pretense that the United States was not at war extended into military recruitment and deployment. Unlike the practice in previous wars, Johnson generally avoided calling up National Guard and Reserve units. Guard and Reserves tended to have older, married soldiers who were settled in their communities. If deployed to Vietnam, they would be missed. Instead, Johnson relied on Selective Service to draft young men.

Given that the post–World War II "baby boom" cohort was (at that time) the largest generation in U.S. history, the draft pool was enormous. That allowed the federal government to do three things. First, focus on the eighteen- and nineteen-year-old end of the draft-eligible cohort. Such young men were less likely to be married or established in careers—and, consequently, less likely to have their absence noted in their communities. Second, rotate soldiers out of the combat theater after one year, rather than have them fight until victory (as in the case of World War II and Korea). Short tours also decreased the likelihood that soldiers' absence would be noted outside their immediate family. Third, provide II-S draft deferments for college, graduate, law, and medical students. No one would have their higher education disrupted—unless they left school or flunked out.

It took little time before the flaws in Defense Department manpower mobilization became obvious. In combat, newly arrived soldiers are the most likely to become casualties because of their lack of experience. Once teenaged troops acquired sufficient experience, they were discharged. Johnson had inadvertently increased the probability that U.S. troops would become casualties—and thus drew unwanted public and media attention to the war.

Although the number of college students tripled in the 1960s, only 17 percent came from working- and lower-middle-class backgrounds. Eighty percent of U.S. troops fighting in Vietnam came from blue-collar families. The student draft deferment became a middle- and upper-class entitlement. Americans noticed that even as defense secretary Robert

McNamara was drafting more working-class teenagers, his son Craig had a draft deferment while attending Stanford. The younger McNamara flew a North Vietnamese flag in his dorm room and smashed shop windows as part of his involvement in antiwar protests.[16]

While becoming a perpetual student was a good way to avoid Vietnam, the danger of failing courses and being expelled loomed large. Students, often with the support of liberal arts faculty, launched protests against the draft and the war. A number of campuses engaged in military-related research, hosted corporate recruiters whose companies manufactured weapons, and housed a Reserve Officers' Training Corps (ROTC) program, all three activities became targets of protest. Violent campus confrontations grew and often spilled over into local communities. In response, many campuses became radicalized, even as public resentment of higher education grew.

Campus and urban unrest divided the national Democratic Party. The antiwar faction, which drew from campus and white-collar constituencies, grew impatient with Johnson. More Democrats not only opposed the Vietnam War but also rejected Truman-based, Cold War policy of communist containment. Such Democrats also regarded working-class whites as racists who had baseless fears of crime. Other Democrats, especially in the South and in northern urban ethnic and Catholic enclaves, resented urban and campus rioters. Johnson was already buckling under domestic political pressure when North Vietnam launched the January 1968 Tet Offensive, which gave lie to his insistence that the war was nearly over.

Whereas 1960s social disorder torched Johnson's presidency, it lit Reagan's path to the White House. Since his 1964 fundraising appeal, Reagan had watched Governor Brown implode. Student unrest at the University of California at Berkeley, which had commenced prior to the 1964 election, increased. Protesting university restrictions on political speech on the campus, hundreds of students seized a campus building. Massive arrests followed. Once the Vietnam War escalated in 1965, Berkeley and Stanford students tried to prevent troop trains from moving through nearby Oakland. Brown, who had the power to appoint and fire University of California and California State University regents (and by extension presidents and chancellors), appeared unwilling to rein in student and faculty protest.

In Los Angeles, when a white police officer arrested a drunken African American motorist, a rumor spread that cops had killed their prisoner, and a "race riot" ensued. The 1965 Watts neighborhood riot led to 34 deaths and 977 burnt buildings over a 150-block area. A flustered Brown condemned the rioters but gave the impression that he blamed racism and poverty for making African Americans suspect the worst about the police. His sense that there was plenty of blame to go around did not sit well with "law-and-order" white Democrats and Republicans.

Conservatives urged Reagan to run for governor in 1966. At first, journalists and studio heads mocked Reagan, confident that he could not win the Republican primary. As Jack Warner quipped, "Jimmy Stewart for governor. Ronald Reagan for his best friend." Then Reagan won the primary. Reagan latched on to welfare spending in California. Between 1946 and 1966, welfare had gone from 2.5 percent of the California state budget to 15 percent. The number of welfare recipients went from 375,000 in 1963 to 1.5 million by 1966. Brown was not only responsible for loosening welfare eligibility requirements and therefore increasing rolls but had also led efforts to eliminate work expectations.[17]

Riding an electoral backlash against Pat Brown, Ronald Reagan won the California governorship in 1966 on a vow to crack down on urban and campus violence. (Ronald Reagan Presidential Library and Museum)

Brown and his allies were as confident as they were contemptuous of Reagan. After all, Nixon had been a former senator, vice president, and presidential candidate, and Brown destroyed him. In comparison, Reagan was an amateur who had never held a state or federal political office. Moreover, Brown believed, Reagan was an unelectable "right-wing extremist."

As Reagan gained in polling, however, the Brown campaign panicked. At first, California Democrats argued that when Reagan criticized welfare, he was really making a racist appeal to white voters. When that line of attacked failed, Brown revealed a vicious side of his character that he had hidden for years. He filmed a campaign commercial that featured children in a classroom setting. Brown told an African American child that like Reagan, Lincoln assassin John Wilkes Booth was an actor. Comparing Reagan to Booth was cringeworthy; insinuating that Reagan shared Booth's proslavery views repelled voters. Reagan benefited by Brown's commission of an unforced error. Brown lost by a million votes, with Reagan claiming 57 percent of the electorate.[18]

Democrats and Republicans alike in Washington, DC, were shocked by Reagan's victory. California had thirty-two Electoral College votes, a population of nearly sixteen million, and an economy so large that it dwarfed nearly all other countries in the world. As governor, Reagan could influence who received the Republican presidential nomination and affect the outcome of the national election. Worse, Reagan, if successful, could use the governor's office as a way station to the White House.

Governor Reagan, who served from 1967 to 1975, demonstrated that he was as much a pragmatic compromiser as he was a politician with firm convictions. Although that mixture had the potential for disaster, Reagan easily won reelection in 1970.

A "conviction" politician, Reagan believed in limiting government power over individuals. He opposed both the 1964 Civil Rights Act and the 1965 Voting Rights Act, arguing that the federal government had no constitutional right to force businesses to cater to African Americans or to monitor local elections. At the same time, Reagan argued that public school administrators had no right to investigate teachers' sexual preferences so long as the teachers did not have relations with students. Reagan vocally opposed a conservative initiative to ban gay and lesbian teachers from the public schools. He also signed a Democratic-sponsored bill to loosen restrictions on abortion in California.

Reagan alienated nearly all Black voters and aggravated moral (or social) conservatives. Conservatives, including Reagan, believed that the majority of Black voters would never leave the Democratic Party. As far as social conservatives were concerned, if they were upset with Reagan, there was no one else to support. California Democrats were embracing a morally looser political philosophy that made them even more distasteful to religious conservatives.

As a "pragmatic politician," Reagan compromised on numerous occasions. He insisted that the abortion bill would have been passed over his veto, so it made sense to get some concessions before signing it into law. Reagan had made welfare reform central to his 1966 campaign, and as governor he removed two hundred thousand people from the rolls. Statistically, however, that meant Reagan had cut the number of welfare recipients by 13 percent after Brown had increased their number by several hundred percent. Facing a deficit left behind by Brown, Reagan raised taxes.[19]

In 1966, Reagan had vowed to crack down on violent campus disrupters. In a sly put-down that circulated nationally, Reagan asserted that student radicals "act like Tarzan, look like Jane, and smell like Cheetah." (Like Bonzo, Cheetah was a chimpanzee, though not a former Reagan costar.[20])

Beyond insulting quips and an occasional show of force, Reagan's confrontation with the campus was subtle. By reducing financial support for the University of California and California State University systems, Reagan forced colleges to levy tuition on students and their parents to pay. Politically, this was a masterstroke. Working-class voters did not tend to go to college, but their tax dollars subsidized tuition. Now the upper-middle class, whose children figured prominently in radical ranks in the University of California system, had to pay. (Middle-class students at that time were more likely to enroll in the California State University system.) Reagan's higher education policy pleased white working-class voters while placing universities in the uncomfortable position of raising tuition to cover escalating operation costs.

The implosion of Johnson's presidency in 1968 gave Republicans a chance to regain the White House. Conservatives were not entirely pleased by Reagan's record but recognized that he was their best candidate. Moreover, they did not trust Nixon, who had been mapping his path back to national power for the past two years. Nixon, who saw Reagan as more of a nuisance than a threat, had the nomination sewn up in spite of conservative rumbling. The general election, however, proved challenging, and Nixon only won because former Alabama governor George Wallace ran as an independent. A self-professed segregationist, Wallace ran on a pledge to crack down on urban and campus rioting. He siphoned off a few million voters from Democratic presidential nominee Hubert Humphrey to throw the election to Nixon.

From Sacramento, Reagan watched as Nixon angered politicians across the ideological spectrum—and, in the process, gained public support. Shrewdly, Nixon abolished student draft deferments but adopted a Selective Service lottery. Once enough students knew that their draft number was high enough that they would not end up in Vietnam, campus antiwar protest largely evaporated.

Meanwhile, Nixon slowly withdrew U.S. troops from South Vietnam, while covertly bombing communist supply routes in "neutral" Laos and Cambodia. He then separated North Vietnam from its Soviet and Chinese patrons. The communist superpowers were more interested in American consumer goods and investment than in protecting North Vietnam from increased U.S. bombing. North Vietnam had no alternative but to negotiate a cease-fire. Antiwar Democrats lost one of their most important campaign issues as the Vietnam conflict faded away.

On the domestic front, Nixon claimed a few liberal Democratic policy initiatives as his own while promising law-and-order advocates a "war on drugs." In 1970, Nixon signed the bill creating the Environmental Protection Agency (EPA), establishing regulations on businesses to prevent air and water pollution and to make violators pay for cleanups, court costs, and payments to victims. A year later, Nixon endorsed Congress's creation of the Occupational Safety and Health Administration (OSHA) to protect workers from negligent employers. In 1973, Nixon announced a new federal anticrime initiative, the Drug Enforcement Administration (DEA). Taken together, the DEA, EPA, and OSHA represented an enormous expansion of federal power over corporations and a usurpation of states' authority. Conservatives complained, but his initiatives were popular, while Democrats seethed because Nixon had outmaneuvered them.

Nixon's 1972 landslide reelection victory proved to be the high point of his presidency. Campaign workers, without Nixon's knowledge, had wiretapped the Democratic National Committee headquarters at Washington's Watergate hotel. Caught in the act of replacing a defective wiretap, Nixon aides feared the news media would track the workers back to the White House. Learning of the break-in, Nixon ordered a cover-up. The problem was that he had wiretapped the Oval Office (just as Johnson had done) with Dictaphones recording phone conversations. A bipartisan congressional committee and a special prosecutor uncovered the cover-up and other Nixon crimes and abuses of power along with crimes committed by members of Nixon's staff and his reelection committee.

Members of Congress and the special prosecutor learned of the existence of the "Watergate tapes" and demanded their release. When Nixon challenged that demand, the Supreme Court unanimously ruled he had to turn over the tapes. Beyond the cover-up conversation, the recordings were a treasure trove of revelations about the bare-knuckled political nastiness of the Nixon administration. They included a1971 conversation between National Security Council head Henry Kissinger and Nixon. Nixon had observed that Governor Reagan was "shallow" and had a "limited mental capacity." Kissinger agreed and noted that Reagan's "brains are negligible." Having embarrassed and incriminated himself, Nixon resigned in 1974 rather than face impeachment and a subsequent Senate trial and conviction.[21]

Conservatives were not heartbroken when Nixon resigned. They soon found, however, that the elevation of Vice President Gerald Ford (1913–2006) to the presidency was a worse alternative. Social conservatives were horrified to learn that Ford, and his wife, Betty, were supporters of abortion and ratification of the Equal Rights Amendment (ERA). Many were convinced that the ERA would open the door to gay marriage and the drafting of women into the military—even though the draft had ended in 1973.

On the international stage, Ford, unable to rally American public opinion for a last-ditch effort to save South Vietnam and claiming that he could not defy a Democratic Congress, stood by when communists conquered South Vietnam, Cambodia, and Laos. Believing that the United States had lost its will to resist communist expansion, the Soviet Union backed insurgencies in El Salvador, Nicaragua, Guatemala, Angola,

Somalia, Ethiopia, and Yemen. The Soviets also gained a sympathetic government in bordering Afghanistan.

In 1973, prior to Nixon's resignation, the Organization of Petroleum Exporting Countries (OPEC) embargoed oil to the United States in retaliation for U.S. support of Israel during its war with Egypt and Syria. The oil embargo was yet another blow to an American economy already experiencing inflation and stagnant wage growth. As if that had not been bad enough, many U.S. industries were struggling to avoid bankruptcy. The best Ford could come up with in response was to distribute buttons with the logo, "Whip Inflation Now," or "WIN." By 1976, many Americans did not think they were winning.

Since leaving the governorship after two terms, Reagan had been delivering daily radio commentaries and enlarging his national following. Friends urged him to challenge Ford for the Republican presidential nomination. Normally, an incumbent president did not face a primary challenge, but Ford's situation was peculiar: he was an appointed, not an elected, vice president. When Vice President Spiro Agnew resigned in 1973 as bribery indictments loomed, Nixon had appointed Ford, the House minority leader from Michigan, to replace him. Ford had a legitimacy problem.

In advance of the primaries, Gerald and Betty Ford visited the Reagans in California. They tried to dissuade Reagan from running for president, but they failed. To the Fords, Reagan was a cultural reactionary and covert racist outside the Eisenhower wing of the Republican Party. President Ford asserted that whenever Reagan criticized welfare spending and singled out "welfare queens" who bore children out of wedlock in order to collect federal assistance, he was using racially coded language. Moreover, Reagan's supporters wanted to change the Republican Party platform to oppose abortion rights and the ratification of the ERA. When Ford's chief of staff, Richard Cheney, asked if he would consider a compromise and name Reagan as his running mate, his boss thundered, "Absolutely not! I don't want anything to do with that son of a b—!"[22]

The Republican primaries, beyond exposing divisions between the party's conservative and moderate factions, pointed to the formation of a new electoral coalition. Where state primaries were restricted, or closed, to registered Republican voters, Ford won. In state primaries that were "open," working-class southern white and northern Catholic Democrats handed Reagan a slew of victories. Ford insisted that Reagan's supporters would not vote for a Republican presidential nominee in the fall. He was half right: they would not vote for Ford. Reagan was picking apart the remnants of the New Deal Democratic coalition that had become alienated in the 1960s and 1970s. Such voters would become known as "Reagan Democrats."[23]

At the Republican National Convention, conservatives, led by North Carolina Republican senator Jesse Helms (1921–2008) and anti-ERA activist Phyllis Stewart Schlafly (1924–2016), partially succeeded in moving the party to the right. Ford, however, had no intention of signing off on the changes, while Betty deserved credit for denying Schlafly a platform victory.

Ford may have narrowly won the presidential nomination, but he desperately needed Reagan to make a nationally televised speech and endorse his campaign. There were similarities between Reagan's 1976 Republican National Convention address and his "Time for Choosing" speech given on behalf of Goldwater. As in 1964, Reagan barely mentioned the Republican nominee. Out of 774 words, Reagan referred to Ford by name once and three other times simply called him "president." Reagan did not discuss the nominee's proposed domestic and foreign policies. Instead, Reagan decried "the erosion of freedom taken place under Democratic rule in this country, the invasion of private rights, the controls and restrictions on the vitality of the great free economy that we enjoy." The United States needed a leader; reading between the lines made it obvious that the leader Reagan referring to was himself.[24]

Journalists and moderate Republican leaders believed that Reagan's political career had ended in 1976. It would turn out that losing the Republican presidential nomination eased the way for Reagan to win the nomination and general election for president four years later. Given the hangover Republicans still suffered from Nixon's disgrace, it would have been difficult for any party nominee to have won—though Ford ran a competitive race. Moreover, even if Reagan had won the nomination and the general election, he would have suffered what ancient China had called "the death of a thousand cuts" as president. Instead, a Democratic president would be blamed for the United States' enormous economic disruption and overseas humiliation in the late seventies.

Jimmy Carter had billed himself during the Democratic primaries and general election as an "outsider." He was a product of Georgia, far from the corrupting environment of Washington, DC. He was not a professional politician but rather a man with an established business who had entered politics later in life. Carter underscored the fact that he had been a governor, not a member of the U.S. House or Senate. That meant he had administrative experience and was used to getting results; he was not a legislator who talked and talked but achieved little. Carter also emphasized that he had been in the military during World War II, though as a Naval Academy cadet, he was not deployed. Reagan's resume was remarkably similar, except that he served two terms, not just one, as governor and spent the war in Hollywood rather than Annapolis.

Unlike many other southern Democrats, Carter repudiated the Truman Doctrine of communist containment and wanted to decrease U.S. military spending. Speaking at the 1977 University of Notre Dame commencement, Carter proclaimed, "'We are now free of that inordinate fear of communism which once led us to embrace any dictator who joined us in that fear." In the future, Carter pledged, the United States would negotiate arms reductions with the Soviet Union, criticize allies who abused their citizens' human rights, and support the liberation of oppressed people around the world.[25]

Unfortunately for Carter, the Soviet Union read Carter's words as signs of American political weakness and military retreat. Soviet leader Leonid Brezhnev (1906–1982) continued to provide advisers and weapons to communist insurgents in Latin America, Africa, the Middle East, and Asia. He also deployed more conventional weapons facing Western Europe and increased spending on nuclear missiles and delivery systems.

American allies, confronting communist insurgencies, religious uprisings, and noncommunist protest, felt betrayed by Carter. The Carter administration had failed to consider the different kinds of opposition that U.S.-aligned nations faced. In South Korea and the Philippines, quasi-military–backed dictatorships beat, tortured, and sometimes murdered dissidents. The United States had the economic and military leverage to force those two countries to reform and, given that most of their dissidents wanted democracy, not theocracy or communism, South Korea and the Philippines would emerge more politically stable and friendlier to America.

In Central America, however, there was generally not much of a democratic alternative to dictatorship. Soviet-backed insurgents in El Salvador,

Guatemala, and Nicaragua intended to replace one form of dictatorship with another but be aligned with the Soviet Union, not the United States. Carter's criticism and political pressure on Nicaragua undermined a U.S.-backed dictator and left the Soviet-supported "Sandinistas" in charge. Encouraged with their progress in Nicaragua, Soviet and Cuban advisers provided greater aid to other Central American insurgents.

Iran proved to be Carter's worst foreign policy disaster. Carter had pressured the Shah of Iran to release political prisoners and recognize the legitimacy of dissident organizations. The problem in Iran was that criticism of the Shah centered around his secular rule and desire to westernize the nation's economy and social relations—the latter of which included ensuring the right of women to vote and acquire an education. When the Shah fled, clerics, led by the exiled Ayatollah Khomeini, established an Islamic Republic. Human rights abuses soared in Iran, women's political status sharply declined, and thousands were executed. In 1979, Islamic radicals seized the U.S. Embassy in Tehran, holding 52 Americans hostage for 444 days. The news media broadcast the Iranian disaster around the world.

On the domestic economic front, Carter saw both inflation and unemployment hit double digits, leading to a stagnant, inflated economy, or "stagflation." Adding the unemployment and inflation rates together created what conservatives called "the Misery Index." As steel mills closed in the industrial heartland and Chrysler went bankrupt, Carter appeared to dart from one policy extreme to another. With Chrysler, the federal government used taxpayers' funds to bail out the automobile corporation. Other industries, however, faced a Federal Reserve policy of tight credit and higher interest rates intended to squeeze out inflation. The effect of Federal Reserve policy was to force companies to go bankrupt, fire workers and replace them with robots, or relocate their operations overseas where they could avoid U.S. taxes and environmental and safety regulations.

During the 1976 election, Carter had successfully appealed to fellow white Southern Baptists, helping him to bring back the South, which had defected to Republicans four years earlier. Carter had cultivated Jerry Falwell, the influential pastor of Virginia's enormous Thomas Road Baptist Church, as well as Virginia Pentecostal cable broadcaster Pat Robertson. Both Falwell and Robertson were disappointed when Carter failed to challenge abortion and gay rights. In 1979, Falwell founded the Moral

Majority to "educate" voters on the need to remove Carter from the White House.

Reeling under the weight of economic and foreign policy crises, confronting defections from his southern base, and barely surviving a primary challenge from the left wing of the Democratic Party, Carter believed he could defeat the Republican presidential nominee in 1980: Ronald Reagan. Most political pollsters and journalists also discounted Reagan, citing his age, extremism, and ignorance.

The late October 1980 televised debate between Carter and Reagan turned out to be an exclamation point to the president's losing campaign. Reagan was already making inroads among white, working-class Democrats in the South as well as in Michigan, Ohio, and Pennsylvania. A desperate Carter tried to use the Johnson playbook and depict Reagan as an unhinged extremist who would launch World War III. Rather than take the bait, as Goldwater had done, Reagan smiled and dismissively said, "There you go again." Those four words proved devasting: "There you go again" implied that Carter was a shrill, dishonest, and desperate man unwilling to admit his failure.

Reagan won 489 electoral votes to Carter's 49 and defeated him by 8.5 million popular votes. The son of an alcoholic, impoverished Irish Catholic shoe salesman had improbably made it to Hollywood and then the White House. Clark Clifford, who had been a legal adviser to Truman and a fixture on the Washington cocktail circuit, sneered that Reagan was an "amiable dunce" who was destined to be "a hopeless failure."[26]

NOTES

1. H. W. Brands, *Reagan: The Life* (New York: Doubleday, 2015), 11.

2. Michael Barone, *Our Country: The Shaping of America from Roosevelt to Reagan* (New York: Free Press, 1990), 43–49; William D. Leuchtenburg, *Franklin D. Roosevelt and the New Deal, 1932–1940* (New York: Harper & Row, 1963), 1, 19; Sean Dennis Cashman, *America in the Twenties and Thirties: The Olympian Age of Franklin Delano Roosevelt* (New York: New York University Press, 1989), 146.

3. "Ronald Reagan Televised Presidential Campaign Address, March 31, 1976," Ronald Reagan Presidential Library and Museum.

4. See Geoffrey C. Ward, *A First-Class Temperament: The Emergence of Franklin Roosevelt, 1905–1928* (New York: Vintage, 2014).

5. William E. Pemberton, *Exit with Honor: The Life and Presidency of Ronald Reagan* (Armonk, NY: M. E. Sharpe, 1988), 16; Steven F. Hayward, "Will the Real Ronald Reagan Please Stand Up?" *Claremont Review of Books*, August 17, 2017; Henry Olsen, "How the Right Gets Reagan Wrong," *Politico*, June 26, 2017.

6. Ronald Reagan, "Remarks at a White House Luncheon Celebrating the Centennial of the Birth of Franklin Delano Roosevelt," in *Public Papers of the Presidents of the United States: Ronald Reagan, 1982,* January 28, 1982 (Washington, DC: U.S. Government Printing Office, 1983), 89.

7. "Ronald Reagan Testimony," in House Committee on Un-American Activities, *Hearings regarding the Communist Infiltration of the Motion Picture Industry*, 80th Congress, 1st Session, October 23–24, 1947 (Washington, DC: Government Printing Office, 1947).

8. Joseph Crespino, *Strom Thurmond's America* (New York: Hill and Wang, 2012), 71; Kenneth J. Heineman, "Catholics, Communists, and Conservatives: The Making of Cold War Democrats on the Pittsburgh Front," *U.S. Catholic Historian* 34 (Fall 2016): 25–54.

9. Matthew Dallek, *The Right Moment: Ronald Reagan's First Victory and the Decisive Turning Point in American Politics* (New York: Free Press, 2000), 32.

10. Lou Cannon, "Nancy Reagan, an Influential and Protective First Lady, Dies at 94," *New York Times*, March 6, 2016.

11. Ibid.

12. Pemberton, *Exit with Honor*, 51.

13. Robert Alan Goldberg, *Barry Goldwater* (New Haven, CT: Yale University Press, 1995), 50, 99; Rick Perlstein, *Before the Storm: Barry Goldwater and the Unmaking of the American Consensus* (New York: Nation Books, 2009), 20–21, 27, 29, 84.

14. Dallek, *Right Moment*, 67–68.

15. Stephen Lesher, *George Wallace: American Populist* (Reading, MA: Addison-Wesley, 1994), 350.

16. Tom Wells, *The War Within: America's Battle over Vietnam* (Berkeley: University of California Press, 1994), 107–8.

17. Dallek, *Right Moment*, 180.

18. Andrew Glass, "Republicans Nominate Reagan for Governor, June 7, 1966," *Politico*, June 7, 2010.

19. John Ehrman, *The Eighties: America in the Age of Reagan* (New Haven, CT: Yale University Press, 2005), 17–18.

20. Pemberton, *Exit with Honor*, 69.

21. David Corn, "Nixon on Tape: Reagan was 'Shallow' and of 'Limited Mental Capacity,'" *Mother Jones*, November 16, 2007.

22. Kenneth J. Heineman, *God Is a Conservative: Religion, Politics, and Morality in Contemporary America* (New York: New York University Press, 2005), 76–78; Craig Shirley, "How Gerald Ford Beat Ronald Reagan at the Last Contested Convention," *Washington Post*, April 22, 2016.

23. Heineman, *God Is a Conservative*, 78.

24. Ronald Reagan, "Republican National Convention Speech, August 19, 1976," Ronald Reagan Presidential Library and Museum.

25. "Text of President's Commencement Address at Notre Dame," *New York Times*, May 23, 1977.

26. Heineman, *God Is a Conservative*, 124.

CHAPTER 2

"TEAR DOWN THIS WALL!": FOREIGN POLICY IN THE TIME OF REAGAN

Like Jack Reagan, Welcher Jordan led a nomadic existence in search of work, though he ranged much wider—from Oklahoma to Illinois. Jordan did not have much financial success in the 1920s, a common outcome for all but a few oil wildcatters. Although Jordan wanted to strike it rich, he maintained an abiding suspicion of the wealthy—especially those who made their money on Wall Street. His Oklahoma forebears had been active in the Peoples' (Populist) Party in the 1890s, advocating for the federal regulation of financiers and the nationalization of railroads.

In 1926, Welcher and wife Leona welcomed a daughter into the family—Jeane Jordan. Ten years later, they had a son. By the time Jeane graduated from high school in Illinois, Welcher and Leona recognized that their daughter was uncommonly bright. Jeane Jordan enrolled in a two-year program of study at Stephens College, a women's school in Columbia, Missouri. She exhibited a keen passion for politics—both as a student and as an activist.

Jeane Jordan's academic performance at Stephens opened the door for her to move to New York City and enroll at Barnard College—one of the most elite women's colleges in the United States. As a political science major, she intently watched the 1948 presidential election. More than half of Progressive Party nominee Henry Wallace's voters, and nearly all his campaign contributions, came from New York City, so young Jordan had an ideal perch from which to watch the election unfold.

She regarded Wallace as a naïve, unwitting tool of the Soviet Union. Segregationist Strom Thurmond was repulsive, and Republican presidential nominee Thomas Dewey seemed inauthentic. Harry Truman, however, not only had a smart foreign policy but also knew how to speak plainly to people. Jordan enthusiastically cast her first presidential ballot for Truman.

Two years after Truman's victory, Jordan earned a master's in political science from Columbia University. Mentors were impressed with Jordan's analytical skills and recommended her for a position in the Intelligence and Research Bureau of the U.S. State Department. Jordan joined a Washington agency that had only come into existence in 1947. Prior to 1947, the bureau had been a part of the Office of Strategic Services (OSS), the United States' first centralized intelligence collection and covert operations agency, created during World War II. When the OSS became the Central Intelligence Agency (CIA) in 1947, the State Department got its own analytical and operations division.

Jordan was not only one of the few women in the bureau but also among a handful who had not served in the OSS or the military. The OSS had been a peculiar fraternity of academics and adventurers. Its membership ranged from the dissolute sons of billionaires (Paul Mellon) to scrappy middle-class Irish Catholics who were not welcome at New York City's "white shoe" law firms (William J. Casey, 1913–1987). OSS operatives had infiltrated German and Japanese lines, coordinated guerrilla operations, and brought Nazi war criminals to trial at Nuremberg. Some returned to their playboy ways after the war, but others reenlisted to fight the Cold War.

While working at the bureau, Jeane Jordan met Evron Kirkpatrick, an OSS veteran fifteen years her senior. They married, had three sons together, and rose in their respective careers. He became the head of the American Political Science Association, while she finished her doctorate in political science at Columbia in 1968, a year after accepting an assistant professorship at Georgetown University in Washington.

Jeane Kirkpatrick (1926–2006) had entered academe at a time when thousands of students and faculty were protesting the role higher education had been playing in Cold War military and intelligence research. Georgetown had been training students in diplomacy and global politics for decades. The Cold War, and proximity to the U.S. diplomatic and intelligence community, transformed sleepy Catholic Georgetown into a major player in the formulation of U.S. foreign policy. Now Georgetown had hired a well-rounded Cold Warrior with hands-on experience as an intelligence analyst as well as a dissertation on Latin American politics.

The violent antiwar protests at the 1968 Democratic National Convention aroused disgust among Kirkpatrick and her circle of friends in the academic and intelligence communities. Four years later, antiwar forces won, nominating South Dakota senator George McGovern for president. McGovern, as a graduate student in history at Northwestern University in 1948, had campaigned for Henry Wallace. The Vietnam War, in

UN Ambassador Jeane Kirkpatrick. Kirkpatrick was one of the key architects of Reagan's foreign policy. (Courtesy of Kenneth Heineman)

McGovern's mind, was part of a larger evil: the Truman Doctrine of communist containment. Although McGovern suffered a crushing defeat at the hands of Richard Nixon in 1972, he commanded a legion of followers in the Democratic Party who had renounced American Cold War foreign policy. Like Ronald Reagan, Kirkpatrick felt that a wrong-headed Democratic Party had left her without a political home.

Despite Jimmy Carter's overtures to Kirkpatrick in 1976 to join his team, she remained unconvinced that he would bring the Democratic Party back to its senses. Henry Fowler, Truman's former secretary of the treasury, shared Kirkpatrick's concerns. Operating out of Washington's Metropolitan Club, an exclusive organization of public officials founded in 1863, Fowler helped establish the Committee on the Present Danger. The committee's 182 members included veteran Democrats such as Fowler, Kirkpatrick, and Johnson administration adviser Eugene Rostow. There were also Republicans—notably Richard Allen, William Casey, and John Lehman.[1]

President Jimmy Carter (1977–1981). Little went right for Jimmy Carter, and much went wrong during his presidency, resulting in his defeat for reelection in 1980 and the Republican capture of the Senate for the first time since 1954. (Library of Congress)

Many, but not all, the committee members acquired a news media tagline: neoconservatives, or "neocons." Hostile critics on the Left and the Right regarded the neocon label as an insulting description of Cold War Democrats who had changed parties but never lost their affection for Truman and Roosevelt. The committee attracted a member who, though not a neocon, otherwise perfectly fit that label: Ronald Reagan.

In the 1970s, the Committee on the Present Danger saw little but discouraging trends for national defense. Drug addiction among troops remained high, a legacy of the Vietnam War. Anywhere from thirty-seven thousand to sixty thousand troops in Vietnam had become addicted to heroin on a yearly basis. In 1971, a psychiatrist working at a stateside rehabilitation clinic that treated veterans observed,

> Vietnam in many ways is a ghetto for the enlisted man. The soldiers don't want to be here, their living conditions are bad, they are surrounded by privileged classes, namely their officers; there is accepted use of violence and there is promiscuous sex. They react the way they do in the ghetto. They take drugs and try to forget.[2]

Although the Vietnam War had ended, and the United States adopted an all-volunteer military in 1973, drug abuse, as well as violent crime, continued to be endemic within the armed forces. Additionally, military pay was so low that spouses often had to find work or go on welfare to support their families. It was no surprise that enlistment in the armed forces fell 32 percent below quota goals even though the military was simultaneously reducing its size. Desperate, the military lowered educational, mental, and physical standards in an effort to make up the shortfall. Fully 28 percent of marines in the 1970s had not graduated from high school—a proportion that was nearly twice the average of their peers.[3]

The class divide that the Vietnam War had exposed between those who went into the armed forces and those who had the financial means to avoid it widened with the creation of the all-volunteer military. Even with the elimination of the draft, students at elite universities in the 1970s continued to fear that it would be reinstated. Berkeley easily rallied two thousand students to participate in demonstrations against a nonexistent draft. At upper-middle-class Northwestern University outside Chicago, 46 percent of male students vowed never to fight for the United States.

At the equally elite University of Michigan, 52 percent of male students opposed the idea of even starting up registration for a draft. The proportion of women at those campuses who were opposed to future wars and drafts was higher.[4]

A Northwestern student captured the spirit of the campus scene in the 1970s: "I don't think the government could ever convince me that the Soviets are on some kind of rampage until they start dropping bombs on us." He was not alone in his suspicion of the military and government. During the 1960s and early 1970s, many elite colleges had either forced the Reserve Officers' Military Training Corps (ROTC) program off campus or eliminated it altogether—as was the case at Columbia and Yale. Overall ROTC enrollment fell 75 percent between 1967 and 1973; it did not recover for the balance of the 1970s.[5]

Participation in ROTC held steady at campuses that enrolled lower-middle-class students, mainly at southern state and public regional universities. Not surprisingly, 60 percent of male students at the University of Oklahoma favored draft registration—even as a prelude to a restoration of compulsory military service. The 1970s gave the United States a working-class, largely impoverished, and heavily southern military led by lower-middle-class officers who were often the first members of their families to go to college. The elites who had filled the ranks of the OSS had few heirs.[6]

Anticommunist Democrats and Republicans identified other troubling trends in U.S. defense and national security. While Carter had not embraced the drastic defense-spending cuts that McGovern had proposed in 1972, he saw unrestrained military spending as a contributor to Cold War tensions. He advocated a modest five- to seven-billion-dollar reduction in overall defense spending—a cut of less than 5 percent. Carter saved tens of billions of dollars by not contracting for the construction of the B-1 bomber to replace the aging B-52 fleet. He also envisioned savings by proposing to hand the Panama Canal, and responsibility for its defense, over to the Panamanian government and drawing down U.S. forces in South Korea.[7]

Carter had followed Nixon's lead by staging a second round of Strategic Arms Limitations Talks (SALT) with the Soviet Union. One of the key agreements Carter reached with Soviet leader Leonid Brezhnev was to build no more than one antiballistic missile (ABM) site in their respective countries. By limiting the ability of both sides to shoot down incoming nuclear missiles, Carter believed, the superpowers would not try to overwhelm each other's defense by procuring and then firing more missiles. The Soviet Union and the United States could turn away from nuclear escalation secure in the knowledge that each nation held the other hostage. Carter reaffirmed the doctrine of "mutual assured destruction" (MAD).

Most disturbing, at least to the activists in the Committee on the Present Danger, Carter delivered a speech in 1977 at the University of Notre Dame commencement in which he declared that the struggle for universal human rights and democracy had begun: "I believe we can have a foreign policy that is democratic, that is based on fundamental values, and that uses power and influence, which we have, for humane purposes. We can also have a foreign policy that the American people both support and, for a change, know about and understand." Very few pro-American nations could live up to Carter's high moral standards; it was doubtful that even the United States could.[8]

One sentence of Carter's speech landed like a punch in the gut to anticommunists because it seemed as if he had declared that the Cold War was over: "Being confident of our own future, we are now free of that inordinate fear of communism which once led us to embrace any dictator who joined us in that fear." As the Cold Warriors viewed matters, Carter had minimized Soviet abuses while condemning valued, though less-than-democratic, allies.[9]

President Gerald Ford had tried to outflank neoconservative foreign policy critics in 1975 by authorizing CIA director George Herbert Walker Bush (1924–2018) to form a sixteen-member "Team B" to access Soviet military capabilities and expenditures. "Team A," the career government analysts who spanned the administrations of Kennedy, Johnson, Nixon, and Ford, argued in their National Intelligence Estimates that the Soviet Union devoted less than 14 percent of its Gross National Product (GNP) to the military. Given that the Soviet GNP was much lower than the U.S. GNP, its military expenditures, Team A concluded, were minimal and posed little threat to the United States and its allies.

Team B, led by Harvard historian and neoconservative Richard Pipes, argued that the Soviet Union was spending at least a quarter of its GNP on the military. Ford had hoped that allowing Team B's outsiders access to classified information would convince them of the error of their ways. It had just the opposite outcome, and Ford left Carter to deal with Team B's escalating criticism of U.S. defense spending. As for Pipes, he joined the Committee on the Present Danger. He was still a Democrat, holding out the hope that Cold Warriors such as his friend Senator Henry Jackson of Washington would defeat the party's McGovern faction.

Team A's and Team B's sharply contrasting analyses of Soviet military capabilities and economic resources devoted to weapons' expenditures were partly a product of clashing ideological agendas. But the fundamental reason both sides disputed the other's assessments was simple: getting reliable intelligence out of the Soviet Union was difficult. The Soviet Union maintained tight control over information and kept its own citizens in the dark. U.S. diplomat George Kennan, who was an architect of communist containment in the Truman administration, had warned that the Soviet Union reliably produced just three products: bluster, paranoia, and secrecy. Foreigners, as well as lower-ranking Soviet officials, could never be entirely certain whether military contractors produced quality weapons, what the government spent (on anything), and how much money disappeared in a vodka-induced haze of corruption.

Although anticommunist Republicans and Democrats were unified behind Team B's assessment, they were less so when it came to the issue of surrendering U.S. control over the Panama Canal. William F. Buckley Jr. (1925–2008), the editor and founder of the leading conservative magazine in the United States, the *National Review*, regarded the handover of the Panama Canal to be the smart diplomatic initiative. Republican Senate minority leader Howard Baker of Tennessee and former Nixon adviser Henry Kissinger supported Ford, and then Carter, in negotiating new treaty arrangements with Panama.

Reagan, in contrast, was a vocal opponent. A major part of Reagan's opposition to the Ford-Carter Panama deal drew upon a vast reservoir of anticommunism: "It should never surprise us that whenever the United States withdraws its presence or its strong interest from any areas, the Soviets are ready, willing, and often able to exploit the situation. Can we believe that the Panama Canal is any exception?" The other factors driving Reagan's opposition received less attention. He feared that a future Panamanian government, whether it was a military dictatorship or under communist control, would neglect maintenance of the canal, extort bribes from shippers, and allow passage of South American narcotics to the United States.[10]

Although the Democratic Senate ratified the new treaty arrangements with Panama in 1978, Carter's foreign policy triumph came with a cost. Most Americans opposed the deal, seeing it, as Reagan did, as just another post-Vietnam retreat for the United States. Baker, who had presidential ambitions in 1980, made himself unacceptable to the Republican Party's conservative faction. Moreover, several of the Democratic senators who were most active in the Panama Canal negotiations would go down in defeat in 1980. Their position on the Panama Canal gave conservatives an effective line of attack. While the public might not follow the bureaucratic struggle between Team A and Team B over Soviet GNP priorities, Americans could understand Reagan when he said of the canal, "We bought it. We built it. We paid for it. We intend to keep it."[11]

Carter did score one foreign policy success in the Camp David Accords of 1978 that brought together Israeli Prime Minister Menachem Begin (1913–1992) and President Anwar Sadat (1918–1981) of Egypt and resulted in Egypt's recognition of Israel's legitimacy as a nation, a framework for peace that included Israel allowing Palestinians in the West Bank and Gaza to govern themselves, and the restoration of Israel's access to the Suez Canal, among several agreements. Although Israel reneged in part regarding Palestinian governance and Sadat was assassinated in 1981 by Islamic extremists, the basic accord held during Reagan's presidency and allowed for attention elsewhere in the region.

That said, the seemingly endless series of foreign policy crises Carter experienced in 1979 not only undermined his presidency but also set the stage for Reagan to launch a fundamental overhaul in American strategic thinking. In February 1979, revolutionaries forced the terminally ill Shah of Iran into exile and then proclaimed an Islamic Republic. The new Iranian government, when not staging anti-American demonstrations for the international news media, tortured and often executed its citizens for listening to American music, for dancing, and, if they were women, for insisting that they had equal rights.

A world away, in the Central American nation of Nicaragua, Cuban-backed insurgents seized power in July 1979 from a pro-American dictator. The "Sandinistas," who named themselves for an assassinated Nicaraguan revolutionary in the 1920s, built up their military with Soviet and Cuban aid. Soon, Sandinistas were funneling weapons and advisers to comrades in El Salvador and Guatemala.

Jeane Kirkpatrick looked upon the Iranian and Nicaraguan revolutions with horror, convinced that they were of a piece of Carter's flawed foreign policy vision. She labored over an essay that the neoconservative magazine *Commentary* published on November 1, 1979. Her essay, "Dictatorships and Double Standards," confirmed Reagan's dim view of Carter and helped him formulate a foreign policy vision that he would take to the White House.

Kirkpatrick began with the contention that the "crowning achievement" of Carter's foreign policy had been the "transfer of the Panama Canal from the United States to a swaggering Latin dictator of Castroite [Cuban communist] bent." That early line in her influential essay grabbed Reagan's attention. She then went on to observe that "the 'Marxist' presence [in the world] is ignored and/or minimized by American officials and by the elite media." That formulation lumped McGovern, Ford, Carter, the CIA, and the *New York Times* together as an indistinguishable mass of incompetency and mediocrity.[12]

Her most important point, however, was this: the United States had to distinguish between pro-American authoritarians and communist totalitarians. Condemning the human rights abuses of America's allies, while soft-pedaling communists' human rights abuses in the name of global cooperation, was a self-defeating double standard. Moreover, authoritarian regimes, while perhaps abusive of their own people, did not typically subvert and invade their neighbors. Totalitarian regimes, on the other hand, financed insurgencies and invaded neighbors. The Shah of Iran was preferable to Cuba's Fidel Castro and should have been supported, not undermined, by Carter.

It was a quirk of history that Kirkpatrick's essay appeared just as two major events rocked the international order. Three days after the publication of "Dictatorships and Double Standards," Iranian militants seized the U.S. Embassy in Tehran and took fifty-two hostages. Although international law regarded the seizure of embassies as an act of war, Carter preferred negotiation to confrontation. The world media showed up to film American hostages and joyous demonstrations on U.S. Embassy grounds. Carter, and by extension, America, appeared to have been terrorized into submission. When Carter finally attempted a military rescue of the hostages, the effort failed before it began—making the United States appear to be even weaker.

On Christmas Day, 1979, the Soviet Union invaded neighboring Afghanistan. Reagan, Kirkpatrick, and even a shocked Carter interpreted the invasion as an exercise in Soviet imperialism. Since World War II, the Soviet Union had had proxies, whether China in the 1950s or Cuba in the 1970s, do its fighting. Although the Soviet Union had militarily intervened to put down uprisings in Hungary (1956) and Czechoslovakia (1968), those two nations had been part of its Eastern European empire. Afghanistan had not been behind the "Iron Curtain," nor did the Soviet Union send proxies. Soviet military intervention in Afghanistan, according to American anticommunists, had to be part of a larger strategy to move into the Middle East and gain control of the region's oil fields.

American policy, first tentatively under Carter and then fiercely under Reagan, would be fixed on driving the Soviet Union out of Afghanistan. In this instance, however, anticommunists had misread Soviet intentions. Brezhnev had wanted to maintain a pro-Soviet regime in Afghanistan but not necessarily because he planned to conquer the Middle East. He feared that Iran's Islamic Revolution would spread to Afghanistan and then to the forty million Muslims who lived in the Soviet Union. The Soviets could not afford to have another radicalized nation on its borders. Additionally, Afghanistan was a major producer of opium, which, when refined, became the heroin smuggled into the Soviet Union. Brezhnev believed that if Afghanistan became destabilized, Islamic revolutionaries and narcotics traffickers would next undermine the Soviet Empire.

The Soviet invasion of Afghanistan and the Iranian hostage crisis were not the only issues that doomed Carter's reelection—there were also damaging economic and social developments. In the 1950s, conservatives who clustered around the *National Review* had argued that anticommunism could be the ideological glue to fuse together a coalition of economic, social, and foreign policy conservatives. The essence of communism, after all, was its insistence on the creation of an all-powerful state bureaucracy. Economic conservatives who championed a free market were fundamentally anticommunist. Although social conservatives often considered moral issues to be more important than economic matters, they feared Soviet (or possibly U.S. government) imposition of secular values on society.

So long as there was a Cold War, Republican conservatives believed that they had a chance to build a winning electoral coalition and peel away morally traditional, anticommunist Democrats. Reagan was the leader, as well as the embodiment, of such a coalition.

Political pundits offered a key insight into what was first required to build a successful presidency: "Personnel is policy." From a Hollywood perspective, which had served Reagan well over the decades, that meant a good film had to have a solid cast. One star might draw the public's attention to the production, but if you wanted to keep the audience's attention and sell more tickets, you had to have strong, appealing figures in the supporting roles. Prima donnas, however, were not welcome, though sometimes they did not reveal their bad behavior until after production began.

For the core of his foreign policy personnel, Reagan selected fifty-one members from the Committee on the Present Danger. Richard Pipes became a National Security Council adviser on Soviet Affairs and William Casey headed the CIA. Two figures who had served time in the Nixon administration, investment banker John Lehman and Hoover Institution think tank analyst Richard Allen became, respectively, secretary of the navy and national security adviser. Allen had been advising Reagan on foreign affairs since 1977. Although born in 1942, Lehman's background did have an OSS flair about it. He was a Jesuit-educated aircraft carrier pilot and financial expert who had earned a doctorate in international relations from the University of Pennsylvania.

Kirkpatrick's title of U.S. ambassador to the United Nations (UN) appeared to be modest when compared to the offices Allen, Casey, Lehman, and Pipes received. That impression was mistaken. She was the vocal "big-picture" strategist in the Reagan cabinet and used the UN as a world stage from which to defend U.S. foreign policy and denounce communist totalitarians. Kirkpatrick's public stature became so great she received a recurring role in Berkeley Breathed's popular comic strip, *Bloom County*. In *Bloom County*, Kirkpatrick pursued a love affair with "Bill the Cat," sending him a large chocolate shaped like Nicaragua and a note that read, "Let's devour it together." (Flattered, Kirkpatrick requested, and received from Breathed, an autographed original of the template "celluloid" to display in her office.)[13]

Of the multiple foreign policy issues that loomed large in the early 1980s, Reagan and Kirkpatrick worked most closely on countering Soviet, Cuban, and Nicaraguan influence in Central America. Reagan dedicated

CIA director William J. Casey and Ronald Reagan. Casey's role in covert operations in Central America and Afghanistan was an important part of Reagan's strategy of exerting military pressure on the Soviet Union. (Ronald Reagan Presidential Library and Museum)

economic support to Central American countries resisting communist insurgents, provided funds for weapons procurement, and directed the U.S. military to train soldiers in El Salvador, Guatemala, and Honduras. The Reagan administration made it clear that while Nicaragua may have allied with the Soviet Union, it might still be wrested back by supporting the Contras, a counterrevolutionary band covertly aided by the CIA. In 1983, Reagan demonstrated that communist revolutions could be reversed, sending 7,600 troops to the Caribbean island of Grenada, where they routed several hundred Cubans.

In addresses to Congress and the public, Reagan urged Americans to pay closer attention to their backyard. He observed that "El Salvador is nearer to Texas than Texas is to Massachusetts," just as San Antonio was closer to Nicaragua than that it was to Washington. If the communists won in Central America, a cycle of violence and misery would send millions of refugees flooding into the United States—mostly to border states such as Texas. Americans living in the Southwest understood the stakes, even if elites living in far-off New England did not.[14]

Reagan argued, "Violence has been Nicaragua's most important export to the world" and that "Nicaragua is a communist dictatorship armed to the teeth, tied to Cuba and the Soviet Union, which oppresses its people and threatens its neighbors." The people of El Salvador, Reagan contended, wanted to have democratic elections but found it difficult, given that Nicaraguan-backed communist insurgents were murdering those who stood for freedom.[15]

At the UN, Kirkpatrick insisted that the best way for America to promote human rights in El Salvador was to crush the communist insurgents. She also argued that "the legitimate democratic government" of El Salvador was winning the insurgency. There was, however, a threat to Central American democracy just as menacing as Nicaragua and Cuba: congressional Democrats. Kirkpatrick observed that there were members of Congress aiding "Marxist forces" in Central America. Other Democrats were embracing a policy of "self-defeating appeasement" when it came to communist Nicaragua.[16]

Four of the five leading Democratic "appeasers," whom Kirkpatrick did not name, came from Massachusetts—the only state McGovern had carried in 1972. That was the reason Reagan had pointedly informed the American people that Texas was closer to the combat theater in Central America than faraway Massachusetts.

Congressman Edward Boland amended funding legislation for the Department of Defense in 1982, 1983, and 1984 to prohibit Reagan from providing military aid to the Nicaraguan Contras. Speaker of the House Thomas "Tip" O'Neill (1912–1994) supported Boland, arguing that the Contras were "murderers, marauders, and rapists." Lieutenant Governor, and soon-to-be U.S. senator, John Kerry warned that Nicaragua would become another Vietnam War. Governor Michael Dukakis refused to allow the Massachusetts National Guard to participate in military exercises in Central America. He unsuccessfully sued the federal government, contending that Reagan, unlike Presidents Wilson, Roosevelt, Truman, and Eisenhower, did not have the constitutional authority to deploy the Guard outside the United States. (Both Dukakis and Kerry became unsuccessful Democratic presidential nominees.)[17]

The fifth prominent Democratic critic of Reagan's Central American policy was Carter's CIA director, Stansfield Turner. Turner argued that Reagan and CIA head Casey were "politicizing intelligence" to advance their anticommunist ideological agenda. He also informed anyone within earshot that Reagan was "stupid." Before the 1980s, it had been rare for officials from a previous administration to attack their successors in public. It was especially rare for someone highly placed in the intelligence community to be vocally partisan.[18]

Although Reagan scored some successes against the communists in Central America, he was less successful in dealing with revolutionary Iran in particular and the Middle East in general. Iran had released its American hostages before Reagan's 1981 inauguration. While Iranian leaders believed that Reagan would have launched an attack if they had not turned over their prisoners, there were other considerations in play. First, and foremost, Iranian revolutionaries had achieved their primary objective: humiliate the United States and destroy the credibility of its president. Second, Iraqi dictator Saddam Hussein had launched an invasion of Iran in the fall of 1980. Hussein, who led a secular, nationalist regime, feared the spread of Iran's brand of revolutionary Islam into Iraq. Iran had to turn its attention to fighting a war that killed hundreds of thousands of people on both sides.

The Iranian-Iraqi War (1980–1988) posed its own set of problems for the United States. Reagan, along with the rulers of Kuwait and Saudi Arabia, leaned toward Iraq, with Arab leaders providing weapons to Hussein. Meanwhile, France, a longtime U.S. ally, gave Iraq technical aid, which included the construction of a nuclear reactor to help provide the nation with electrical power since Iran was threatening its ability to drill and export oil. In 1981, Israel, which was also a U.S. friend, used American-built warplanes to bomb Iraq's reactor. Israeli leaders did not inform Reagan of their intentions, fearful that the United States would warn Hussein. The Israeli government claimed that Iraq's nuclear power program was a front for the development of atomic weapons that it would use against Israel. America's Arab allies were outraged, blaming Reagan for not reining in Israel. At the UN, Kirkpatrick joined the Security Council in condemning Israel's military action and praising Iraq's restraint and "cooperative spirit."[19]

Reagan's difficulties with Israel escalated. In 1975, a civil war had broken out in Lebanon, pitting Muslims against Christians (mainly Eastern Rite Catholics). Taking advantage of the chaos, Yasser Arafat, the leader of the Palestinian Liberation Organization (PLO), set up operations in Lebanon. Founded in 1964, the PLO dedicated itself to bringing down Israel and replacing it with a Palestinian state. PLO tactics included terror bombings, airplane hijackings, and assassinations. In 1972, a PLO affiliate,

Black September, had staged a dramatic operation that captured world attention: the slaughter of eleven Israelis at the Munich Summer Olympics.

Wishing to deprive the PLO of a major operating base, Israel invaded Lebanon in 1982. Caught between the Israeli military and the PLO were tens of thousands of Lebanese who were killed or wounded. Reagan contacted Israeli leader Menachem Begin and denounced the "holocaust" he had unleashed on the Lebanese people. Begin furiously reacted to Reagan's use of the term "holocaust," to which the president replied that he had deployed it deliberately. Privately, Reagan noted, "Israel has lost a lot of world sympathy." He instructed Kirkpatrick to say nothing while the UN Security Council called for a cease-fire. Officially, the United States hoped to avoid an outright condemnation of the Israeli invasion, though unofficially Reagan wanted Israel out of Lebanon.[20]

Israeli prime minister Menachem Begin, whose attack on Iraq and invasion of Lebanon in the early 1980s made it difficult for Ronald Reagan to conduct a productive foreign policy in the Middle East. (Library of Congress)

In an attempt to impose stability in the capital city of Beirut, Reagan dispatched several hundred troops to Lebanon's capital. France, which had colonial-era ties to Lebanon, also sent peacekeeping forces. What Reagan did not appreciate, however, was that while the Israeli victory against the PLO may have slayed the Arab nationalist dragon, the invasion had rallied tens of thousands to the cause of radicalized Islam. An Iranian-backed organization, *Hezbollah* ("Party of God") formed in 1982 and became a political player in Lebanon. A year later, in the fall of 1983, *Hezbollah* fighters drove trucks laden with explosives into the American and French military compounds. The suicide bombers killed 58 French troops and 241 U.S. service members. It was the worst loss of U.S. military personnel since the Vietnam War.

Unlike Johnson, who would have seen the *Hezbollah* attack as a compelling reason to deploy more troops, Reagan withdrew from Lebanon. Secretary of Defense Caspar Weinberger, along with most of Reagan's military advisers, had never held out much hope that Lebanon could be salvaged. They favored withdrawal. Many Democrats who had been accusing Reagan of being a militarist were caught off guard. They found themselves in the uncomfortable position of denouncing a policy decision that they had been advocating. Most disconcerting to Democratic critics, public opinion polls showed that Americans blamed Islamic terrorists, not Reagan, for the loss of U.S. troops.

Israel's actions in Iraq and Lebanon exposed divisions within the Democratic and Republican parties. In 1978, the Congressional Black Caucus, which was a growing political force inside the Democratic Party, had denounced Israel as an ally of racism in Africa, the Middle East, and the United States. This was one of the many reasons Cold War Democrats such as Kirkpatrick had become neoconservative supporters of Reagan. Many neoconservatives, though not all, were Jews as well as Zionists; in their eyes, Israel could do no wrong. Any criticism of Israel was, to neoconservatives, anti-Semitic.

Kirkpatrick walked a fine line: she considered herself to be a staunch friend of Israel but believed it served no one's interest to not tell an ally when it was behaving badly. She avoided being labeled an anti-Semite by *Commentary*, the *Public Interest*, and other neoconservative media outlets. There could be no doubt that Kirkpatrick wanted to protect Israel from its enemies.

Other Reagan officials, however, were hostile to Israel and earned neoconservative scorn. Former Nixon administration staffer and journalist Patrick J. Buchanan became a lightning rod as soon as he accepted the offer to become Reagan's director of communications in 1985. He had complained in 1976 of a "Jewish lobby" influencing U.S. foreign policy. Buchanan subsequently argued that the PLO had legitimate grievances and was harshly critical of Israel's invasion of Lebanon. He lasted two years before resigning and never held another White House appointment.[21]

Domestic politics aside, the Lebanese disaster had given Iran a successful follow-up to its triumphant seizure of the U.S. Embassy in Tehran. *Hezbollah* became the Lebanese government in all but name and operated with impunity. With Iranian financing and personnel, *Hezbollah* kidnapped, tortured, and executed American intelligence agents—making sure that Reagan obtained recordings of the proceedings. Iran's operatives also assassinated political rivals in Lebanon, often with car bombs.

In spite of the United States' poor record in dealing with revolutionary Iran, National Security Council staffer Oliver North (1943–) and National Security Advisor Robert McFarlane concocted a plan that they believed would curry favor with Tehran and circumvent the congressional prohibition against funding the Contras in Nicaragua. Both North and McFarlane had served in the U.S. Marines in Vietnam. While their combat experiences had affected them profoundly, their reaction to antiwar protestors was even greater. Despite Reagan's insistence that he could get congressional Democrats to lift Boland's restrictions on Contra funding, North and McFarlane did not share his optimism.

Their scheme was one part James Bond and one part Wile E. Coyote. Although the United States had labeled Iran a terrorist state and prohibited weapons sales to the regime, North and McFarlane knew Tehran was desperate for missiles in its war with Iraq. Using Israel as a conduit, North and McFarlane moved hundreds of antitank and antiaircraft missiles to Iran. In 1985, McFarlane and North made a secret trip to Iran, where they charged dearly for the weapons. They insisted that American hostages held in Lebanon would be released in exchange for the missiles. With the proceeds from the weapons sale, North and McFarlane purchased weapons for the Contras. North even brought a cake to the Iranian negotiating table as a sign of friendship.

It did not take long for North and McFarlane's plan to sour. First, Reagan was able to convince House Democrats to remove restrictions on Contra funding, meaning that North and McFarlane had broken the law for no reason—and armed a terrorist regime to boot. Second, Iran's allies in Lebanon, after releasing the hostages whose freedom North and McFarlane had negotiated, simply took a fresh batch of American prisoners. And third, in 1986 Iranian government officials leaked the entire story to *Al Shiraa*, a receptive Arabic magazine published in Beirut. It took North and McFarlane by surprise that an anti-American, anti-Zionist Iranian government would want to embarrass the United States and Israel and set off a political firestorm in Washington.

After an internal investigation, Reagan administration officials discovered that the principal players had diverted funds from the Iranian arms sales to purchase weapons for the Contras. Congressional Democrats seized upon what became known as the "Iran-Contra Scandal." Highly publicized congressional hearings forced Reagan to admit that he knew about the arms deal with Iran but not the Contra aspect of the operation. As with the 1983 Beirut disaster, Reagan's public approval ratings briefly slipped and then dramatically rebounded. While some Democrats, mainly in the news media and in higher education, talked about impeaching Reagan, there was no groundswell of congressional or public support for such an action.

There was one bright spot for Reagan's foreign policy in the Middle East: Afghanistan. The Soviet invasion had provoked exactly what Brezhnev had feared: a revolutionary Islamic *jihad*, a religious war. Holy Warriors (*mujahideen*) mobilized for action. Many were from the ethnic Pashtun region that bordered Pakistan. Islamic radicals from across the Middle East traveled to Pakistan, Iran, and Afghanistan to fight the Soviet Union; among them was the son of a wealthy Saudi contractor, Osama Bin Laden. Like the United States in Vietnam, the Soviet Union fought an insurgency with massive artillery barrages and aerial bombing. Perhaps as many as one million Afghanis died. The more Afghanis killed in indiscriminate Soviet attacks, the more people joined the mujahideen. Many resistance fighters funded their Holy War with the heroin they smuggled into the Soviet Union, Europe, and the United States.

In the United States, the Heritage Foundation, a Washington, DC–based, conservative think tank, urged Reagan to provide military aid to the mujahideen. Reagan directed the CIA to funnel aid to Afghanistan but to make sure that the weapons they sent were older, surplus arms readily available on the international market. He wanted to make it difficult for the Soviet Union to prove that the United States was covertly arming the mujahideen—though Brezhnev and his successors knew the truth.

By 1985, White House officials decided to raise the stakes for the Soviet Union in Afghanistan. The metrics, or body count, of the war seemed to be in the Soviets' favor—ultimately there were fifteen thousand Soviet soldiers killed to ninety thousand mujahideen. Thanks to Soviet helicopter gunships, insurgents found it difficult to move outside their caves. Recognizing that the Soviets might win, Reagan authorized the CIA to send a newly developed high-tech weapon: the shoulder-fired, heat-seeking Stinger missile. Firing the Stinger required no advanced technical skills, and operators did not have to worry about their own accuracy—the missile frequently found its target. The United States sent three hundred Stingers to the mujahedeen in 1986 and another seven hundred in 1987.

The Soviets lost 270 aircraft to the Stingers, leading pilots to fly at ever higher altitudes. Such heights all but removed helicopter gunships from convoy escort and close-combat support roles. The deployment of Stingers meant that Reagan not only did not care if the Soviets knew that the United States was supporting the insurgency but also wanted Kremlin leaders to know that the United States was committed to their defeat in Afghanistan.

The United States' proxy war in Afghanistan and U.S. support of anticommunist forces in Central America were not the only foreign policy stresses the Soviet Union faced in the 1980s. In 1978, a Polish national and Roman Catholic cardinal, Karol Wojtyla (1920–2005), became Pope John Paul II. Wojtyla had endured both the Nazi and Soviet occupations of his homeland. As the first non-Italian pope in several centuries, and the first from a communist nation, Pope John Paul II instilled fear in the Kremlin. Soviet intelligence (KGB) chief Yuri Andropov was outraged. Andropov, who subsequently became Soviet leader in 1982 following Brezhnev's death, ordered Polish officials to print pamphlets warning school children that "the Pope is our enemy." He was right to be frightened. Pope John Paul II came to Poland in 1979, said Mass to millions of Poles, and told them, "Be not afraid!"[22]

"Tear Down This Wall!": Foreign Policy in the Time of Reagan

Polish-born Pope John Paul II (1978–2005) proved to be a key ally to Ronald Reagan, with both determined to end the Soviet occupation of Eastern Europe. (Library of Congress)

A year after the Pope's visit, an electrician named Lech Walesa (1943–), who worked in the Lenin Shipyard in Gdansk, organized an illegal strike. Walesa, whose father had been a forced laborer in a Nazi work camp, defied Polish and Russian communists to establish a trade union, Solidarity. Since the Communist Party proclaimed itself to be the embodiment of the working class, it was not ideologically permissible for laborers to form independent trade unions.

Under pressure from the Soviet Union, Polish communists suppressed Solidarity, arrested Walesa, and imposed martial law between 1981 and 1983. Andropov was convinced that Pope John Paul II was pulling Walesa's strings. At the same time, American anticommunists were equally convinced that Andropov was behind the failed 1981 effort to assassinate the Pope.

Poland posed a fundamental problem for the Soviet Union. At the end of World War II, Stalin had seen the occupation of Poland as a linchpin in the Soviet domination of Eastern Europe. Poland was a piece of real estate vital to Soviet national security. Germany, after all, had invaded Russia twice (1914 and 1941) through Poland. Moreover, Poland was the gateway to the Baltic nations of Lithuania, Latvia, and Estonia—whose citizens, like the Poles, resented Soviet domination. If Poland broke free of Soviet control, it might inspire the Baltic nations to rise up. Worse, a free Poland would separate the Soviet Union geographically from its East German dependency, potentially inspiring yet another nation to revolt. Poland had an even greater potential to undermine the Soviet Empire than Afghanistan had. Like Stalin, Andropov (and Reagan) understood that Poland could be the first falling domino in a chain that led to Moscow.

While Poland grew restive and Afghanistan bled, Reagan opened yet another front to exert pressure on the Soviet Union. To begin with, Reagan rejuvenated the military. To improve military recruitment, both in quality and quantity, Reagan raised soldiers' pay. Given the technological sophistication of most modern weaponry, the U.S. military increasingly functioned in all but name as a two-year vocational school. Since most public high schools were in the process of abandoning vocational education in favor of a college preparation curriculum, the military became the place for working-class youths to learn electronics, mechanics, welding, and computer operations. After the dismal 1970s, the American military once again became an avenue of upward social mobility for working-class teenagers. There was also no longer a need to maintain low physical and education recruitment standards.

U.S. defense spending went from $165 billion in 1981 to $336 billion in 1984. (In 2019 dollars, 1984 defense spending would be the equivalent of $814 billion.) The number of troops rose by 100,000, and the U.S. Navy added 46 ships in pursuit of Secretary John Lehman's vision of a 500-strong fleet.

Enlistment in ROTC also surged. In 1974, the Army had thirty-two thousand enrolled in ROTC programs. By 1983, there were seventy-three thousand Army ROTC cadets. Better pay and vocational training opportunities certainly helped ROTC enrollment and enlistment in the ranks, but credit went to Reagan's rhetorical leadership as well. He championed patriotism, honored veterans, refused to apologize, by contrast with Carter, for past mistakes in U.S. foreign policy, and successfully ran for reelection with the slogan, "Let's make America great again." Reagan also promised that the United States would never again fight with self-imposed limitations as it had in Vietnam: "Young Americans must never again be sent to fight and die unless we are prepared to let them win."[23]

It should be noted, however, that class division remained between the military and American elites. Few ROTC officers came from upper-class state universities and private schools. Nearly all the enlisted ranks were filled with the children of laborers, northern urban Catholics, small-town southerners and midwesterners, and African Americans. New Englanders were minimally represented, as were the offspring of doctors and lawyers and other professionals.

When it came to nuclear weapons, Reagan pursued several strategies that confounded friend and foe alike. First, he deployed more nuclear missiles in West Germany, decreasing the amount of time the Soviet Union would have to react to an American strike. Second, Reagan wanted to develop antimissile technology, throwing aside earlier antiballistic missile treaty limitations. He did not believe that the United States should leave itself incapable of shielding Americans from a possible Soviet attack. Third, Reagan found the policy of Mutual Assured Destruction to be morally repellent. He wanted to eliminate nuclear weapons altogether.

Peace activists in Europe and the United States regarded Reagan's first two strategies as repulsive and largely failed to appreciate his commitment to the third strategy. A "nuclear freeze movement" grew in West Germany and the United States. Most German peace activists regarded Reagan as Hitler reincarnate, which blinded them to the fact that the Soviet Union was covertly helping to finance their demonstrations outside American military bases. In the United States, Senator Ted Kennedy of Massachusetts called for freezing the development of nuclear weapons. Public opinion polls indicated that 70 percent of Americans also supported a moratorium on nuclear weapons' research, development, and deployment. At the same time, however, they did not embrace unilateral disarmament.

Reagan carefully explained to voters that he, too, in an ideal world (one that he hoped to live in), would like to stop making atomic bombs. Until then, however, he wanted to develop antimissile technology. In an address to the UN General Assembly in 1985, Reagan laid out his rationale for what he called the Strategic Defense Initiative (SDI):

> We do not ask that the Soviet leaders, whose country has suffered so much from war, to leave their people defenseless against foreign attack. Why then do they insist that we remain undefended? Who is threatened if Western

research and Soviet research, that is itself well-advanced, should develop a nonnuclear system which would threaten not human beings but only ballistic missiles? Surely, the world will sleep more secure when these missiles have been rendered useless, militarily and politically; when the sword of Damocles that has hung over our planet for too many decades is lifted by Western and Russian scientists working to shield their citizens and one day shutdown space as an avenue of weapons of mass destruction. If we're destined by history to compete, militarily, to keep the peace, then let us compete in systems that defend our societies rather than weapons which can destroy us both and much of God's creation along with us.[24]

Critics in the mass media, the Democratic Party, and the universities ridiculed Reagan's SDI proposal when he initially shared it with the American people in 1983. They mockingly called it "Star Wars," after the popular science fiction film series. Numerous academics and journalists claimed that Reagan had been inspired by cheesy 1940s and 1950s movies about space aliens. To critics' dismay, however, public opinion was firmly behind Reagan. If Americans could not ban the bomb, they would at least like to be able to shoot it down prior to detonation over the United States. Few cared if such technology was feasible; the majority liked the *idea* of having the capability to shoot down incoming missiles.

Reagan's defense and foreign policies were illuminated by sharp anticommunist rhetorical flourishes. In a 1983 address to the conservative National Association of Evangelicals, Reagan warned against a nuclear freeze and the dangers of seeing the Soviet Union as a trustworthy partner:

> So, in your discussions of the nuclear freeze proposals, I urge you to beware the temptation of pride—the temptation of blithely declaring yourselves above it all and label both sides equally at fault, to ignore the facts of history and the aggressive impulses of an evil empire, to simply call the arms race a giant misunderstanding and thereby remove yourself from the struggle between right and wrong and good and evil.[25]

The American and international news media seized on a single phrase from Reagan's speech and capitalized it: Evil Empire. Beyond its *Star Wars* vibe, as a construct "Evil Empire" was jarring. Tom Wicker, the *New York Times*'s ace political reporter, denounced a "smug" Reagan for issuing "a near proclamation of a Holy War." Privately, Reagan's secretary of state,

George Shultz, was appalled. Jeane Kirkpatrick countered that the president had done nothing more than state the obvious.[26]

Reaction to Reagan's "Evil Empire" speech was a product of ideology but also depended upon whether one looked at shorter or longer historical time frames. Neither Ford nor Nixon, in their pursuit of détente with the Soviet Union, had been as vocally anticommunist as Reagan. Kennedy, whose 1961 inaugural address championed global freedom, had been careful not to name the Soviet Union as the enemy. Americans had to go back to Truman to find a president who publicly regarded the Soviet Union as the flip side of Nazi Germany.

As Reagan intuited, there were plenty of voters yearning for the moral clarity of the early Cold War era, before Vietnam and the dispiriting 1970s. The Truman Doctrine of communist containment had been reincarnated as the "Reagan Doctrine" of pushback against communists on all fronts.

The Reagan Doctrine had its share of detractors outside the Soviet orbit. William Arkin, an analyst affiliated with the leftist Institute for Policy Studies, warned in the prestigious *Bulletin of the Atomic Scientists* that because of Reagan and the SDI, "nuclear war is now more likely." Robert McGeehan, of the University of Southern California School of International Relations, contemptuously observed that Reagan's "foreign policy pronouncements included so many inanities as to be almost amusing." Harsher still, University of Cape Town (South Africa) religious studies professor David Chidester compared Reagan to cult leader Jim Jones and asserted that he "wanted children to die to save them from communism."[27]

Former Canadian prime minister and Liberal Party leader Pierre Trudeau (1919–2000) warned Soviet leaders that Reagan was a tool of reactionaries and would never negotiate in good faith. Pope John Paul II, though generally supportive of Reagan, worried that the SDI would force a paranoid Soviet Union into a nuclear war. He did, however, refrain from criticizing Reagan, overruling many of his cardinals and bishops.

Among U.S. allies, British prime minister and Conservative Party head Margaret Thatcher (1925–2013) proved to be Reagan's best friend. She encouraged Reagan to hold firm on developing SDI. Thatcher worried that the British Labour Party was embracing a nuclear freeze as a prelude to unilateral disarmament and an end to the historic alliance with

British prime minister Margaret Thatcher (1979–1990) successfully launched economic reform in the United Kingdom and stood staunchly by Ronald Reagan as he sought to bring about the collapse of the Soviet Empire. (Library of Congress)

the United States. Despite that concern, she informed Reagan that they could both stand up to the critics in their respective countries. The duo could promote free markets at home and liberty overseas—just as Truman and British prime minister Winston Churchill had done in the 1940s. Without Thatcher, Reagan would have stood nearly alone on the international stage.

Meanwhile, in the Soviet Union, communist leaders were thrown off balance. Brezhnev's two decades of rule had given the Soviet Union its greatest foreign policy successes since 1945. Moreover, the Soviet Union had enhanced its arsenal both in quantity and quality. Soviet missiles could strike deep into the United States. Brezhnev had accomplished something that Stalin could have only dreamed of: global military power and a rough parity with the United States. For all that, however, the Soviet Empire was dying.

Brezhnev had held tight to power, drawing to him a few aging associates who had risen in the bureaucracy like characters in a Gilbert & Sullivan production. Andropov died after just fifteen months as Soviet leader. As a product of the secret police, Andropov's nature was to be distrustful and cautious, even though he knew the Soviet economic and political system had to be reformed. Konstantin Chernenko, who was three years older than Andropov, expired after thirteen months as leader. His specialties were propaganda and political surveillance. He was not going to embrace change.

Reagan argued that he could not negotiate serious arms reduction talks with the Soviet Union as long as its leaders kept dying every few months. He was being, in equal parts, defensive, darkly humorous, and entirely accurate. There was neither political stability nor continuity at the top in the Soviet Union.

By 1985, many members of the Soviet Old Guard who had come up through the ranks under Stalin were dead. A new generation, represented by Mikhail Gorbachev (1931–), the least senior member of the governing *Politburo*, came to power. A devout communist, Gorbachev did two things that separated him from his predecessors. First, he had obtained a law degree, learning to analyze things from a perspective other than what could be gleaned from a wiretap. Second, he married a philosophy and sociology lecturer. Raisa Gorbachev was a career woman who discussed policy issues with her husband. She did not remain in the shadows like the other communist politicians' wives. Moreover, she also believed that just because people were communist did not mean they had to dress themselves in sackcloth and ashes. In some ways, Raisa Gorbachev was a Russian Nancy Reagan.

The Gorbachevs recognized an essential fact that Vladimir Lenin had also (resentfully) understood: a vibrant economy required a degree of political freedom from state interference. (In the early 1920s, Lenin had called this reality the "New Economic Policy." Stalin subsequently killed Lenin's initiative, along with its supporters.) In order to achieve *perestroika*, a restructuring of the Soviet economy, Gorbachev argued that there had to be *glasnost*, an openness to the free exchange of ideas—even if those ideas did not follow the Communist Party line. Gorbachev's dilemma boiled down to one fundamental question: Could the Soviet Union continue to exist if its citizens were free to embrace different economic and political beliefs? He believed it was possible; history would prove otherwise.

Soviet leader Mikhail Gorbachev (1985–1991), the last head of the Soviet state, pushed for economic reform and negotiated nuclear arms reductions with Ronald Reagan. Gorbachev also presided over the disintegration of the Soviet Union. (Library of Congress)

On the international stage, Gorbachev had to convince Reagan of his sincere desire to de-escalate the Cold War in order to reallocate scarce Soviet economic resources. He wanted Reagan's trust that glasnost was a policy, not a tactic. "Openness," however, whether at home or abroad, was not a natural impulse for Soviet bureaucrats. In 1986, a nuclear accident occurred at the Chernobyl plant in the Soviet Ukraine. Moscow at first denied that there was a problem and then tried to minimize it. At least seventy thousand Soviet citizens were poisoned, and untold numbers died. Soviet denials proved untenable once the immense radioactive cloud moved into Europe. Gorbachev often complained that Reagan repeated one Russian proverb to him at their summits: "Trust but verify." Chernobyl meant that Reagan was not going to stop saying that anytime soon.

Reagan was nearly alone among conservatives and establishment Republicans in believing that Gorbachev had the potential to become a friend of the United States. Although Richard Nixon and Henry Kissinger

"Tear Down This Wall!": Foreign Policy in the Time of Reagan

Nancy Reagan and Raisa Gorbachev at the White House. (Ronald Reagan Presidential Library and Museum)

had negotiated with the aggressive Brezhnev, neither trusted Gorbachev. Reagan informed Nixon that he planned to negotiate with Gorbachev on the elimination of as many American and Soviet nuclear weapons as possible. Nixon, who had long held Reagan in contempt, complained that Gorbachev had duped the foolish actor. Kissinger concurred. Both Kissinger and Nixon wrote newspaper articles criticizing Reagan and did their best to undermine him publicly and privately.

Conservative activists were particularly aggravated with Reagan. Social conservative leader Phyllis Schlafly, the head of the American Eagle Forum, visited Reagan in the White House to denounce him for negotiating with Gorbachev. Howard Phillips, the leader of the Conservative Caucus, argued that Reagan was "a useful idiot for Soviet propaganda" as well as "a weak man with a strong wife and a strong staff"—qualities that served to engineer his capitulation to communism. The venerable *National Review* warned that Reagan was destroying American national security. Journalists George Will and Charles Krauthammer, both devout anticommunists, attacked Reagan's judgment. As Will contended,

"Reagan has accelerated the moral disarmament of the West—actual disarmament will follow—by elevating wishful thinking to the status of political philosophy."[28]

Kirkpatrick, along with George Shultz, loyally backed Reagan through the three summits he held with Gorbachev between 1985 and 1987. Among foreign policy experts, she was one of the few to understand that Gorbachev had little choice but to enact domestic economic and political reforms and come to terms with the United States. In a 1987 trip to the Soviet Union sponsored by the Council on Foreign Relations, Kirkpatrick and Kissinger jousted privately. Publicly, Kirkpatrick weighed in with her assessment: "The leaders of the Soviet Union, including Mikhail Gorbachev, attach a great deal of importance at this stage to what they are calling in English 'the new thinking.' The specifics of change are less clear at this point than what is apparently a will to new approaches." For a veteran Cold Warrior such as Kirkpatrick, that statement was the equivalent of a box of chocolates delivered to Gorbachev's front door.[29]

To the stunned surprise of many, and to the dismay of quite a few conservatives, Reagan and Gorbachev worked out a major arms control agreement at their 1987 meeting. The Intermediate-Range Nuclear Forces Treaty of 1987 led the Soviet Union to withdraw 1,500 missiles from Eastern Europe, while the United States took out 750 from West Germany. This was the beginning of a drawdown of forces in Europe. It also led both superpowers to rethink their targeting of each other's homelands. Reagan wanted to end the nuclear strategy of Mutual Assured Destruction, and Gorbachev concurred.[30]

What Gorbachev painfully learned, and what conservative activists largely failed to understand, was that Reagan was capable of separating foreign policy strands even as he wove together a tightly knit strategy. In other words, the mere fact that Reagan wanted to reduce, if not eliminate, nuclear weapons and found Gorbachev to be an exceptional partner did not mean he was going to cut the Soviet Union slack on other foreign policy issues. The United States would continue to arm Afghan's Holy Warriors until Gorbachev withdrew Soviet forces. So, too, did Reagan seek to weaken Soviet control of Eastern Europe.

In 1987 Reagan went to West Berlin, using the Berlin Wall and Brandenburg Gate as the world's largest stage prop. Twenty-six years earlier, communist leaders had erected the Berlin Wall in order to close off an escape route to the West. Kennedy had gone to West Berlin to assure Germans that he stood with them, even if he was unwilling to risk a war by knocking down the wall. He had even tried his hand at speaking German, *"Ich bin ein Berliner,"* by which he meant, "I am a Berliner!" Unfortunately, by incorrectly inserting *"ein"* into the phrase, Kennedy actually said, "I am a jelly donut!" West Berliners, however, appreciated Kennedy's intent if not his execution.

Reagan proved to be more assertive than Kennedy—and more careful with his German phrasing. He aimed a challenge directly at Gorbachev:

> We hear much from Moscow about a new policy of reform and openness. Some political prisoners have been released. Certain foreign news broadcasts are no longer being jammed. Some economic enterprises have been permitted to operate with greater freedom from state control. Are these the beginnings of profound changes in the Soviet state? Or are they token gestures, intended to raise false hopes in the West, or to strengthen the Soviet system without changing it? We welcome change and openness; for we believe that freedom and security go together, that the advance of human liberty can only strengthen the cause of world peace.
>
> There is one sign the Soviets can make that would be unmistakable, that would advance dramatically the cause of freedom and peace. General Secretary Gorbachev, if you seek peace, if you seek prosperity for the Soviet Union and Eastern Europe, if you seek liberalization: Come here to this gate! Mr. Gorbachev, open this gate! Mr. Gorbachev, tear down this wall![31]

Gorbachev could give no convincing response to Reagan. After all, the Berlin Wall's construction had been a Soviet admission that if people were able to flee communism, they would do so in droves. On the other hand, Gorbachev knew what Reagan knew: if the walls came tumbling down in Berlin, there was a possibility that the process of collapse could not be contained.

Reagan's Berlin Wall speech put an exclamation point on an incredible journey in U.S. foreign relations. Few Americans, regardless of political party or relative level of foreign policy expertise, would have predicted in 1981 that within six years Reagan would have largely achieved his defense and diplomatic objectives. Citizens went from fearing a nuclear war with the Soviet Union to relegating that concern much further down the list of their worries. While his Middle Eastern policy failed, he enjoyed a level of success elsewhere that had not been seen in previous decades. It helped Reagan that he had an honorable, well-intentioned Soviet counterpart—something that none of his predecessors had ever enjoyed. Still, Reagan placed sufficient economic and military pressure on the Soviet Union to give Gorbachev the opening he needed to bring about reforms. From there, the clock was ticking down on the life expectancy of the Soviet Empire.

NOTES

1. Jeffrey H. Michaels, "Waging 'Protracted Conflict' behind the Scenes: The Cold War Activism of Frank R. Barnett," *Journal of Cold War Studies* 19 (Winter 2017): 70–98; David Shribman, "Group Goes from Exile to Influence," *New York Times*, November 23, 1981.

2. Alvin M. Shuster, "GI Heroin Addiction Epidemic in Vietnam," *New York Times*, May 16, 1971.

3. Michael Barone, *Hard America, Soft America: Competition vs. Coddling and the Battle for the Nation's Future* (New York: Crown Publishing, 2004), 129–34.

4. Jonathan Kaufman, "Quiescent Campuses of Post-Vietnam Era Stir with Draft Talk," *Wall Street Journal*, January 31, 1981.

5. Ibid.; Marc Lindemann, "Storming the Ivory Tower: The Military's Return to America's Campuses," *Parameters* 37 (Winter 2006–2007): 44–57.

6. Kaufman, "Quiescent Campuses"; Lindemann, "Storming the Ivory Tower."

7. John Otis, "Harold Brown, Secretary of Defense during Carter Administration, Dies at 91," *Washington Post*, January 5, 2019.

8. "Text of President's Commencement Address at Notre Dame," *New York Times*, May 23, 1977.

9. Ibid.

10. Glen S. Krutz and Jeffrey S. Peake, *Treaty Politics and the Rise of Executive Agreements: International Commitments in a System of Shared Powers* (Ann Arbor: University of Michigan Press, 2009), 116–17; Adam Clymer, "A Movement, a Plan, a Canal," *New York Times*, March 15, 2008.

11. Clymer, "A Movement."

12. Jeane J. Kirkpatrick, "Dictatorships and Double Standards," *Commentary* 68 (November 1, 1979): 34–45.

13. Richard Allen, "Jeane Kirkpatrick and the Great Democratic Defector," *New York Times*, December 16, 2006; Charles Solomon, "Strip that Split the Cartoonists," *Los Angeles Times*, November 26, 1987.

14. Ronald Reagan, "Address to Joint Session of Congress on Central America," April 27, 1983, Ronald Reagan Presidential Library and Museum.

15. Ibid.; Ronald Reagan, "Radio Address to the Nation on Central America," March 24, 1984, Ronald Reagan Presidential Library and Museum.

16. "El Salvador Winning, Mrs. Kirkpatrick Says," *New York Times*, February 10, 1983; "Congressmen Attacked over El Salvador Stand," *New York Times*, May 5, 1983; Shirley Christian, "Nicaragua Week in the Capital," *New York Times*, April 19, 1985.

17. Robert Surbrug, *Beyond Vietnam: The Politics of Protest in Massachusetts, 1974–1990* (Amherst: University of Massachusetts Press, 2009), 235; David Evans, "Supreme Court Confirms U.S. Control over Guard," *Chicago Tribune*, June 12, 1990.

18. Stansfield Turner, "Avoidable Damage to the CIA," *New York Times*, October 24, 1984; William E. Pemberton, *Exit with Honor: The Life and Presidency of Ronald Reagan* (Armonk, NY: M. E. Sharpe, 1988), 111.

19. David K. Shipler, "Israeli Jets Destroy Iraqi Atomic Reactor: Attack Condemned by U.S. and Arab Nations," *New York Times*, June 9, 1981; Bernard D. Nossiter, "Israelis Condemned by Security Council for Attack on Iraq," *New York Times*, June 20, 1981.

20. Bernard D. Nossiter, "UN Council Calls for Cease-Fire in Lebanon," *New York Times*, June 6, 1982; George C. Herring, *From Colony to Superpower: U.S. Foreign Relations since 1775* (New York: Oxford University Press, 2008), 872–73.

21. Joshua Muravchik, "Patrick J. Buchanan and the Jews," *Commentary* 78 (January 1991): 19–26.

22. David Remick, "John Paul II," *New Yorker Magazine*, April 11, 2005.

23. Richard Halloran, "ROTC, Shunned No More, Grows Increasingly Selective," *New York Times*, July 20, 1987; Gregory L. Schneider, *Cadres for Conservatism: Young Americans for Freedom and the Rise of the Contemporary Right* (New York: New York University Press, 1999), 93.

24. Ronald Reagan, "Address to the 40th Session of the United Nations General Assembly, New York, New York," October 24, 1985, Ronald Reagan Presidential Library and Museum.

25. Ronald Reagan, "Remarks at the Annual Convention of the National Association of Evangelicals, Orlando, Florida," March 8, 1983, Ronald Reagan Presidential Library and Museum.

26. Tom Wicker, "In the Nation; 2 Dangerous Doctrines," *New York Times*, March 15, 1983.

27. David Chidester, "Saving the Children by Killing Them: Redemptive Sacrifice in the Ideologies of Jim Jones and Ronald Reagan," *Religion and American Culture* 1 (Summer 1991): 177–201; Robert McGeehan, "Carter's Crises: Iran, Afghanistan, and Presidential Politics," *World Today* 36 (May 1980): 163–71; William M. Arkin, "SDI—Pie in the Sky?" *Bulletin of the Atomic Scientists* 40 (April 1984): 9–10.

28. James Mann, *The Rebellion of Ronald Reagan: A History of the End of the Cold War* (New York: Viking, 2009), 49–51; Robert Shogan, "Conservatives Hit Reagan on Treaty: One Calls President 'a Useful Idiot' of Soviets; Criticism of Accord Mounts," *Los Angeles Times*, December 5, 1987.

29. Jeane Kirkpatrick, "Transforming Soviet Communism from Within," *Washington Post*, December 12, 1987; Philip Taubman, "Gorbachev Said to Support Talks Despite His Doubts about Reagan," *New York Times*, February 7, 1987.

30. Andrew Glass, "Gorbachev Calls for Nuclear Weapons Treaty, February 28, 1987," *Politico*, February 28, 2019.

31. Ronald Reagan, "Remarks on East-West Relations at the Brandenburg Gate on West Berlin," June 12, 1987, Ronald Reagan Presidential Library and Museum.

CHAPTER 3

TRICKLE-DOWN PROSPERITY: ECONOMIC POLICY DURING THE REAGAN REVOLUTION

Economic theories often resemble religions; they begin as heresy and may end up as dogma. Before the Great Depression, it was a tenet of economic faith in Europe and the United States that balanced budgets were good and that government spending was evil—unless the funds were devoted to national defense, though that exception was not universally embraced. Then British economist John Maynard Keynes argued that the Great Depression was the bitter fruit of austere government budgets and the poor distribution of wealth. Citizens needed increased purchasing power to stimulate economic growth. Governments could provide that power through what was euphemistically called "income transfers." Fundamentally, that meant redistributing income from the few to the many, often through increased taxes on the affluent to pay for government work programs and entitlements for the less well off.

In the United States, President Franklin Roosevelt may not have fully accepted Keynes as an apostle of prosperity, but federal taxation, deficit spending, and expansion of aid programs moved the British economist's ideas from heresy to dogma. Along with that transformation came an idea whose time had come: fully empowering the Federal Reserve to exert leverage over the national economy. If the United States faced a stagnant economy, the Federal Reserve could lower the prime interest rate to make borrowing more attractive and increase the amount of money in circulation. Conversely, if inflation was the problem, the Federal Reserve could raise the prime interest rate to discourage borrowing and decrease the amount of money available for loans.

After World War II, American economists and policy analysts were convinced that they had found the sacred texts to guide them away from inflation and economic stagnation. Of course, there was an underlying assumption behind such economic optimism: it would be impossible to have high inflation and unemployment at the same time. An overheated, stagnant economy was a contradiction in terms and, therefore, an impossibility.

The Eisenhower faction in the Republican Party embraced much of Roosevelt's Keynesian economic policy agenda. Indeed, Richard Nixon famously observed in 1971 that "we are all Keynesians now." It was hard to argue with Keynesian economic theory given the apparent fruits it bore. In the 1950s, American wages (adjusted for inflation) averaged an annual rate of growth of over 8 percent. Though that rate of growth slowed in the early 1960s, U.S. workers still saw their wages increase by nearly 6 percent in 1965. Meanwhile, the unemployment rate through the 1950s and early 1960s was typically below 5 percent and frequently less than 4 percent. According to Keynesians, such figures were close to "full employment" since most of the core unemployed were either disabled or single mothers at home caring for children.[1]

As the postwar U.S. economy boomed, federal spending, along with the growth of government at all levels of society, increased. In 1950, the U.S. government spent $41 billion. Twenty years later (adjusted for inflation), Washington spent nearly $208 billion—five times its expenditures in 1950. In those same years, the national debt went from $257 billion to $383 billion (as adjusted for inflation). Between 1950 and 1970, the federal government increased defense and social welfare spending several times over. Federal, state, and municipal government employment also expanded. In 1940, all levels of government employed 4.2 million people at a cost of $20 billion. By 1976, the number of federal, state, and municipal employees stood at 15 million with a payroll of $575 billion (which, in 1940 inflation-adjusted dollars would have been the equivalent of $364 billion).[2]

Increased federal spending and government employment spurred greater taxation. In 1953, median income earners ($4,200 annually) devoted nearly 12 percent of their income to financing the operations of the federal government. By 1975, median income earners ($12,000 annually) paid nearly 23 percent of their income to Washington. Their tax burden had almost doubled. Those who earned four times the median annual income in 1953 paid 20 percent of their earnings to the federal government. Twenty-two years later, this same cohort was devoting roughly 30 percent of their annual income to federal taxes. Their proportionate tax burden had risen by a third while those less well-off had seen their federal taxes increased by almost 50 percent.[3]

One of the tenets of the Keynesian faith had been that the wealthier members of society, not the middle and working classes, would bear the brunt of taxation. Two developments, however, changed that calculation. First, the escalating size and cost of government required finding additional sources of revenue. The tax net had to be cast wider. Second, in the era of the Great Depression, when the Keynesian doctrine became codified, just 3 percent of Americans had sufficient income to be required to pay federal taxes. A few years later, nearly all Americans had sufficiently sized incomes to be required to pay federal taxes. (The Social Security payroll deduction, for instance, was a federal tax in a different guise.) Given the rising cost of government, Washington was not going to adjust tax rates for inflation or real increases in blue-collar income. A steelworker in 1970 was paying at a federal tax rate that in 1935 would have been reserved for a corporate lawyer.

Keynesian economic theory was the product of an industrial era and came of age in the United States at a time when most of the world huddled among the ruins left behind by a destructive global war. In 1945, it was difficult to tell the winners and losers apart—with the notable exception of the U.S. presidents Roosevelt and Truman, who understood that the United States essentially had the only functioning economy remaining on the planet. To alleviate suffering, and hopefully prevent future global wars, the United States committed itself to reconstructing its allies and onetime foes. Restoring global trade and finance required that the U.S. dollar become a universal currency with which to value other nations' money and goods. The "dollar standard" replaced the "gold standard," which many nations had dropped at the beginning of the Great

Depression. New York City emerged as the global finance center as much as Washington became the world's political capital.

Although Americans only recognized it in retrospect, the U.S. economy in 1950 had begun a transition away from an industrial to a postindustrial or "knowledge" economy. In the 1940s and early 1950s, there had been 650,000 steelworkers and 854,000 miners. By the 1970s the number of steelworkers was reduced by half, while there were 80 percent fewer miners. Conversely, in 1940 there had been 111,000 college professors. Thirty years later, the United States had 551,000 college professors. More post–World War II jobs required advanced education, often in mathematics and the sciences. Automation contributed to the reduction in industrial employment, as did the relocation of American manufacturing overseas where there were no labor unions, corporate taxes, or expensive environmental and safety regulations to follow.[4]

Foreign competition, aided by postwar U.S. reconstruction policy and the lowering of tariff barriers to promote global trade, placed enormous pressure on American manufacturing. In the early 1950s, Pittsburgh made more steel than the entire nation of France, while Chicago produced more steel than all of Great Britain. West Germany, in comparison, was in ruins. By 1960, West Germany was making 31 million tons of steel, much of it exported to the United States. Meanwhile, West German (and Japanese) cars began to enter the U.S. market. In 1955, the United States received 58,000 auto imports; four years later, 615,000 imported cars came into the United States and accounted for 10 percent of the American automobile market. By 1979, 9 million imported cars came into the United States, with Japan claiming 18 percent of the American market.[5]

The United States' industrial economy began its reckoning in the 1970s. Between 1977 and 1980, the three steel mills in Youngstown, Ohio, closed, resulting in the disappearance of 38 percent of the city's well-paying, unionized manufacturing jobs. Pittsburgh steel mills began closing, casting nearly seventy thousand workers into the growing ranks of Pennsylvania's unemployed. Chrysler announced that it was bankrupt, threatening to close up shop unless the federal government bailed it out with taxpayers' money. President Jimmy Carter and a Democratic Congress, in part as a recognition of the importance of the autoworkers' union vote and ability to generate campaign contributions, rushed to save Chrysler but did not do the same for other corporations.

Nationally, both unemployment and inflation rose in tandem—a Keynesian improbability that became known as "stagflation." The United States remained dependent on oil from Middle Eastern nations opposed to America's Israeli ally. Oil embargoes continued to be a potential threat to the U.S. economy. Inflation reached 18 percent by the end of the 1970s—a rate not seen in decades. Unemployment hit 7 percent—twice what it had been in the 1960s. In hard-hit industrial communities such as Flint, Michigan, which was part of the General Motors' empire, the unemployment rate was 20 percent.

In response to escalating inflation, the Federal Reserve resorted to its traditional tactic of raising the prime interest rate—to 20 percent. With the cost of borrowing becoming prohibitive, Americans stopped buying homes and renting new office space. Those who were looking to purchase a new automobile turned to less expensive imports. Subsequently, contractors stopped building houses and offices, and American automakers saw their inventories of unsold cars mount. Inevitably, automobile plants and steel mills cut back or closed—leading to higher levels of unemployment.

Abandoned mill, Duquesne (Pennsylvania) Steel Works. Hundreds of thousands of unionized jobs disappeared in the 1970s and 1980s as steel mills and automobile plants shut down. While industrial states such as Illinois, Michigan, Ohio, and Pennsylvania suffered, the low-wage, high-tech Sunbelt prospered. (Library of Congress)

While the American economy suffered its worst years since the Great Depression, economist Arthur Laffer (1940–) was formulating a post-Keynesian response. The son of a Youngstown corporate executive, Laffer displayed a keen aptitude for mathematics and had the ability to see the nexus between policy ideas and real-world consequences. He went on to Yale and then to graduate school at Stanford, where he earned a doctorate in economics. Laffer joined the economics faculty at the University of Chicago, a center of "free market" studies, and did a stint as chief economist in Nixon's Office of Management in Budget (OMB). His experiences in Washington convinced him that nearly everyone involved in formulating federal economic policy, whether Democrat or Republican, was wrong. The Keynesian faith had to be exorcised from the American soul.

Working his way through mountains of economic data, Laffer argued that raising U.S. tax rates resulted in *lower*, not higher, federal receipts as citizens and corporations "sheltered" (hid) their money or pulled back from investing. U.S. Treasury secretary Andrew Mellon had called the correct play in the 1920s, though perhaps at the wrong time. Few Americans paid federal taxes in the 1920s; by the 1970s nearly everyone paid federal taxes. Reducing their tax burden would place a great deal of money into Americans' hands to stimulate consumer spending and corporate expansion. Contrary to Keynes, the best thing the federal government could do for the economy was to get out of the way.

Laffer's challenge in the 1970s was not so much that his ideas were heretical (which they were) as they were indecipherable to most people. To read his 1971 *Journal of Business* article, "A Formal Model of the Economy," required a journey down a rabbit hole lined with mathematical calculations that few Americans had ever encountered. Laffer may have been a prophet of economic salvation, but he needed a John the Baptist to interpret his teachings to the masses.[6]

Luckily for Laffer, he found his messenger in Jude Wanniski (1936–2005), a *Wall Street Journal* editor. The grandson of a Polish immigrant coal miner in eastern Pennsylvania, Wanniski made his way to UCLA, where he studied politics and journalism. In 1974, while dining with Laffer, Wanniski was able to extract from the economist a simplified "cocktail napkin" (literally) illustration of his taxation theory. The "Laffer Curve," or what Wanniski rebranded as "supply-side economics," demonstrated that raising taxes was often economically counterproductive. Wanniski's

Trickle-Down Prosperity: Economic Policy during the Reagan Revolution

Andrew Mellon, secretary of the treasury (1921–1932) and author of a tax plan that became a precursor to supply-side economics in the 1980s. (Library of Congress)

easy-to-understand analysis caught Ronald Reagan's eye. During World War II, Reagan, in response to a high marginal tax rate, had done exactly what Laffer discussed: he cut back on his work, which resulted in him sending less, not more, income to the federal treasury.

Wanniski was so convinced of Laffer's insights on human economic behavior that in 1978 he published a landmark book, *How the World Works*. As the title suggested, Wanniski believed that Laffer had found one big truth that explained not just economics but also history, politics, psychology, and social organization. In effect, Wanniski had proclaimed a belief system that, like a religion, explained everything about how people operate.

Laffer and Wanniski argued that the conservative fixation on deficits and federal spending made them vulnerable to liberal attack. A wiser political strategy, they insisted, was to emphasize tax reduction and to say less about spending. That did not mean, however, that deficits were not important. Laffer offered the possibility that his proposed tax policy would "grow" the economy at a fast rate and, therefore, generate more tax revenue than what the government spent. However, Laffer cautioned, there was no guarantee that tax cuts would "pay for themselves," as some new converts were arguing. He understood that federal spending had to be prioritized and reduced.

Neither Laffer nor Wanniski lacked for critics on the Left and the Right. Conservative writer George Gilder authored a dismissive essay, "Laffing Gas," for the *National Review* in 1978. Gilder caricaturized Laffer, arguing this is what the economist believed: "Balanced budgets are a disabling fetish of conservatism; government spending is here to stay, so why fight it? Fund it with the lower taxes that the people love." On the liberal side of the aisle, the *New York Times* editorialized in 1980 that Laffer's supply-side economics was "the nostrum of the ideological Right." Perhaps most disturbing to the *New York Times* and Gilder was

(From left) Arthur Laffer (at far left) and Ronald Reagan's Economic Policy Advisory Board, 1981. Laffer adapted Andrew Mellon's policies and created supply-side economics. (Ronald Reagan Presidential Library and Museum)

the fact that more politicians, notably northern Republicans and southern *Democrats*, were taking Laffer and Wanniski seriously. Some even made supply-side economics the centerpiece of their 1978 congressional campaigns.[7]

Reagan embraced Laffer and Wanniski during the 1980 Republican Party primaries. Former CIA director George H. W. Bush, whose father had been an Eisenhower loyalist while in the U.S. Senate, was contemptuous of Reagan's economic views. Bush waved aside Laffer's ideas as little more than "voodoo economic policies." Tennessean Howard Baker, the leader of the Senate's Republican minority, described tax cuts as a "riverboat gamble" unworthy of consideration. Given the opposition Reagan faced from his party's leadership, there was seemingly little need for the *New York Times* to join the battle; he could not possibly win the Republican nomination, let alone the general election.[8]

Not only did Reagan defy expectations by winning both the nomination and presidential election but he also successfully "managed" (co-opted) Bush and Baker. He offered Bush the vice presidency. Reagan's advisers had suspected that Bush's political ambitions outweighed his principles, and Bush became a convert to "Reaganomics" as he later glided toward the 1988 Republican presidential nomination. As for Baker, Reagan handed him a Senate majority, which made him a point person for legislating Reaganomics. Baker could not refuse Reagan an accommodation after elevating him to a position he likely would have never had held but for the president. Moreover, back home in Baker's Tennessee, Reagan was as popular as Davy Crockett and Jack Daniels.

Reaganomics had its share of champions, most especially the Heritage Foundation. In 1973, beer baron Joseph Coors and Pittsburgh corporate heir Richard Mellon Scaife (the grandnephew of Andrew Mellon) helped found the Heritage Foundation in Washington. Coors and his allies were concerned that the oldest Right-leaning think tank in the nation's capital, the neoconservative American Enterprise Institute (AEI), had become too accepting of Keynesian economics and was more "academic" than action oriented. The Heritage Foundation would issue short policy position papers for an intended audience of politicians and sympathetic journalists. Although Heritage had a federal tax exemption as an "educational" institution, there was no doubt that its "curriculum" was partisan.

The Heritage Foundation became for conservative economic policy what the Committee on the Present Danger was for foreign policy: a source of Reagan administration personnel and ideas. Washington insiders referred to the Heritage Foundation as "Reagan's think tank." Dozens of individuals affiliated with Heritage passed through the Reagan White House. Most importantly, in 1980 Heritage issued its first "Mandate for Leadership." Well over a thousand pages long, the Mandate for Leadership contained two thousand proposals and served as a blueprint for Reagan's domestic policies. The Reagan White House adopted 60 percent of the Heritage Foundation's policy proposals. Conservative activists, however, complained that Reagan should have adopted 100 percent of the Mandate for Leadership's agenda.[9]

Two pieces of legislation, and a core belief in limiting federal regulations on business, served as the centerpiece of Reagan's economic agenda: the Omnibus Budget Reconciliation Act of 1981 and the Economic Recovery Tax Act of 1981. The first bill laid out Reagan's funding priorities, which included reductions in social welfare spending and greater allocations to national defense. Reagan's economic advisers had hoped to make a sizable cut to the food stamps program, which helped poor families on welfare to eat. However, they came up against more opposition than just the anticipated welfare rights' activists. Heartland farmers regarded food stamps as a well-deserved agricultural subsidy—and they let their Republican senators know their feelings. In 1964, Republican presidential nominee Barry Goldwater had gone down in crushing defeat after antagonizing the "farm lobby." Reagan had no intention of repeating history.

Reagan had endorsed conservatives' calls to eliminate the U.S. Departments of Commerce, Education, and Energy. He quickly discovered, though, that two of the three agencies performed vital tasks for the United States that could not be trusted to the private sector or state governments.

Antigovernment activists had thought that it would be easy to eliminate smaller federal entities such as National Public Radio, Public Television, the National Endowment for Arts, and the National Endowment for the Humanities. Although few Americans received much direct benefit from any of these public-sector initiatives, those who did were largely upper-middle class and college educated. Many were also *Republican* voters. Antagonizing white-collar professionals in Republican-leaning suburban districts did not appeal to Reagan. Big Bird would continue to live in his federally subsidized nest on *Sesame Street*.

The Economic Recovery Tax Act had initially proposed a 30 percent tax reduction, but Reagan indicated that he would settle for 25 percent spread out over three years. Meanwhile, the top tax marginal rate went from 70 percent to 50 percent on incomes above $200,000. The tax on capital gains, or profits, dropped to 20 percent from 28 percent. Drawing on Laffer's theories, and the recommendations of the Heritage Foundation, Reagan's tax reform also indexed incomes for inflation. This was a significant change, since an income of $200,000 in 1940 was, as a result of inflation, the equivalent of $1.2 million forty years later. The tax system in place since World War II hit wage earners hard as well as penalized profitable businesses. Unintentionally, Roosevelt's heirs had created a taxation system that discouraged domestic investment and punished Americans whose incomes artificially rose due to inflation.

Along with tax and budget legislation, Reagan argued that federal regulations and an all-powerful Washington bureaucracy hampered economic growth. There was ample cause to believe that this was true. At the end of the 1970s, federal regulations on business, including those created by Nixon's EPA and OSHA, added $100 billion annually to operational expenses. (Adjusted for inflation, that would be $358 billion in 2019.) Choosing to issue an executive order rather than take another fight to the Democratic House, Reagan ordered regular reviews of federal regulations, a reduction in paperwork, and a cost-benefit analysis. The latter was to determine if regulations did more damage than good to the economy. It was noteworthy that Reagan singled out Nixon's and Johnson's regulatory legacies for chastisement but not Roosevelt's.[10]

Reagan believed that the federal government should reduce its regulatory role in the U.S. economy while empowering the states to determine which policies would work best for them. At a 1976 meeting of the Chicago Executive Club, Reagan had championed the need for "a systematic transfer of authority and resources to the states—a program of creative federalism for America's third century." If the federal government got out of the way, Reagan insisted, business and states would thrive.[11]

Whether or not a devolution of economic authority to the states was practical, Reagan was correct in calling attention to how many resources the federal government consumed. Between 1950 and 1980, the share of the nation's Gross Domestic Product (GDP) that went to Washington increased from 14 percent to nearly 23 percent. Reagan vowed to reverse that trend and reduce the federal government's portion of the GDP to 19 percent. While Reagan envisioned a significant reduction, he was still giving the federal government a considerable role in Americans' lives.

Pushback against Reagan's budget and taxation proposals came swiftly. Democratic Speaker of the House Tip O'Neill went to the White House and told Reagan that he would accomplish nothing. O'Neill informed Reagan that while he may have been a successful governor, he was "in the big leagues now" and out of his depth. Privately, O'Neill complained that Reagan was merely "an actor reading lines," incapable of making intelligent decisions. His opposition to Reagan, however, went even deeper: he believed that Reagan was not just stupid but evil. As O'Neill argued, it was "sinful that Ronald Reagan ever became president."[12]

Democratic Speaker of the House (1977–1987) Thomas "Tip" O'Neill. (O'Neill is center, shaking hands, facing front.) O'Neill faced massive defections among southern Democrats on a number of legislative votes and proved unable to derail Ronald Reagan's economic and foreign policy agendas. (Library of Congress)

Michigan's Democratic congressional delegation, whose twelve members included some of the most senior, powerful members of Congress, declared their opposition to Reagan's proposed economic policies. In response to the growing economic crisis of the 1970s, Michigan Democrats, along with their moderate Republican counterparts, had increased state government employment by 53 percent. To pay for that, the legislature had raised the state income tax that a moderate Republican governor, George Romney, had created in 1967. Michigan's state representatives had also pushed for increases in welfare payments, which by 1980 were 52 percent above the national average. Despite their efforts to create government jobs and increase welfare, Michigan's economy worsened. Its unemployment rate stood at 16 percent in 1980, twice the national average. Given this state of affairs, Michigan's congressional Democrats argued, the federal government needed to increase taxes and aid programs—just the opposite of what Reagan advocated.[13]

Former Carter administration officials weighed in on the economic policy debate. C. Fred Bergsten, the assistant secretary of the treasury for internal affairs, warned that supply-side economics would destroy the value of the American dollar and present a greater "threat to U.S. global interests . . . than do the Soviets or anybody else." Hodding Carter III, a journalist and former assistant secretary of state for public affairs, argued that Reagan was "substituting the garrison state for the welfare state." Moreover, he continued, Reagan was the worst of "the barbarians who now threaten" the destruction of the United States and the end of "equal rights." The president was nothing more than a "political snake oil" salesman.[14]

The *New York Times*, whose editorials and stories shaped the content and analysis of the three national television networks (ABC, CBS, and NBC), fell in behind House Democrats. Its editors dismissed Laffer's economic theories as "amateurish" and assured Americans that well-informed Republican businesspeople on Wall Street opposed Reagan. Even before the passage of Reagan's tax cuts, the *New York Times* insisted that supply-side economic policies had failed. It was clear that after four months in office, Reagan had not brought about any economic improvement. His was a failed presidency.[15]

More worrisome to the Reagan White House than the *New York Times* was the critical coverage provided by the *Washington Post*. Someone close to Reagan was feeding sensitive, politically embarrassing information to *Washington Post* editor William Greider. In its coverage, the *Washington Post* showed an administration divided over tax cuts, entitlement spending, and the military buildup. Greider's source was openly contemptuous of rivals within the administration and convinced that Reaganomics was unworkable.

Greider eventually revealed that his source was Reagan's director of the Office of Management and Budget, David Stockman (1946–). The OMB director was one of the youngest members of the administration, a "baby boomer" who came of age in the 1960s. Unlike most conservatives, Stockman's introduction to politics had come from the Left, first as a member of the Michigan State University Christian Movement and then as an ally of the Students for a Democratic Society (SDS). He protested against the Vietnam War and secured a continuation of his student draft deferment by going to Harvard Divinity School.

Office of Management and Budget director David Stockman and Ronald Reagan sharing a moment in early 1981, before knowledge that Stockman was leaking derogatory information to the news media became public. (Ronald Reagan Presidential Library and Museum)

Stockman abandoned his clerical studies to make a successful run for Congress from Michigan. By then, he had moved to the libertarian Right. He opposed the federal bailout of Chrysler—and was the only member of Michigan's Republican congressional delegation to do so. Once in the OMB, Stockman complained to Greider that Reagan refused to eliminate entitlement programs, undo the New Deal, and stop throwing money at a spendthrift Pentagon. That last issue was the reason defense secretary Caspar Weinberger, a World War II veteran, called Stockman "the blow-dried draft dodger." In an administration filled with middle-aged males with close-cropped, marine-style haircuts, Stockman's long, well-groomed locks were the subject of ridicule.[16]

Rather than fire Stockman, Reagan kept him around, where he became an isolated, untrusted figurehead. In part, Reagan did not like personal confrontation—a common reaction among people who grew up in troubled families and who saw themselves as peacekeepers. Reagan was also a shrewd enough politician to know that the national news media would make Stockman a martyr if he fired him. It was, in public relations terms, better to let Stockman, like the stump of a fallen tree, quietly rot in place.

In the face of a hostile press, much publicized dissension within White House ranks, and a Democratic House leadership determined to thwart his budget and tax reforms, Reagan still came out the winner. Reagan's success was due to two factors: his own political skills and a Democratic opposition that was more divided than Tip O'Neill or the news media appreciated.

On March 30, 1981, a delusional gunman, John Hinckley Jr., attempted to assassinate Reagan. Hinckley gravely wounded Reagan—more gravely than the American public knew at the time. He also wounded Reagan's press secretary, a Secret Service agent, and a District of Columbia police officer. (Press secretary James Brady suffered permanent brain damage.) Most of the American people rallied behind Reagan, who did not let the public know how slow his recovery would be from a bullet-pierced, collapsed lung.

Reagan's political skills went far beyond garnering sympathy for having nearly died. He already had a strategy in motion before the assassination attempt to move public opinion behind his economic policies. Three weeks after his inauguration, Reagan had gone on national television to address the nation. He used straightforward language as he informed the public, "We're in the worst economic mess since the Great Depression." Although he did not name Keynesian economics as a contributor to the United States' economic woes, there was no mistaking that he had a new gospel to propound: "Our aim is to increase our national wealth so all will have more, not just redistribute what we already have which is just a sharing of scarcity."[17]

Having warmed up to his subject, Reagan took direct aim at the politicians and journalists who called for tax increases rather than tax cuts:

> Some say shift the tax burden to business and industry, but business doesn't pay taxes. Oh, don't get the wrong idea. Business is being taxed, so much so that we're being priced out of the world market. But business must pass its costs of operations—and that includes taxes—on to the customer in the price of the product. Only people pay taxes, all the taxes. Government just uses business in a kind of sneaky way to help collect the taxes. They're hidden in the price; we aren't aware of how much tax we actually pay.

Reagan's observation was true, but it was one seldom heard outside the confines of the U.S. Chamber of Commerce and conservative think tanks and media outlets. Most Americans had never seen a politician connect the dots, let alone walk them through the intricacies of economic policy in such a congenial, easy-to-understand manner.[18]

Shortly after his national address on the economy, Reagan scheduled a televised joint session of Congress, where he further outlined his budget and tax agenda. He also delivered Saturday morning radio talks—and showed that the skills he had acquired forty years earlier at WHO in Des Moines remained sharp. (Reagan delivered 326 radio broadcasts during his presidency.) From behind the scenes at the White House, conservative intellectual Martin Anderson in the Office of Policy Development generated economic talking points for widespread distribution. Reagan participated in these meetings which formulated "The Issue of the Day." Regardless of what journalists or political rivals wanted to discuss, the White House relentlessly pushed its issues.

Only those advisers closest to him knew that Reagan was more involved in shaping domestic policy than had been true of his three immediate predecessors. In a very calculated manner, Reagan let a critical news media and House Democrats believe that he was detached from policy making, hazy on details, and lazy. Little did they know that Reagan was fighting an insurgency, not a conventional political war. Only too late would O'Neill realize he had walked into an ambush. To his credit as a political analyst, Hodding Carter had warned congressional Democrats that they needed "to learn guerrilla warfare."[19]

O'Neill's policy defeat was the product of an erroneous assumption. He assumed that if House members had "Democrat" next to their names, then they would follow his lead. While that may have remained true in northern urban districts, it was becoming problematic in the South. Since the 1968, southern whites had been splitting their ballots, voting Democratic at the local and congressional level but supporting Republican presidential candidates (with the exception of Ford). In part, southern whites were reacting against the civil rights revolution, but that was not the whole story. Southern whites recoiled against the 1960s cultural revolution (namely drugs and free love), antiwar protests, and rising violent crime rates. In 1980, Reagan had crushed Carter among Southern Baptists—the Georgian's own people. Political survival required southern white officeholders to support Reagan.

Reagan targeted southern congressional Democrats, making personal telephone calls and inviting them to the Oval Office. Watching their charmed Dixie colleagues, a few concerned northern Democrats warned O'Neill that Reagan had the power of mind control. Some also fretted that Reagan was smarter than they had thought. O'Neill was skeptical—until House Democrat Phil Gramm (1942–) of Fort Worth, Texas, announced that he had forged a bloc of pro-Reagan southerners. Although Gramm lacked seniority, which in Congress translated into deference and power, as a former Texas A&M economics professor, he had credibility on tax and budget policies. Gramm was a disciple of Laffer. Outraged, northern Democrats and journalists labeled Gramm's followers "Boll Weevils." The boll weevil was a parasite that had nearly destroyed the southern cotton industry decades earlier.

Forty-eight House Democrats voted for Reagan's tax cut, providing him with a 238 to 195 victory. They had earlier passed Reagan's budget proposal, which Gramm carried through the House. In the Republican-controlled Senate, 37 Democrats supported the Reagan tax reform. Nearly all the Democratic defectors in the House and Senate were southerners. Tellingly, however, in follow-up votes, 3 Michigan Democrats in the

Economist, Democratic representative, and then Republican senator from Texas Phil Gramm. In the early 1980s, Gramm organized southern Democratic support for Ronald Reagan's legislative agenda, leading congressional and news media liberals to denounce him and his allies as "Boll Weevil Democrats." (Library of Congress)

House fell in line behind Reagan. Like their southern counterparts, they were sensitive to electoral outcomes back home. In 1980, 40 percent of the membership of the United Automobile Workers of America (UAW) had voted for Reagan. The UAW in Michigan was interchangeable with the state Democratic Party. Where the UAW went, Michigan's Democratic leadership followed.

Reaganomics did not perform overnight miracles. Indeed, the United States' economic disruption continued through 1981 and into 1982. Although Reagan repudiated many of Carter's policies, he had embraced at least one: supporting Federal Reserve chair Paul Volcker as he hiked prime interest rates in an effort to squeeze inflation out of the U.S.

economy. Reagan and Volcker believed that escalating inflation, if not reversed, would undermine the United States' economic and political institutions much as it had in the 1920s German Weimar Republic. For people such as Reagan and Volcker, who lived through the Great Depression and World War II, it was an article of faith that German hyperinflation in the 1920s had contributed to the rise of Nazi Germany several years later.

The economic (and political) cost of fighting inflation effectively, however, was steep. Industries had to decide whether to relocate overseas to reduce production expenses, fire workers and favor automation, or close. Akron, Ohio, which was once a center for the production of automobile tires, saw its workforce decline from fifty-five thousand after World War II to ten thousand by 1982. Michigan lost a quarter of a million autoworker jobs between 1979 and 1982. Pittsburgh, which despite losing steelworker jobs was still able to retain ninety thousand in 1980, saw that number cut in half by 1984. All these industrial jobs were unionized, meaning that workers lost generous wages as well as health-care benefits.[20]

Reagan understood that he had a political problem, especially with the approaching 1982 congressional midterm elections. A voter backlash against Republicans would potentially give O'Neill enough new Democratic seats to eradicate his Boll Weevil problem. Reagan used his Saturday morning radio broadcasts to reassure voters to not lose faith in his economic policies. The advantage of radio was that, like Roosevelt, Reagan could directly speak to Americans without a "media filter" editing his commentary. The disadvantage was that, unlike the 1930s, most Americans watched the television networks for their news; radio listeners were likely already singing in Reagan's choir.

In a private meeting with his Council of Economic Advisers, Reagan rejected recommendations to raise taxes and focus on reducing the growing federal deficit. He countered that "tax increases don't eliminate deficits, they increase government spending." Reagan insisted on maintaining course and giving his tax reforms the time to improve the economy. His economic advisers agreed, but some were worried.[21]

Reagan made the best of a bad situation. As an alcoholic's son, an actor, and California governor, Reagan had a lot of experience doing just that.

In an April 1982 radio broadcast, Reagan defended his economic policies and urged listeners to be patient:

> Now, I know you've been told by some that we should do away with the tax cuts in order to reduce the deficit. That's like trying to pull a game out in the fourth quarter by punting on the third down.
>
> You've also been told our program hasn't worked. Well, of course it hasn't; it hasn't really started yet. Our 5-percent cut in October was almost wiped out by the January increase in the Social Security tax called for in the 1977 tax bill. The reduced budget spending and the 10-percent tax cut in July will be the real beginning of our program.
>
> There's no instant cure, but there is a cure. With your help and your prayers, we'll find it.[22]

O'Neill justifiably went into the 1982 midterm elections confident of victory. The Democrats picked up twenty-six seats in the House, which reduced some of Reagan's legislative leverage but not all of it. Moreover, O'Neill had launched a campaign against Gramm, denying him important committee assignments and supporting challengers in the Fort Worth Democratic primaries. O'Neill not only failed to deny Gramm reelection but he inadvertently raised the Boll Weevil's profile across Texas. Although O'Neill regarded himself, with good reason, as a tribune of working-class people standing against predatory elites, in Texas he was just another Yankee carpetbagger. O'Neill and his Democratic allies never understood that in much of the South and Southwest, white voters viewed them as the predatory elites.

Going into early 1983, O'Neil unveiled the Democrats' budget outline. They proposed to undo Reagan's tax cuts—and then raise taxes by a few hundred billion dollars. Congressional Democrats also advocated reversing Reagan's defense buildup and putting more money into social welfare programs. Reagan confided to his diary that O'Neill had committed two potentially fatal errors. First, House Democrats had asserted control of the National Democratic Party's agenda going into the 1984 presidential election. Any Democrat hoping to win the 1984 presidential nomination would have to embrace O'Neill's policies. Democrats who refused to do so would not win the nomination. Second, O'Neill had laid out economic and foreign policy initiatives that were less popular than the congressman realized. The only thing that could be more damaging to Democrats in

1984 than harkening back to Jimmy Carter's policies would be to nominate someone closely associated with Carter.[23]

Reagan was confident that O'Neill had set the Democrats up for a massive electoral defeat. Still, he would not sit back and wait for the anticipated victory. Reagan needed to insulate himself politically—and it helped that the policies he embraced as a result were ones in which he believed.

While Reagan accepted that America had entered a postindustrial era, he drew a line as to how far economic restructuring would go. The United States still needed industry to produce military-related materials, and people needed good-paying manufacturing jobs. Not everyone was going to become an electrical engineer. In 1981, Reagan informed the Japanese and West German governments that they were going to accept self-imposed, "voluntary" trade quotas or face tariff hikes. He was not going to oversee the destruction of America's entire automobile and steel industries. German and Japanese companies, seeking to avoid tariffs and quotas, relocated some production to the United States. No fools, they went to the lower-wage, nonunion South or rural Midwest. While German and Japanese automakers typically paid less than the American automakers, their wages were higher than what service and retail employers offered.[24]

Reagan had worked with congressional Democrats in 1982 to pass the Tax Equity and Fiscal Responsibility Act. In exchange for eliminating a few tax deductions for businesses, Reagan got Democrats to cut some domestic program spending. Democrats were eager to look tough against Wall Street and had been loudly denouncing Reagan for increasing federal deficits. Only upon further reflection did they realize that they were now on record for having cut social welfare programs in the name of deficit reduction—which made them look like Goldwater Republicans. Desperate, congressional Democrats turned to Social Security, certain that Reagan would fall into their trap.

Democrats miscalculated. Having waved the flag of economic nationalism in the politically critical, economically stressed industrial heartland, Reagan was happy to salvage a Social Security program headed toward insolvency. Millions of senior citizens relied on Social Security to carry them through retirement; few had savings, though Reagan wanted to expand tax-sheltered investment opportunities for working Americans.

Since its creation in 1935, Social Security had become a Democratic weapon with which to threaten Republicans. President Eisenhower had observed that "should any political party attempt to abolish Social Security and eliminate labor laws and farm programs, you would not hear of that party again in our political history." In 1964, Democrats had, accurately, branded Goldwater as an enemy of Social Security and successfully roused millions of voters against his presidential candidacy. Carter had tried the same Social Security scare tactics against Reagan in 1980, but he failed. Reagan did not seem mean enough (unlike Goldwater) to take away seniors' retirement checks and reduce them to eating cat food.[25]

Privately, Reagan complained that O'Neill's allies were willing to see Social Security collapse if it meant they could use it as a club to beat him up. Reagan had to maneuver congressional Democrats into cooperating with the White House. His solution was not original, though that did not diminish its effectiveness. He announced the creation of a fifteen-member National Commission on Social Security Reform. Reagan would select five members, and Senate Republicans would nominate five. House Democrats could opt to fill out their nominee list or decline and risk looking obstructionist. O'Neill caved. In 1983, acting on the commission's recommendations, Reagan and Congress hiked the Social Security payroll tax and, for future generations, raised the retirement age required to receive full benefits, to stabilize the program. Cheerfully twisting a rhetorical knife into O'Neill's back, Reagan hailed Social Security reform by quoting Roosevelt: "The future lies with those wise leaders who realize that the great public is more interested in government than in politics."[26]

Economist Lester Thurow, of the Massachusetts Institute of Technology (MIT), had earlier led off the Democratic attack on Reaganomics. Both the *New York Times* and the *Washington Post* gave Thurow a platform from which to attack Reagan's economic policies. According to Thurow, Reagan's military spending was diverting vital financial resources away from the U.S. economy. Although Cold War Democrats had once regarded defense spending as a Keynesian economic stimulus, post-Vietnam Democrats regarded the military with suspicion. They were not wrong to be leery of Pentagon waste and inefficiency.[27]

From the perspective of the early 1980s it was difficult for congressional Democrats and economists such as Thurow to imagine how increased spending on military research could eventually benefit the economy.

Networking computers into what the military called an "internet" and developing electronic computer communication, or "email," had no apparent civilian economic application.

Other Democratic critics dismissively branded Reagan's tax policies as "trickle-down economics." They had readapted the "trickle down" phrase from William Jennings Bryan, the 1896 Democratic presidential nominee. In his first-ever national convention speech, Bryan had condemned Republican economic policy for benefiting the wealthy while everyone else had to hope that prosperity would "leak through to those below." While "trickle down" was evocative and became a part of the 1980s news and academic narrative on Reaganomics, it ignored the historical context. Bryan ran unsuccessfully for president *three times*, losing by a wider margin each time he ran.

At the 1984 Democratic National Convention in San Francisco, New York governor Mario Cuomo delivered an electrifying keynote speech. He chastised Reagan for arguing, like the Puritans, that America was a "Shining City upon a Hill." Rather, Cuomo insisted, America was Charles Dickens' nightmarish *A Tale of Two Cities*. Reagan took money from starving families and either gave it to the wealthy or wasted it on the military. Worse, Americans starved while Reagan's dictatorial allies in Latin America "murder nuns" and oppress their people.[28]

Americans, Cuomo continued, had to stop seeing Reagan as a friend. In reality, Reagan was callous and indifferent to human suffering. Americans had to vote for "[the] Democratic Party which has saved this nation from depression, from fascism, from racism, from corruption, [and] is called upon to do it again—this time to save the nation from confusion and division, from the threat of eventual fiscal disaster, and most of all from the fear of a nuclear holocaust."[29]

Although Cuomo captured the Democratic convention's heart, he was not its presidential nominee. O'Neill and the Democratic leadership wanted Carter's vice president, former Minnesota senator Walter Mondale (1928–). A few disgruntled Democrats challenged Mondale in the primaries, but party officeholders held hundreds of convention seats and largely controlled their state delegations. A product of Congress and a party loyalist for decades, Mondale could be relied upon to follow his leaders' agenda. O'Neill had mapped out the strategy; Mondale would not deviate from it.

Ronald Reagan and Democratic presidential nominee Walter Mondale face off in debate in 1984. Mondale went on to lose in a historic landslide. (Ronald Reagan Presidential Library and Museum)

While Mondale and Cuomo had no significant policy differences, their rhetorical skills were light-years apart. Cuomo could read the content label on a bottle of aspirin and make it sound like Abraham Lincoln's Gettysburg Address. Mondale could do the opposite. What Mondale's acceptance speech lacked in eloquence, however, was made up for in provocative promises. Voters had to go back to Goldwater in 1964 to find another presidential nominee who pledged to inflict pain if elected: "Mr. Reagan will raise taxes, and so will I. He won't tell you. I just did." Mondale thought voters would admire his candor. Instead, he alienated many—and those three lines became the only ones voters remembered from his convention speech.[30]

By the time of the 1984 Republican presidential convention, the economy had moved toward recovery and expansion. Unemployment fell from

10.8 percent in December 1982 to 7.2 percent. Inflation had declined to 5 percent, allowing the Federal Reserve to lower the prime interest rate and make it easier for people to afford home mortgages and businesses to borrow money to finance expansion. The Gross Domestic Product growth rate hit 7.2 percent in 1984, up from a negative 1.8 percent in 1982. Expansion continued through the 1980s, adding $30 trillion of goods and services to the nation along with 18.7 million jobs.[31]

If the presidential election had been held in 1982, Reagan very likely would have lost. Public opinion polls showed that only 36 percent wanted to see him reelected. Since then, the economic context had changed dramatically. O'Neill, Cuomo, and Mondale, however, failed to adjust their rhetoric and strategy. Worse, they had failed to look more deeply into various polls on economic policy. Even if Americans were expressing dismay with Reagan in 1982 and early 1983, 78 percent opposed raising taxes. They believed Reagan when he explained why tax hikes were economically counterproductive and hurt consumers.

Reagan had been a stage actor at Eureka College before he became a radio announcer. He thrived in live theater, feeding off the audience's energy and emotions. The economically dynamic city of Dallas, Texas, was the perfect locale for Reagan's performance. While Reagan avoided calling Mondale by name, he invoked the memory of Roosevelt and identified him as his guidepost. Reagan then took aim at Mondale's pledge to raise taxes and reduce defense spending:

> Is there any doubt that they will raise our taxes? That they will send inflation into orbit again? That they will make government bigger than ever and deficits even worse? Raise unemployment? Cut back our defense preparedness? Raise interest rates? Make unilateral and unwise concessions to the Soviet Union?
>
> And they'll do all that in the name of compassion.
>
> It's what they've done to America in the past. But if we do our job right, they won't be able to do it again.[32]

On the campaign trail, Reagan expressed glee as he watched Mondale cultivate union leaders. Meanwhile, Reagan spoke to thousands of cheering industrial workers in such hard-hit states as Ohio. His campaign focused on smaller communities that had emerged from the recession with new, high-tech facilities that, though greatly automated, still offered employment opportunities. It was a wise strategy, since an appearance in Pittsburgh attracted hundreds of protestors and negative television coverage. Continuing to suffer from the closure of the steel mills, it was not surprising that some Pittsburghers drove cars with a provocative bumper sticker that must have alarmed the Secret Service: "Give Hinckley a Second Chance."

Mondale was confident that union members would follow their leaders. In the Democrats' narrative, Reagan had proved himself to be an enemy of working people in 1981. That year the Professional Air Traffic Controllers' Union (PATCO) declared a strike against its employer, the federal government. The union demanded a $10,000 raise for each of its members and a reduction in the workweek from 40 hours to 32 hours. PATCO's leadership did indicate that it would settle for just a $4,000 pay raise, but the rank and file insisted on the original demands. Reagan warned PATCO that it was illegal to strike against the U.S. government. When 11,359 of 13,000 PATCO members refused to return to work, having disrupted thousands of flights, Reagan fired them.

To the Democrats' shock, a majority of Americans, including *private-sector* union members, supported Reagan's PATCO decision. Industrial workers resented the fact that government employees were demanding that the taxpayers give them pay raises and workload reductions far greater than what the industrial workers could ever receive. Moreover, working in a steel mill or automobile plant, no matter how modernized and equipped with safety features, remained a dirty, dangerous way to earn a living. Staring at computer screens in a temperature-controlled facility did not compare. PATCO's members also earned far more than unionized industrial workers.

There was a brief moment prior to the election when Reagan appeared vulnerable. In his first presidential debate, Reagan seemed confused. He privately confessed that he had "flattened out" by trying to squeeze too many "facts and figures" into rebuttals to Mondale. Seeing an opening, Reagan's critics charged that he was too old to serve as president. Slyly, at the second debate, Reagan delivered a zinger: "I want you to know that also I will not make age an issue of this campaign. I am not going to exploit, for political purposes, my opponent's youth and inexperience." Mondale could be seen on television screens laughing in spite of himself.[33]

The 1984 election was a referendum on Reagan's economic and foreign policies. Reagan scored a reelection victory so immense that it placed him in the rarefied company of Lyndon Johnson (1964) and Franklin Roosevelt (1936). He received nearly 59 percent of the popular vote and carried forty-nine of the fifty states in the Electoral College. Reagan lost Mondale's home state of Minnesota by less than four thousand votes.

An analysis of the 1984 election results yielded data that shocked the Democratic Party leadership. A quarter of registered Democrats voted for Reagan. Generally, "Reagan Democrats," as the media dubbed them, were either northern working-class whites or southern white Protestants. Compared to 1980, Reagan increased his support among northern white Protestants and Catholics, winning solid majorities in both groups—and most especially among lower-income earners. Union members also continued to give Reagan significant support. Despite the Democratic Party's efforts in 1984 to depict Reagan as the champion of wealthy elites, it failed to connect with white, working-class voters. One anecdote said much. A Democratic brewery worker from Texas told reporters that "[Reagan] isn't like a Republican. He's more like an American."[34]

Reagan's 1984 landslide victory did not provide much in the way of what political analysts refer to as "electoral coattails." Unlike 1980, Reagan largely failed to boost congressional Republicans. Although Texas congressman Phil Gramm, who declared himself a Republican, won a U.S. Senate seat, the overall news was mixed. Republicans gained sixteen seats in the House but were far short of a majority. In the Senate, Republicans lost two seats but managed to retain control. As had been true since 1968, while growing numbers of white Democrats voted Republican at the presidential level, they continued to support Democrats down ticket.

The great irony of the 1984 referendum on Reaganomics was that Cuomo's *A Tale of Two Cities* was a credible analogy. Some sectors and regions of the United States prospered just as others suffered. Looking at the hard-hit Midwest, Goodyear vice president Stanley Mihelick pulled no punches in his economic prognosis for the region: "Until we get real wage levels down much closer to those of the Brazils and Koreas," there was little hope for recovery. Workers in Mexico and South Korea earned three dollars an hour compared to an average U.S. industrial wage of fourteen dollars an hour. Americans had to learn to live on less money—and expect fewer health and safety protocols in the workplace. If not, American employers would continue to relocate overseas. Mihelick could have added that the security forces in many of the countries playing host to U.S. industry had a history of beating or killing workers who complained about low wages and shop-floor conditions.[35]

In contrast to the Midwest, many southern and western states, often collectively referred to as the "Sunbelt," experienced an economic boom in the 1980s. Defense contractors, energy producers (oil and natural gas), and assembly facilities blossomed in the Sunbelt. Given the region's history of low wages, weak or nonexistent unions, and a political leadership resistant to environmental and safety regulation, the Sunbelt was the one American region that most closely resembled Brazil, Mexico, or South Korea. Many prospered in the Sunbelt, but many remained mired in poverty—even if employed.

The postindustrial economy spawned its winners and losers. Computer programmers were in high demand, but they were outnumbered five-to-one by low-wage, fast-food workers. For every well-paid computer system analyst, there were four nonunion janitors scraping by. Middle-income jobs, mainly in manufacturing, declined 20 percent in the 1980s. Low-wage jobs increased 50 percent. A third of the new jobs created in 1983, at the start of the Reagan boom, were part-time positions. As had long been the practice, the U.S. Labor Department did not include part-time workers in its unemployment rate calculations.[36]

Millions of Americans experienced upward social mobility and became upper-middle class just as millions of others lost income and social status. Critics coined a new phrase in the 1980s, "Brazilification," to describe the United States' postindustrial economic order. There was, however, a significant difference between the United States and Brazil. In Rio de Janeiro, busloads of tourists would visit its slums in search of "authentic" food and music. Next to no one in the United States was lining up to tour North Philadelphia or East Los Angeles. Poverty in the United States might have been a political issue, but it was not a reality middle-class Americans wanted to experience personally.

Objectively, Laffer's economic vision fell short of the national revival he had prophesied. Then again, going back to the economic policies of the 1970s, as Mondale and O'Neill wanted, was no panacea either. Hourly wages, as adjusted for inflation, had fallen 0.2 percent in 1980. A decade later, inflation-adjusted wages had grown 0.9 percent. This was improvement, though nothing compared to the 1950s or 1960s.[37]

Reagan had pledged to reduce the proportion of the GDP that went to Washington—aiming for a figure of 19 percent. At the end of his second term, the federal government consumed 22.3 percent of the nation's GDP. There had been little change from the Carter years—except that since the GDP in 1988 was larger than it had been in 1981, more money was going to Washington, not less. Moreover, it was important to keep in mind that Reagan *slowed* the rate of domestic social spending but did not reduce it. Rising military spending, meanwhile, ensured that Washington continued to consume a significant portion of the national wealth.

Americans, whether as individuals, as business owners, or as a nation, took on increased debt load in the 1980s. Personal savings fell while people, along with the federal government, financed their spending with borrowed money. Between 1980 and 1986, consumer debt, as adjusted for inflation, more than doubled, increasing from $371 billion to $740 billion. Home mortgage debt grew 65 percent in those same years.

In 1980, the federal government spent $615 billion. At the end of the 1980s, as adjusted for inflation, the federal government was spending $1.2 *trillion*. Much of America's spending came from debt, which other nations increasingly financed. In 1980, the national debt was $900 billion. Two years later, national debt had grown to $1.1 trillion. By 1984, the national debt was $1.5 trillion, and the United States was running annual deficits of $200 billion. With borrowed money came interest payments. In 1980, 8.8 percent of the federal budget went toward interest payments on national debt. Six years later, 13.7 percent of the U.S. budget had to be set aside to make interest payments.[38]

The federal government had no choice but to make interest payments on its debt; default would mean no more money beyond what Washington took in from taxes. As interest payments ballooned, there was less money available to spend elsewhere. Politically, it had proven impossible to cut domestic social spending—and entitlement programs such as Social Security were not only sacrosanct but also guaranteed to increase in cost as the U.S. population aged. Military spending was the only area that could be cut significantly but not as long as the Cold War raged. The Democrats' call to cut defense spending in 1984 had contributed to their rout in the presidential election.

Perhaps the greatest economic irony of the 1980s stemmed from the lessons Reagan learned, and failed not to learn, from Roosevelt. Reagan not only quoted Roosevelt but he even held a party in the White House in 1982 to mark what would have been the late president's hundredth birthday. Conservatives were appalled; Reagan just smiled and handed out cake.

If Reagan had been more thorough in his study of his political idol, he would have known that in 1933 Roosevelt had opposed the creation of the Federal Deposit Insurance Corporation (FDIC). While Roosevelt felt sympathy for Americans who saw their savings vanish when banks failed, he worried that federal insurance of deposits would allow shiftless bankers to force the taxpayers to cover their poor business decisions. But when Roosevelt saw how politically popular the FDIC would be, he agreed—on the condition that the federal government would keep strict oversight of banks.

In 1982, Republican and Democratic members of Congress teamed up to pass legislation to allow savings and loan institutions (S&Ls) to offer loans beyond home mortgages, keep less cash on reserve for emergencies, and overall, be under less federal oversight. Consumers needed more money to borrow, and the thinking was that S&Ls were ideally suited for that purpose. The problem was that the S&L industry began to speculate in real estate and construction with little realistic thought to prospects for profits, and it handed out money to people with little ability to make interest payments. By 1986, S&Ls began to collapse. One-third ultimately failed. Because they were covered by FDIC, taxpayers had to shell out $124 billion.

Roosevelt had left behind a warning. His heir, in a desire to fuel consumer spending, foster economic growth, and deregulate business, had unintentionally added to Americans' economic woes. A panicked Wall Street reacted to the mounting S&L crisis on October 19, 1987, erasing $560 billion in assets. Businesses, and markets, were only as good, and as stable, as the people who ran them. That truism was not one that Laffer and Wanniski had fully assimilated into their belief system. Reagan had known better but had set aside his common sense in the pursuit of economic growth.

NOTES

1. Peter B. Levy, *America in the Sixties—Right, Left, and Center: A Documentary History* (Westport, ed., CT: Praeger, 1998), 284–85.

2. Ibid., 285–86; Everett Carll Ladd Jr., *Where Have All the Voters Gone? The Fracturing of America's Political Parties* (New York: W. W. Norton, 1978), 15.

3. Ladd, *Where Have All the Voters Gone?*, 47.

4. Ibid., 14; Floyd Norris, "Today's Titans Can Learn from the Fall of US Steel," *New York Times*, July 3, 2014; Philip Jenkins, "The Postindustrial Age: 1950–2000," in *Pennsylvania: A History of the Commonwealth*, edited by Randall M. Miller and William Pencak (University Park: Pennsylvania State University Press, 2002), 321.

5. Jon C. Teaford, *Cities of the Heartland: The Rise and Fall of the Industrial Midwest* (Bloomington: Indiana University Press, 1994), 217; Gunnar Anderson, "Changes in Location Pattern of the Anglo-American Steel Industry: 1948–1959," *Economic Geography* 37 (April 1961): 95–114.

6. Arthur B. Laffer, "A Formal Model of the Economy," *Journal of Business* 44 (July 1971): 247–70.

7. George Gilder, "Laffing Gas," *National Review* 30 (September 1978): 1090–92; Joseph F. Sullivan, "Sliding Down the Laffer Curve," *New York Times*, May 7, 1978; "The Tax-Cut Lunch Just Can't Be Free," *New York Times*, June 23, 1980.

8. Brian Domitrovic, "George H. W. Bush's Voodoo Rhetoric," *Forbes*, December 2, 2018, https://www.forbes.com/sites/briandomitrovic/2018/12/02/george-h-w-bushs-voodoo-rhetoric/#6102dc0f798a; "Howard Baker, 88, Posed Famous Watergate Query," *New York Times*, June 26, 2014; John Ehrman, *The Eighties: America in the Age of Reagan* (New Haven, CT: Yale University Press, 2005), 45.

9. John Stahl, *Right Moves: The Conservative Think Tank in American Political Culture Since 1945* (Chapel Hill: University of North Carolina Press, 2016), 120; Phil Gailey, "Heritage Foundation Disappointed by Reagan," *New York Times*, November 22, 1981; Brad Knickerbocker, "Heritage Foundation's Ideas Permeate Reagan Administration," *Christian Science Monitor*, December 7, 1984.

10. Richard S. Williamson, "A New Federalism: Proposals and Achievements of President Reagan's First Three Years," *Publius* 16 (Winter 1986): 11–28.

11. Ibid., 11–28.

12. William E. Pemberton, *Exit with Honor: The Life and Presidency of Ronald Reagan* (Armonk, NY: M. E. Sharpe, 1988), 100, 111.

13. Charles Press and Bernard Klein, "The Political Response in Michigan to Reaganomics and the New Federalism," *Publius* 12 (1983): 139–49.

14. Hodding Carter III, "The Democrats Need to Learn Guerrilla Warfare," *Wall Street Journal*, May 14, 1981; C. Fred Bergsten, "The Costs of Reaganomics," *Foreign Policy*, no. 44 (Autumn 1981): 24–36.

15. "In Defense of Wall Street," *New York Times*, June 2, 1981.

16. William Greider, "The Education of David Stockman," *The Atlantic*, December 1981, https://www.theatlantic.com/magazine/archive/1981/12/the-education-of-david-stockman/305760; Kenneth J. Heineman, *God Is a Conservative: Religion, Politics, and Morality in Contemporary America* (New York: New York University Press, 2005), 126–27.

17. Ronald Reagan, "Address to the Nation on the Economy," February 5, 1981, Ronald Reagan Presidential Library and Museum.

18. Ibid.

19. Carter III, "The Democrats Need to Learn Guerrilla Warfare"; Shirley Anne Warshaw, "White House Control of Domestic Policy Making: The Reagan Years," *Public Administration Review* 55 (May–June 1995): 247–53.

20. Teaford, *Cities of the Heartland*, 217; Philip Jenkins, *Decade of Nightmares: The End of the Sixties and the Making of Eighties America* (New York: Oxford University Press, 2006), 182.

21. Douglas Brinkley, ed., *The Reagan Diaries* (New York: HarperCollins, 2007), 54.

22. Ronald Reagan, "Radio Address to the Nation on the Program for Economic Recovery," April 3, 1982, Ronald Reagan Presidential Library and Museum.

23. Brinkley, ed., *Reagan Diaries*, 137–38.

24. Ehrman, *The Eighties*, 93; "The Auto Quotas: We Asked for It," *New York Times*, March 6, 1985.

25. Lewis L. Gould, *Grand Old Party: A History of Republicans* (New York: Random House, 2003), 335–36.

26. H. W. Brands, *Reagan: The Life* (New York: Doubleday, 2015), 425–27; Brinkley, ed., *Reagan Diaries*, 39.

27. Lester C. Thurow, "Beware of Reagan's Military Spending," *New York Times*, May 31, 1981.

28. Michael Oreskes, "Rising Voice in Democratic Ranks: Mario Matthew Cuomo, Man in the News," *New York Times*, July 17, 1984; Jeff Shesol, "Mario Cuomo's Finest Moment," *New Yorker*, January 2, 2015, https://www.newyorker.com/news/news-desk/mario-cuomos-finest-moment.

29. Oreskes, "Rising Voice in Democratic Ranks"; Shesol, "Mario Cuomo's Finest Moment."

30. "Transcript of Mondale Accepting Party Nomination," *New York Times*, July 20, 1984.

31. Richard C. Auxier, "Reagan's Recession," Pew Research Center, December 14, 2010, https://www.pewresearch.org/2010/12/14/reagans-recession; Martin Anderson, "The Reagan Boom—Greatest Ever," *New York Times*, January 17,

1990; Tim Sablik, Federal Reserve Board of Richmond, "Recession of 1981–82," *Federal Reserve History*, November 22, 2013; Michael Comiskey, "The Promise and Performance of Reaganomics," *Polity* 20 (Winter 1987): 316–31.

32. "Convention in Dallas: The Republicans; Transcript of Reagan's Speech Accepting GOP Nomination," *New York Times*, August 24, 1984; Gould, *Grand Old Party*, 426.

33. Brinkley, ed., *Reagan Diaries*, 271; Brands, *Reagan*, 454–56.

34. Jenkins, *Decade of Nightmares*, 186; Seymour Martin Lipset, "The Elections, the Economy, and Public Opinion: 1984," *Political Science* 18 (Winter 1985): 28–38; Heineman, *God Is a Conservative*, 148.

35. Michael Moffitt, "Shocks, Deadlocks, and Scorched Earth: Reaganomics and the Decline of U.S. Hegemony," *World Policy Journal* 4 (Fall 1987): 553–82.

36. Heineman, *God Is a Conservative*, 134.

37. Levy, *America in the Sixties*, 284–85.

38. Ehrman, *The Eighties*, 67; Moffitt, "Shocks, Deadlocks, and Scorched Earth," 553–82.

CHAPTER 4

"JUST SAY NO": SOCIAL POLICY IN REAGAN'S AMERICA

The expansion of railroad lines after the Civil War transformed isolated Lynchburg, Virginia, into a dynamic regional transportation hub. Lynchburg grew from six thousand residents in 1865 to forty thousand residents by 1930. A booming economy and population growth meant that there was a market for local entertainment. With the adoption of Prohibition in the 1920s, legal supplies of alcohol dried up, and licensed taverns closed. Carey Falwell and his brother Garland realized that they could make a fortune manufacturing and transporting illegal alcohol. Even more money could be made by opening up a nightclub where they would serve their moonshine. The Falwell brothers also established a hotel so that their nightclub customers could continue the party into the morning hours.

Unfortunately for the Falwells, while their illicit businesses prospered, they began sampling too much of their product. Neither brother could hold his liquor, as the saying went, and, unlike Jack Reagan, Carey and Garland were mean drunks. In 1931, during a fight, Carey shot his brother dead. Carey successfully pleaded in court that the murder was in self-defense, but he never forgave himself—and he kept drinking heavily. Even the birth of a son, Jerry, in 1933, did not turn Carey's life around. By the time Jerry Falwell (1933–2007) reached his fifteenth birthday in 1948, Carey had drunk himself to death.

If Carey Falwell built an empire of sin, his son would build an empire of salvation. After attending the Baptist Bible College in Springfield,

Missouri, Jerry Falwell returned to Lynchburg. In 1956, Falwell established the Thomas Road Baptist Church. He began with thirty-five members. Thomas Road grew to over ten thousand congregants and reached thousands more with Falwell's radio broadcasts, *The Old-Time Gospel Hour*. He even established his own college (Liberty Baptist) in 1971, fearful that secular humanism might corrupt Southern Baptist youths if they went to a public university.

The social upheavals of the 1960s appalled Falwell. He was especially repelled by civil rights activist Martin Luther King Jr. In 1965, Falwell delivered a ringing sermon, "Ministers and Marches," which detailed his disgust with King and the Southern Christian Leadership Conference. It was wrong, Falwell argued, for clergy such as King to use their pulpits to advance a secular political agenda: religion was about saving the individual, not transforming society. Worse, Falwell insisted, was the fact that civil rights groups were focusing on the wrong agenda. After all, Falwell concluded, "the alleged discrimination against Negroes in the South" paled in comparison to the problem of alcoholism. In truth, Falwell knew more alcoholics than African Americans, which blinded him to the injustice of racial segregation and electoral disenfranchisement.[1]

By the 1970s, Falwell reconsidered his opposition to political engagement. Crime, divorce, narcotics usage, and premarital sex had escalated in the 1960s. The homicide rate had nearly doubled in the 1960s, while divorces increased by over 100 percent. Marijuana smoking had become commonplace among high school and junior high school students. Antidrug activists were convinced that marijuana smoking was a gateway drug to more dangerous narcotics, including heroin and cocaine. Less affluent junkies frequently financed their addiction through theft and prostitution—with the latter leading to an increase in sexually transmitted diseases.

Campus antiwar protest and an expansionist Soviet Union further alarmed Falwell. Then the U.S. Supreme Court, in *Roe v. Wade* (1973), removed most state-level restrictions on abortion. Falwell concluded that King had made a good point. If you do not engage society and work toward its betterment, then you will find yourself living in a hell on earth. By 1980, Falwell was prepared to apologize to Black church members and clergy in Lynchburg; segregation and disenfranchisement were sins that he had once wrongly embraced.

Falwell had placed a great deal of faith in Jimmy Carter in 1976, convinced that a fellow Southern Baptist could redeem America's soul. He was mistaken. To begin with, Carter, unlike Falwell, was not a religious fundamentalist. Although most Southern Baptists were socially and economically conservative, Carter identified with a minority liberal faction within the church.

Even if Carter had wanted to restore American morality to its pre-1960s incarnation, the Democratic Party had become more culturally open to different lifestyles and values. Public opinion polls consistently showed that as income and education levels rose, so, too, did support for abortion, civil rights, divorce, and gay rights. For example, nearly three-quarters of college-educated, upper-middle-class Democrats in the 1970s supported abortion, compared to 32 percent of high school–educated, working-class Democrats. Social liberals, whose ranks increased for a variety of reasons—from the expansion of higher education to disdain for anticommunist, anti–civil rights white Democrats—became more influential within party ranks.[2]

Antiabortion protest, Washington, DC, 1978. After the U.S. Supreme Court in 1973, with *Roe v. Wade*, recognized abortion as a right, social conservatives mounted a cultural counteroffensive. (Library of Congress)

The price of winning the Democratic presidential nomination in 1976, and securing renomination in the face of challengers on the Left, was steep. There was no way Carter could appease Falwell and social liberals—one or the other would be disappointed. The question then became, Who was more politically important to Carter in the Democratic primaries? While Falwell was clearly not the answer to that question, there was still the matter of winning reelection.

In 1979, Falwell announced that he had founded a new organization, the Moral Majority. To maintain its tax-exempt status as a "voter education" organization, the Moral Majority did not officially endorse candidates. Instead, churchgoers would receive a "scorecard" detailing the positions of candidates on abortion, crime, federal economic policy, gay rights, and Soviet expansionism. To no one's surprise, Carter scored badly, as did many Democrats in general.

Falwell cited King as his inspiration. If the civil rights movement could mobilize Black Protestants in the struggle for equality, why not have white Protestants band together to promote a socially conservative agenda? In short order, the Moral Majority enrolled two million members. Half were Baptists, and nearly all were Protestant and white. Few Catholics or Jews joined the Moral Majority, and it retained a strong southern accent—including areas of the North where Dixie migrants had settled during and immediately after World War II in search of industrial jobs. Just as southern Black migration in the World War II era had helped transform race relations into a national electoral issue, southern white migration moved Dixie's traditionalist religious values out of their regional home.

In his best-selling 1980 manifesto, *Listen, America!*, Falwell named America's enemies. First, there were gays. Falwell warned the faithful that "we are losing the war against homosexuals." Gays were taking over the nation's public schools, universities, and the news media, he claimed. Second, the United States was threatened by the growth of the federal government and the regulation of business. As Falwell argued, "Our Founding Fathers knew that free enterprise was the best economic organization to maintain the free society they had created." Third, U.S. leaders had betrayed the nation to international communism. Falwell observed, "Most of our leaders have been blinded by the intention of the communists because these leaders are in spiritual darkness." Carter may have claimed to

Moral Majority leader Jerry Falwell. Disillusioned with fellow Southern Baptist Jimmy Carter, Falwell founded the Moral Majority in 1979 with the hope of influencing the Republican Party. (Courtesy of Kenneth Heineman)

have been a Christian, but his foreign policy revealed the truth. At best, Carter was an unwitting Soviet tool.[3]

Falwell was not the only leader of what would become known as the "New Christian Right." While Falwell was the product of a dysfunctional family in search of upward mobility, Marion "Pat" Robertson (1930–) came from a position of wealth and high social station. His father, Virginia senator A. Willis Robertson, had been among the 101 Dixie Democrats in Congress who signed the 1956 "Southern Manifesto" pledging "massive resistance" against racial integration.

After serving in the Korean War and graduating from Yale Law School, Robertson had a religious awakening. Though a nominal Southern Baptist, Robertson wanted something deeper to give his life meaning. He and his wife became Pentecostal missionaries and moved into the struggling, increasingly African American Bedford-Stuyvesant neighborhood of New York. After New York, Robertson relocated to Norfolk, Virginia, where he began a church. In 1960, Robertson launched a religious cable broadcast service. He named his media outlet the Christian Broadcasting Network (CBN).

The Pentecostal movement had emerged in the early twentieth century, emphasizing that faith could heal peoples' ailments and that the Holy Spirit could possess people and allow them to speak in strange

Religious conservative activist Pat Robertson. The son of a segregationist Democratic senator from Virginia, Robertson believed in racial equality and opposed abortion and gay rights. Appalled by Jimmy Carter, Robertson became a Republican and later a religious political activist. (Courtesy of Kenneth Heineman)

"tongues." Most of its adherents, who were concentrated in the South, were impoverished. To the horror of respectable Southern Baptists, Pentecostals often held interracial services. When southern Democrats imposed electoral disenfranchisement in the late nineteenth century, they had eliminated the voting rights of 90 percent of African Americans and 30 percent of poor whites. Many of the disenfranchised southern whites were Pentecostals.

In 1966, Senator Robertson made a desperate appeal to his son. The passage of the 1965 Voting Rights Act had enfranchised tens of thousands of Black voters in Virginia, who had little use for the senator. Realizing that the Voting Rights Act had also enfranchised poor white Pentecostals, Senator Robertson asked his son to mobilize them on his behalf. Pat Robertson refused to do so, arguing that his father's sinful treatment of God's children required atonement. Senator Robertson ended his political career in 1966.

Like Falwell, Pat Robertson had high hopes for Carter but ended up disappointed. Robertson's estrangement from Carter stemmed from the treatment Pentecostal schools received from the Internal Revenue Service. During the 1960s and 1970s, hundreds of private religious academies, many of them Southern Baptist, were formed. Such schools were often a blatant attempt to avoid the racial integration of the public schools. Carter administration officials wanted to deprive such schools of their tax-exempt status as religious educational institutions. Pentecostal academies, however, were not typically founded with the desire to avoid racial integration. Most Pentecostals wanted to separate themselves from secular society. Carter's appointees, though, failed to distinguish among the southern religious schools with regard to their agendas. Once Carter's people began punishing the Pentecostal schools, Robertson turned against Carter.

By 1980, Robertson claimed to have several million viewers, though those figures were inflated. (Falwell also exaggerated the amount of popular support the Moral Majority enjoyed.) Where Falwell danced around making direct voter appeals to retain the Moral Majority's tax-exempt status, Robertson was less circumspect. He grandly announced before the election, "We have enough votes to run the country . . . and when the people say, 'We've had enough,' we are going to take over."[4]

While Robertson and Falwell shared nearly identical views on social issues, there were differences between the two on economics. Falwell, speaking for the aspiring middle class, was an enthusiastic proponent of unregulated capitalism: "God is in favor of freedom, property, ownership, competition, diligence, work and acquisition. All of this is taught in the Word of God, in both the Old and New Testaments." Robertson, who saw himself as a spokesperson for the poor, was less enthusiastic about the free market: "Communism and capitalism in their most extreme, secular manifestations are equally doomed to failure." It was not that Robertson rejected free enterprise; he believed that while it was the best economic path to improving peoples' lives, capitalism was still morally flawed.[5]

The third prominent figure in the ranks of moral conservatives was female, Catholic, and, in contrast to Robertson and Falwell, a political activist since her youth. Born into a middle-class Catholic family in St. Louis, Phyllis Stewart went to Washington University and then on to graduate school at Radcliffe. The family regarded Franklin Roosevelt with disdain and was staunchly Republican. In 1945, she obtained a job in New York with a conservative think tank, the American Enterprise Association (later renamed the American Enterprise Institute and subsequently relocated to Washington). Prominent corporate foes of the New Deal and labor unions funded the think tank's operations, including Joseph Pew (Gulf Oil), Lewis Brown (Johns Manville), and Tom Girdler (Republic Steel). In 1949, she married a successful St. Louis attorney, John Schlafly, and together they had six children.

Phyllis Schlafly (1924–2016) may have been a champion of traditional gender roles and the centrality of family to Western civilization, but she never lost her taste for politics outside the home. She crusaded at the local level against international communism and made an unsuccessful run for elective office. It was not until 1964, however, that Schlafly found her muse: Arizona senator Barry Goldwater. She wrote and self-published a Goldwater campaign book, *A Choice Not an Echo*, that sold three million copies. Schlafly had done something that few thought possible: she imposed coherency, logic, and order on Goldwater's beliefs. Indeed, Schlafly explained what Goldwater believed better than he ever could. Moreover, unlike Ronald Reagan, Schlafly focused on Goldwater.

Although she could not have known it at the time, Schlafly reached the height of her political influence in the 1970s with her efforts to derail the ratification of the Equal Rights Amendment (ERA) to the U.S. Constitution. The ERA would have enshrined into the Constitution equal

Social conservative activist Phyllis Schlafly. Organizer and leader of opposition to the ratification of the Equal Rights Amendment, Schlafly doggedly attempted to move the Republican Party toward religious conservatism. (Library of Congress)

rights for women, much as the Fourteenth and Fifteenth Amendments had tried to protect African Americans' citizenship and voting rights a century earlier. Schlafly, however, saw sinister intent and potentially objectionable results in a ratification of the ERA by the required thirty-eight state legislatures. (By 1973, thirty-five states had ratified the ERA.)

First through a STOP-ERA campaign and then by founding the Eagle Forum, Schlafly crusaded against ratification. She argued that the ERA would eliminate child support payments to divorced mothers. Additionally, Schlafly predicted, if the draft were ever reinstated, the ERA would require young women to serve in the military. (Schlafly was pro-military but did not want women in uniform.) Worst of all, Schlafly warned, the ERA would give gays and lesbians the right to marry and raise children. Once gays received equal rights, the American family would collapse, and the nation would perish.

Thanks to her lobbying efforts and public relations campaign, Schlafly was able to place sufficient pressure on state legislatures either to rescind their pro-ERA votes or to oppose ratification altogether. At the 1976

Republican National Convention, Schlafly worked with North Carolina senator Jesse Helms to compel Gerald Ford to repudiate the ERA and *Roe v. Wade*. Helms got the Republican Party to back away from abortion rights though not to completely repudiate the practice. Schlafly, however, failed to end the Republican Party's support of the ERA.

Reagan's relationship with Schlafly and Falwell, and with religious conservatives in general, was complicated—though with Robertson it was less so since he did not have the level of access Falwell had with the White House. On the one hand, Reagan needed social conservatives' votes. It was especially important if he could persuade the religious conservatives who had been voting Democratic that it was time to switch loyalties. For that very reason, Reagan traveled to Lynchburg in 1980 and spoke to

Social conservative activist and North Carolina Republican senator Jesse Helms. As a senator, Helms combined anticommunism with a socially conservative cultural agenda. He was also a critic of affirmative action and of Martin Luther King Jr. (Courtesy of Kenneth Heineman)

Falwell's followers. He then went to Dallas where he addressed another church group. In a sly reference to their tax-exempt status as a religious and educational organization, Reagan said, "I know you can't endorse me, but I want you to know that I endorse you and what you are doing."[6]

On the other hand, there was a host of social issues for which Reagan gave religious conservatives a few gestures of support, but little else. He was willing to record talks to groups who came to Washington on the anniversary of *Roe v. Wade* to picket the U.S. Supreme Court. Rhetorically, Reagan regarded abortion as a slide down a slippery moral slope. As he asserted in 1988:

> America was founded on a moral proposition that human life—all human life—is sacred. And this proposition is the bedrock of our national life, the foundation of our laws. It's the wellspring of our Constitution. Courts may ignore it, and they have. They cannot—and I should add—have not denied it. When reverence for life can have no boundaries, when we begin to take some life casually, we threaten all life.[7]

Somewhat more concretely, Reagan gave social conservatives a clear platform victory on abortion at the 1984 Republican National Convention. The Republican Party proclaimed that "the unborn child has a fundamental individual right to life which cannot be infringed." Reagan, however, did not speak at antiabortion rallies in person, expended no political capital to limit abortion rights, and understood that most voters never looked at a party's political platform. Falwell fumed that some of Reagan's advisers "probably couldn't spell abortion." He was even more upset when Reagan nominated Sandra Day O'Connor (1930–), a supporter of abortion rights, to the U.S. Supreme Court. The first woman to serve on the Court, O'Connor had no intention of overturning *Roe v. Wade*.[8]

Neither religious conservatives nor secular liberals understood that Reagan's views on abortion were nuanced and that he did not believe in the euphemisms both sides of the issue deployed: pro-life and pro-choice. When Reagan read a heartfelt letter from a Republican abortion supporter in 1984, he privately called her on the phone. (At first, she thought it was a prank call.) Out of sight of television cameras, Reagan told her that there are "two peoples' rights involved in abortion—the mother and the unborn child." What right did government, whether federal, state, or local, have to force a woman to continue a pregnancy? On the other hand, did the rights of the unborn child outweigh the concerns of a mother who might have compelling reasons to terminate her pregnancy? Serious moral dilemmas could not be adequately addressed on an automobile bumper sticker.[9]

Tied into the abortion issue and the struggle over ratification of the ERA was what political pundits in the 1980s referred to as "the gender gap." Liberal activists argued that more women than men voted Democrat than Republican. They insisted that abortion rights fed into the gender gap, as did the fact that more women were entering the workforce and becoming economically independent of men—though there was a "wage gap" that paralleled the gender gap.

The gender gap voting analysis was incomplete at best. While more women than men voted Democratic beginning in the 1980s, much of that difference could be accounted for by the fact that African Americans, Mexican Americans, and Jews lopsidedly rejected Republicans. If race, ethnicity, and religion were accounted for, then the gender gap nearly disappeared. A majority of white women, excluding Jews, were just as likely to vote Republican as white males.

There was also a social class gap that rendered the gender gap less impressive as a tool of analysis. While the proportion of women in the workforce went from 34 percent in 1950 to nearly 52 percent by 1980, and continued to increase, why that happened, as well as the shape of the labor market, mattered. The declining value of wages in the 1970s had forced larger numbers of women into the workforce to support their families. Further, while hundreds of thousands of women entered lucrative white-collar professions in the 1980s, others took low-wage jobs. For the latter group, especially working-class white women, whichever party promoted economic growth and cut taxes would get their vote. Ratifying the ERA was well down their list of priorities.

Abortion rights did not necessarily fit comfortably into the gender gap. Planned Parenthood, which was the nation's largest provider of contraceptives and abortion services, conducted its own public opinion polling. Their results were consistent through the 1970s and 1980s. Level of education, income, and religious engagement were the best predicators of where one stood on abortion. Tellingly, there was a gender gap of sorts on abortion. Single males in their twenties were the most supportive of abortion rights, while religiously observant Christian women were the most opposed to abortion.

The issue of gay rights was just as messy as that of abortion for the nation—and would have been so even without the advent of acquired immunity disease syndrome (AIDS) in the 1970s. Federal, state, and local public health officials had been bewildered by the outbreak of a lethal disease that they believed was sexually transmitted and confined to a single demographic—hence they originally called the mysterious affliction the "gay-related immune disease," or GRID. Once it became obvious that the infection could be spread through contaminated needles shared among heroin users, as well as by blood transfusions, GRID became AIDS. Ignoring the fact that one could contract AIDS without being a drug user, gay, or sexually promiscuous, Falwell contended that, "AIDS and syphilis and all sexually transmitted diseases are God's judgment upon the total society for embracing what God has condemned: sex outside of marriage."[10]

Democratic activists and the news media attacked Reagan for not responding to the AIDS crisis quickly enough and for failing to provide sufficient federal funding to find a cure. His slow response, however, was not due to any bias against gays. Reagan had known many people in Hollywood who had kept their sexual orientation hidden so that they could continue to work. (His acquaintances included the actor Rock Hudson, who died of AIDS in 1985.) As a union leader, Reagan never discriminated against actors on the basis of sex. More importantly, as California governor, Reagan had opposed efforts to ban gay teachers in the public schools. He had even tried, but failed, to push back against a media-hyped "sex scare" and related FBI investigation after hostile journalists claimed there was a "homosexual ring" in his administration. Finally bowing to political pressure from the FBI, as well as from Republicans *and Democrats*, Reagan fired his gay chief of staff.

As president and leader of his party, Reagan was in a position to know how important gays were to the conservative movement. Terry Dolan (1950–1986), who died of AIDS, was the chair of the National Conservative Political Action Committee (NCPAC). Dolan's brother was Reagan's chief speechwriter on foreign policy issues. Marvin Liebman, who had helped found the American Conservative Union (ACU) in 1964, was gay. The ACU and NCPAC were major fundraisers for the Right.

Schlafly's son John was also gay, though she tried to keep that fact quiet as she crusaded against gay rights.

Gays were not the only people that had an often-strained relationship with religious conservatives. Falwell, along with millions of evangelicals and fundamentalists, embraced Israel. Their support for Zionism, however, often had a catch. Many conservative Protestants believed that Israel was the fulfillment of biblical prophecy—in particular, the countdown to Armageddon. The founding of Israel, such religious conservatives argued, would lead to the apocalyptical struggle between Christ and Satan. During the final battle, many Jews would realize their error in rejecting Christ as their savior. Those Jews would become Christians and be saved; those who did not would burn in hell.

Other Protestant conservatives did not even hold out that much hope that Jews could be redeemed. In 1980, during a political rally that included several Reagan advisers, Bailey Smith, the president of the Southern Baptist Convention, proclaimed, "God does not hear the prayer of a Jew."[11]

Paradoxically, Southern Baptists (and Pentecostals) were often more supportive of Israel than Jews were. In part, the horrors of World War II, followed by the founding of Israel as a "Jewish homeland," were becoming distant memories with the passage of time. Moreover, the 1967 Arab-Israeli War, which led to the Israeli occupation of territories with large Palestinian populations, left a sour taste in the mouths of many American Jews. Factions within the Democratic Party became more critical of Zionism after 1967, forcing Jewish Democrats to choose sides. Some fled to the Republican Party, the "neoconservatives," but most Jews remained Democratic voters. A few defended Israel, but the majority of Jewish Democrats increasingly preferred to discuss anything but Israel.

Southern Baptists and Jews were sharply divided over abortion, gay rights, and the role of the federal government in the economy. As religious groups, Jews were among the most socially and economically liberal, while Southern Baptists were their mirror image. Reagan may have been a staunch, though critical, ally of Israel, but his economic policies, and support from religious conservatives, ensured that few Jews voted for him. Indeed, his embrace of Zionism was often a detriment to gaining greater Jewish support.

The ideological divisions between Southern Baptists and Jews were rooted in theology and historical experience. Jewish religious belief focused on the here and now and spent less time contemplating the afterlife. If life was unjust, then, many Jews believed, it was incumbent upon them to work for social and political change. Moreover, if faced with a hostile local population, then it was important for Jews to make allies among the rulers of the nation, who might protect them from persecution (though elites were often the source of Jews' mistreatment).

Conversely, Southern Baptists were focused on heaven and hell and were convinced that poverty and suffering were the products of individuals' sinful behavior. Southern Baptists were also leery of federal intervention, believing that local government was best suited to ban anything they regarded as immoral. The federal government, many Southern Baptists argued, was too distant from the people to be able to distinguish between the saints and the sinners. Moreover, from the perspective of some Southern Baptists, the federal government had once waged a war on the South, placed it under military occupation, and elevated former slaves into positions of political power. Washington could not be trusted—and that distrust extended to a number of Reagan administration personnel. While it was true that the Moral Majority wanted to use the federal government to advance its political agenda, it was ultimately in pursuit of protecting local and regional economic and social values. Falwell and his followers hoped to exercise power over the federal government in order to diminish federal power.

While conservatives often had strained relations with gays and most Jews, their interactions with African Americans demonstrated an even higher level of dysfunction. Some of that was due to history, some to mutual misunderstanding, and some to Reagan.

In 1955 William F. Buckley Jr., the heir to an oil fortune, launched the *National Review*. Buckley wanted to make the *National Review* the leading voice of post–World War II conservatism and largely succeeded. The *National Review* was not subtle about expressing its reasons for opposing civil rights legislation: "In the Deep South the Negroes are, by comparison with whites, retarded ('unadvanced,' the NAACP might put it). Any effort to ignore the fact is sentimentalism and demagoguery. Leadership in the South, then, quite properly, rests in white hands."[12]

Through the 1950s and early 1960s, the Republican Party's Eisenhower faction had supported civil rights legislation, though Eisenhower was reluctant to use the federal government to compel social or racial change.

Typically, more congressional Republicans than Democrats supported civil rights initiatives. To Goldwater and other conservatives, civil rights proposals were, like Social Security and labor laws, unreasonable intrusions into peoples' lives and businesses. Restaurant owners should be able to deny service to people based upon their skin hue just as much as businesses should be able to operate without labor unions. Goldwater opposed the 1964 Civil Rights Act and, as the Republican presidential nominee, campaigned against such legislative initiatives. Although Goldwater lost in a historic landslide, the Republican Party slowly moved away from championing civil rights in its pursuit of alienated southern white voters.

Reagan's relationship with African Americans was complex. In 1948, Reagan had strongly supported adding a civil rights plank to the Democratic Party platform and endorsed Truman's executive order to integrate the armed forces. Eighteen years later, Reagan still considered himself to be a friend of racial minorities, but nonetheless he owed his election as California governor to a backlash against inner-city protest, disorder, and mounting crime rates. Many working-class whites blamed African Americans for the increased chaos in the cities, often overlooking the fact that most of the victims of violent crime were African American.

During the 1980 campaign, Reagan delivered a speech supportive of states' rights at the Neshoba County, Mississippi, fairgrounds. Critics argued that Reagan was making subtle racist appeals, since three civil rights workers had been murdered sixteen years earlier in the Neshoba County seat of Philadelphia, Mississippi. A thousand activists had participated in the 1964 "Mississippi Freedom Summer," a campaign to register African Americans to vote. Two-thirds of the Freedom Summer volunteers were Jewish, and two of the three civil rights workers murdered in Philadelphia had been Jewish.

Reagan's attackers failed to inflict much damage on him. To begin with, during the 1976 campaign, Jimmy Carter had not only spoken at the Neshoba County fairgrounds but had done so standing alongside the segregationists who had held elective offices during the bloody summer of 1964. If Reagan speaking in Neshoba County in 1980 was racist (or opportunist), then Carter's actions in 1976 were also racist (or opportunist).

Taken at face value, Reagan's Neshoba County speech had nothing to do with race. First, he delivered a well-rehearsed quip to let his southern Democratic audience know that he shared their Roosevelt political lineage: "We've had the New Deal, and then Harry Truman gave us the Fair Deal, and now we have a misdeal." Second, Reagan decried rising taxes and a financially burdensome federal bureaucracy. Then Reagan followed up with the states' rights passage that liberals insisted was a covert racist appeal to whites:

> I believe in state's rights; I believe in people doing as much as they can for themselves at the community level and at the private level. And I believe that we've distorted the balance of our government today by giving powers that were never intended in the constitution to that federal establishment. And if I do get the job I'm looking for, I'm going to devote myself to trying to reorder those priorities and to restore to the states and local communities those functions which properly belong there.[13]

Many of the white voters who liked Reagan could not understand why civil rights activists were accusing him, and, by extension, them, with racism. More than a few did not understand that states' rights' rhetoric and attacks on federal intervention had been shields behind which southern segregationists long denied African Americans equal rights. Others knew and considered it irrelevant since, they believed, past injustices had been corrected with civil rights legislation.

The Neshoba County incident underscored a perceptions gap between liberals and conservatives—one that was as much ideological as racial. To civil rights activists, Philadelphia (Mississippi) and Selma and Montgomery (Alabama) were akin to secular Stations of the Cross. Through them ran the path to salvation. To conservatives, Philadelphia, Selma, and Montgomery were either examples of lawlessness (on the part of civil rights activists) or distractions from more important issues—namely combatting international communism and the out-of-control growth of the federal government. Reagan saw some merit in the first view but more enthusiastically embraced the second line of thought. Senator Helms was less temperate, opposing legislative efforts to make Martin Luther King Jr.'s birthday a federal holiday on the grounds that he was a communist agitator.

In 1984, the Republican Party bluntly took aim at civil rights activists by denouncing racial hiring quotas. Reagan framed affirmative action as a liberal assault on whites: "If you happen to belong to an ethnic group not recognized by the federal government as entitled to special treatment, you are the victim of reverse discrimination." The peculiar thing about Reagan's attack on affirmative action was that he was denouncing a federal policy in a manner to suggest that he was powerless to do anything about it. While hiring quotas had grown out of the 1964 Civil Rights Act and subsequent federal bureaucratic rules and court decisions, the president still had many ways to undermine their imposition—whether through executive or legislative action. A cynic might believe that conservatives found affirmative action to be a useful political tool with which to mobilize white voters rather than a policy to be ended.[14]

It would be decades before Americans obtained one critical piece of evidence indicating that Reagan clearly did not think much of Africans. In 1971, during a phone conversation with Richard Nixon, Reagan vented about the African diplomats at the UN who had voted against U.S. interests: "To see those, those monkeys from these African countries—damn them, they're still uncomfortable wearing shoes!" Reagan was not aware that Nixon was recording their conversation.[15]

Conservatives defended Reagan, making several points, including the fact that nowhere in his personal papers or diaries did he ever use such disparaging racial language. They also observed that Reagan maintained friendships with African Americans from his college years. Moreover, throughout his presidency, Reagan decried bigotry.[16]

A few caveats, however, are in order. Reagan was very self-conscious of his public image, taking care to keep a well-groomed record for posterity. Had he known Nixon was recording him, Reagan would have likely been more discrete. (Nixon had the uncanny ability to bring out the worst in others, just as Reagan on occasion went off script and made verbal gaffes.) Moreover, the records that are given to an archive often depend on who is doing the selecting. Some items may be included but others, if potentially embarrassing, may be omitted. As for Reagan having African American friends, that did not preclude him from having a low opinion of Africans. To paraphrase 1960s Black radical Malcolm X, it was possible for some whites to love the individual African American but to hate the race. What we can conclude with some certainty is that Reagan's racial views, as reflected in his diary and public speeches, were more enlightened than those of many of his contemporaries. Simultaneously, his racial views could be as bad as those of others.

African American activists were not united in their reaction to Reagan. Former Carter official Andrew Young had gone to a rally at Ohio State University in 1980 and argued that if Reagan were elected, "it's going to be all right to kill n—s." Young's over-the-top rhetoric alienated moderates and mobilized angered Reagan supporters. Benjamin Hooks, the executive director of the National Association for the Advancement of Colored Peoples (NAACP), countered after the election that African American fear of Reagan was way "out of proportion to reality." Hooks understood that while Reagan would never be an ally, he did not have to be an enemy either. The NAACP leader embraced the pragmatic political philosophy that had taken Reagan so far. Hooks noted that he would be watching the White House, taking a wary trust-but-verify approach that Reagan later used with Mikhail Gorbachev.[17]

Bound up in civil rights protest and white backlash was the issue of "law and order." Since the 1960s, the phrase was politically charged, and its meaning depended as much on the speaker as on the audience. When former Alabama governor and independent presidential candidate George Wallace called for law and order in 1968, there was no mistaking that he was aiming his rhetoric at inner-city minorities and affluent college protestors. To Wallace, and the voters he siphoned from the Democratic Party, law and order meant a police crackdown. A majority of Americans, mainly white, supported the violent police response to radical antiwar protest at the 1968 Democratic National Convention in Chicago. At Chicago, leftists chanted, "The whole world is watching!" They later understood that the "world" was cheering on the police as they clubbed demonstrators, regardless of whether or not they had thrown rocks.

To many African Americans, "law and order" was a thinly veiled justification for police violence in impoverished urban neighborhoods. Community relations between African Americans and police departments had never been close, but they had grown more distant during the 1960s. Part of the problem was due to midwestern and eastern cities emulating the policing example set by Los Angeles. In Los Angeles, because of its low-density sprawl and enormous area, police had shifted from "walking the beat," and getting to know the people in the neighborhoods, in favor of radio cars dispatched from centralized stations. The Los Angeles policing model made law enforcement officers look more like an alien army of occupation and less like a friend trying to render aid. Of course, it did not help community relations in cities such as Philadelphia where the police leadership did regard itself as commanding an army of occupation.

The other part of the problem in urban race relations went by the label "white flight," though by the 1980s middle-class African Americans had joined the exodus to the suburbs. In 1960, Detroit's population was 29 percent African American. Three years after the 1967 riot, Detroit was 44 percent African American. By 1980, Detroit was 63 percent African American. It was not so much that the Black population was growing as it was that the white, heavily Catholic and ethnic population of the Motor City left. As Detroit lost people and industry shuttered or, like the new General Motors plant built in "Poletown," replaced workers with robots, the city's tax base contracted. As Detroit became poorer, the need for social services and public safety grew enormously. It was as if at the end of the 1970s, many American cities, especially in older northern communities, had become segregated reservations for the poor.

Violent crime, which had increased by over 100 percent in the 1960s, rose another 100 percent in the 1970s and an additional 100 percent in the 1980s. Most of the homicides in the United States were clustered in a handful of cities and drove up national crime rates. By 1990, Los Angeles and New York, which together accounted for 4 percent of the U.S. population, claimed nearly 21 percent of the nation's homicides.

It was no little irony that Reagan, whose political career benefited enormously by mounting public revulsion against urban disorder, oversaw one of the worst escalations of domestic violence and crime in American history. Much of the crime and violence could be tied to the expanding narcotics trade. Although exact figures were difficult to obtain, since U.S. law enforcement agencies only intercepted a fraction of the drugs imported into the country, experts offered a few ballpark figures. The Medellin Cartel in Colombia, for example, netted at least $2 billion shipping cocaine to the United States (or $6.2 billion, adjusted for inflation). By the mid-1980s cocaine had surpassed coffee as Colombia's number one export.

The rising American demand for narcotics gave drug cartels in Mexico, Central America, and South America an enormous incentive to expand production and fight for their market share in the United States. The number of American cocaine users may have increased from fifteen million to twenty million in the first few years of the 1980s—a market expansion that would have astonished, and delighted, any legitimate businessperson.

Law enforcement representatives estimated that 70 percent of the narcotics shipped into the United States came through Miami. In the fight for control of Miami, rival traffickers turned the city into an art deco Wild West. So many corpses piled up in Dade County that the medical examiner had to rent a refrigerated truck to store the bodies until he could perform autopsies.

There was another development that no one in law enforcement had anticipated. The twenty-dollar bill was the denomination of choice for drug traffickers working the Miami-to-South America corridor. So many twenties passed through drug dealers' hands that by the end of the 1980s, nearly every twenty-dollar bill circulated in the United States would have tested positive for cocaine residue. That development made the use of drug-sniffing dogs to locate traffickers' cash more challenging.

Reagan went to Congress in 1982 to request additional funding for antidrug personnel and operations. He also pushed for laws to target drug trafficking. An offender would face enormous penalties if arrested with an amount (by weight) of drugs considered to be more than what would have been taken for personal use. In essence, the federal government treated every drug user as a potential dealer.

The 1984 Comprehensive Crime Control Act was a watershed in law-and-order legislation. Viewing marijuana as a "gateway drug" to cocaine, Republicans and Democrats increased federal penalties for its possession. Violent repeat offenders, including those arrested on narcotics charges, now faced a mandatory minimum prison sentence of fifteen years. The federal government also received the power to seize the property and funds of criminals. Before 1984, the federal government had to prove that a criminal's money or possessions were tied to illegal activities. The 1984 Crime Control Act regarded all of the assets of offenders as fruits of criminal activities, and they became subject to forfeiture. Initially intended to punish large-scale drug dealers, especially the Miami operators, asset forfeiture became increasingly common for other offenses.

In the two years after the passage of the Crime Control Act, the U.S. prison population grew 32 percent. Overall, federal incarceration numbers increased dramatically during the decade. In 1980, the United States had 1.8 million people in prison, on parole, or on probation. At the end of the decade, there were 4.4 million prisoners and ex-convicts in the United States—more than anywhere else in the world. (China's prisoner population would have been larger but for its frequent practice of summarily executing those accused of crimes.)

Critics of Reagan's law-and-order policy charged him with racial bias. Their accusations rested on two points. The first was that the majority of those arrested on narcotics charges belonged to racial minority groups. Minorities were incarcerated at rates that were several times larger than their proportional representation in the population. Second, the 1986 Anti-Drug Abuse Act imposed mandatory minimum prison sentences for all offenders but created greater penalties on crack cocaine addicts than on cocaine powder users. Crack was a relatively cheap drug in which "rocks" were formed by mixing ammonia with a little cocaine. Users could then smoke the rock. Many crack cocaine users belonged to racial minorities, while more expensive powder cocaine tended to be the drug of choice of middle-class and affluent whites.

There was a bias in law enforcement and Reagan's war on drugs, but it was as much a class bias as it was a racial bias. Prosecutors found it difficult to win cases against defendants who had the financial resources to hire good attorneys—though asset forfeiture could financially hamper an effective defense. For the privileged class of offender, prosecutors found it easier, and less expensive, to plea bargain charges down and redirect offenders to rehabilitation facilities. Middle-class offenders could be seen as victims of addiction who could be educated to see the error of their ways.

Inner-city drug offenders, who could not afford a good attorney and relied on overworked public defenders, were fair game. Prosecutors could score relatively easy, and numerous, victories, which improved their political profile (if elected) and earned them rapid promotions. Crack users, whose reasoning skills often suffered by the inhalation of household cleaning agents mixed in the rocks, made self-incriminating statements to the police and were easily misled and intimidated. They would not be going to rehab spas to get "clean"; they would go to prisons where narcotics were readily available.

First Lady Nancy Reagan's public relations campaign, "Just Say No to Drugs," fit well into the spirit of therapeutic education. Children watching Saturday morning television cartoons could view an antidrug

"Just Say No": Social Policy in Reagan's America

advertisement that featured a frying egg and a voice-over saying, "This is your brain on drugs. Any questions?" In addition to the fried egg commercial campaign, Nancy Reagan appeared on various television comedies and dramas, from *Dynasty* to *Different Strokes*, urging youths to say no to drugs. While her appearances were well intentioned, the viewer demographics of such shows skewed toward middle aged and middle class. Such people were unlikely to be regular cocaine users. "Just say no" might have dissuaded some middle-class youths from experimenting with drugs, but it did nothing to stem narcotics trafficking and the resulting violence that washed over American cities in the 1980s.

Urban disorder had another dimension that came to public attention in the 1980s: homelessness. Some on the Left, and in the mainstream news media, tried to link the growing number of homeless, destitute people to Reaganomics and the 1982 recession, but the roots were much deeper and largely found elsewhere.

In 1948, Reagan's anticommunist Hollywood comrade in arms, Olivia de Havilland, had received praise for one of her most searing films—*The*

Nancy Reagan, Just Say No school rally. Convinced that education was the best approach to young children to dissuade them from trying narcotics, First Lady Reagan toured schools. (Ronald Reagan Presidential Library and Museum)

Snake Pit. The film depicted the brutal conditions patients might have experienced inside what were then called "insane asylums." De Havilland's performance inspired renewed political interest in reforming the treatment of psychiatric patients.

By the early 1970s, the American Civil Liberties Union (ACLU) had successfully mounted legal challenges against state governments that placed mental patients under lock and key. In 1975, the U.S. Supreme Court, in O'*Connor v. Donaldson,* ruled that the mentally ill could not be confined against their will. The Supreme Court, however, insisted that no one should be deinstitutionalized if they posed a threat to public safety and if they could not expect assistance from their families.

Most states, looking to reduce their spending on the mentally ill, deinstitutionalized patients by the tens of thousands, regardless of whether they were dangerous or would be abandoned by their families and end up living on the streets. In 1950, psychiatric hospitals and prison hospital wards housed one million mentally ill people. Thirty years later, that number had fallen to one hundred thousand. Many of the deinstitutionalized found themselves alone and adrift. The ACLU had not expected this outcome.

In 1981, the Reagan administration estimated that there were 250,000 homeless people in the United States. Liberal activists countered that there were 3 million living on the streets. While neither of these figures was accurate, there was sufficient data to make several observations. First, many of the homeless had narcotics and alcohol addiction issues. Of the 400,000 cocaine addicts in Los Angeles County in the 1980s, one-quarter were homeless. Second, 73 percent of the homeless across the United States were single men, while 8 percent were married men who had wandered away. The homeless were not, as the broadcast networks depicted them, families who had fallen upon hard times. Finally, while many of the homeless defecated in the streets and others committed theft and assault, most were more likely to be not the perpetuators but the victims of violent crime.[18]

There was one dimension of the homeless problem in which Reaganomics did play a role: urban renewal. Through the 1960s and 1970s, as dozens of major urban centers experienced economic decline, the poor, including the mentally ill, could often find substandard housing rather than live in the streets. Many decrepit hotels and tenements offered cheap single-room-occupancy (SRO) options. If not for Nelle Reagan's patience, and a job courtesy of the New Deal, Jack Reagan would have likely found himself living in a Chicago SRO. Ronald Reagan knew such an outcome had been possible.

As the economy expanded in the 1980s, urban real estate developers began buying SRO hotels and tenements. Many drew on the federal grants programs created during the Johnson administration to promote historic preservation and urban renewal. Speculators converted the SROs into upscale condominiums and apartments, leaving their former occupants to move elsewhere—which frequently meant relocating to the streets. Manhattan led the way in the extinction of SROs and the subsequent increase in the homeless population.

While the U.S. homeless population swelled, prisons overflowed, and narcotics trafficking flourished, yet another issue came to the fore: the five million immigrants living in the country illegally. In 1965, Congress, at Johnson's urging, eliminated the national origins quotas on immigration that had been in place since 1921. The immigration laws of 1921 and 1924 had placed severe restrictions on immigration from Southern and Eastern Europe and continued earlier limitations on the admission of Asians. Prior to World War I, immigration restriction had enjoyed a wide array of support. Labor leaders believed that cheap immigrant workers drove down the wages paid to the native born, while some intellectuals were convinced that the admission of undesirable nationalities would pollute the United States' racial pool. The civil rights revolution of the 1960s made the continued restriction of immigration on the basis of nationality morally unacceptable.

The 1965 immigration reforms opened America's doors wider. Millions of immigrants, largely from Asia, Mexico, and South America, came to the United States. Many arrived after filing federal paperwork. Most sought citizenship. Others came across the border from Mexico without documentation. Both Republican senator Alan Simpson (1931–) of Wyoming and Reagan were concerned about the welfare of what the news media referred to as "the illegals." Simpson, who worked with Reagan on immigration, observed that the president "knew that it was not right for people to be abused. Anybody who's here illegally is going to be abused in some way, either financially [or] physically. They have no rights."[19]

Reagan created a bipartisan panel to study immigration, appointing Father Theodore Hesburgh, the president of Notre Dame University and a former member of the U.S. Civil Rights Commission, as chair. During the 1984 election, Reagan spelled out his position while debating Walter Mondale: "I believe in the idea of amnesty for those who have put down roots and lived here, even though some time back they may have entered illegally."[20]

Democrats were badly divided on immigration reform. House Speaker Tip O'Neill insisted initially that there was "no constituency" for reform. Americans were not concerned about the issue. Representative Kent Hance, a Democrat from Texas, warned that amnesty would encourage more illegal immigration, which would undercut the wages of native Texans. For its part, the Democratic-aligned leadership of the AFL-CIO, speaking on behalf of organized labor, wanted illegal immigrants deported, not given amnesty. The members of the Hispanic Caucus in the Democratic Party, however, disagreed with Hance, O'Neill, and union leaders. They wanted reform—and considerable penalties imposed on employers who hired and exploited illegal immigrants.

The 1986 Immigration and Reform Control Act achieved part of what Simpson, Reagan, and Hesburgh wanted: amnesty for three million immigrants who entered the United States illegally before 1982. Greater federal penalties on large agricultural employers and building contractors who employed illegal immigrants at low wages, however, did not materialize. That development was not surprising. Agribusiness and construction were politically powerful and strongly positioned within the Republican and Democratic parties. Both farmers and contractors wanted undocumented workers who, given their status, could not file grievances with the U.S. Labor Department or the Occupation Safety and Health Administration. If such workers went on strike, employers could inform on them to the federal government and have them deported.

Republicans, like Democrats, were badly divided on immigration reform. In part, the business, or "Wall Street," wing of the Republican Party opposed federal regulation of employers, regarding it as a betrayal of free-market principles. Many businesses also agreed with the AFL-CIO that illegal immigrants were an inexpensive labor force with no rights. They saw that as a good thing.

Some conservatives, however, opposed all immigration from South America and Mexico, regardless of whether it was legal or not. They pointed to the millions of children born of Southern and Eastern European immigrants in the early twentieth century who went on to become Roosevelt voters and union members. That previous demographic deluge, worried conservatives argued, had paved the way for the erection and consolidation of the welfare state. What sort of mischief would the children of new immigrants from Mexico and Latin America inflict upon the United States in the future—beyond destroying the Republican Party's electoral prospects? Conservative intellectuals such as Harvard's Samuel Huntington warned that Spanish-speaking immigrants brought with them a poisonous culture of socialism and violence and could not be assimilated.

Although they played little role in the immigration debate and had next to no success on abortion, social conservatives in the 1980s acquired a voice in the Heritage Foundation, courtesy of the think tank's major benefactor, beer baron Joseph Coors. There was no little irony that the proceeds of alcohol sales were empowering Protestant evangelical political activists.

Coors's support of religious conservatives was often as limited in effectiveness as it was counterproductive. Both Schlafly and the Heritage Foundation learned that lesson. Coors had been a vigorous champion of Schlafly, urging Reagan to recognize her contributions to the conservative cause. Schlafly indicated that she would accept a seat on the U.S. Supreme Court. Instead, Reagan appointed her to a commission to celebrate the bicentennial of the U.S. Constitution. As for the Heritage Foundation, the more influential that religious conservatives such as Falwell became, the fewer corporate donations the think tank received. Corporate leaders were often as socially liberal as they were economically conservative. Silicon Valley nearly produced as many libertarians as computer chips (the latter increasingly being manufactured less expensively overseas).

Libertarians, who had been fighting a losing rearguard action since the New Deal, had rallied to Goldwater in 1964. Though Goldwater lost decisively, he inspired a new generation of libertarians. Sixty thousand college students joined the Young Americans for Freedom (YAF), a conservative campus organization that Buckley had founded in 1960. Young libertarians, who were largely from upper-middle-class, secular families and often concentrated in the nation's elite public and private colleges, expressed themselves on a variety of issues. They opposed the draft and the Vietnam

War while supporting the legalization of narcotics. Libertarians believed that the federal government had no constitutional right to regulate the boardroom or the bedroom.

In 1977, two Wichita, Kansas, businessmen, the brothers Charles (1935–) and David Koch (1940–2019), helped found a libertarian think tank in Washington: the CATO Institute. The Koch siblings were convinced that the American Enterprise Institute had fallen into the hands of neoconservatives who still carried Franklin Roosevelt's banner. As for the Heritage Foundation, its corporate benefactors, the Koches believed, did not really want to decrease the size of the federal government. The Heritage Foundation was actually seeking control of the federal government in order to help businesspeople line their own pockets at the expense of taxpayers. CATO also opposed increasing U.S. defense spending as much as it decried what it regarded as a big government–big business alliance.

David Koch, who was the most politically active member of his family, ran for vice president in 1980 on the Libertarian Party ticket. While he had taken the number two spot, David Koch used his charisma and money to set the libertarians' agenda. The Libertarian Party embraced abortion and gay rights, as well as the legalization of narcotics, while calling for the abolition of Social Security, the FBI, and the CIA. David Koch warned that if Reagan were elected, Americans would experience "no change whatsoever from Jimmy Carter and the Democrats." While the overwhelming majority of voters had no use for the Libertarian Party in 1980, its ideas would subsequently influence hundreds of state and national politicians—albeit subtly, out of sight of the television cameras.[21]

The Reagan administration served as a stage for a low-key power struggle between social conservatives and libertarian-leaning Republicans. It was a battle that began in the 1960s at the University of South Carolina. Connie Marshner (1951–) had become a leader of the campus YAF chapter. A devoutly religious woman, Marshner became associated first with Jerry Falwell and then with Pat Robertson. As a delegate to a White House Conference on Families during the Carter administration, she had led a noisy walkout in protest against supporters of abortion and gay rights. She became an adviser on family policy in the Reagan administration but soon found herself marginalized, and she left Reagan's service deeply disappointed.

While Marshner was championing sexual abstinence and traditional Protestant morality at the University of South Carolina, the innovative good-ole-boy leader of the campus chapter of the College Republicans was building a political profile. Lee Atwater raised money for the College Republicans by charging admission to pornographic films. Such films were then as illegal as they were difficult to obtain, but Atwater knew how to get things done. He became a low-level political adviser in the Reagan administration. His cultivation of Vice President George H. W. Bush earned Atwater promotions and a leading role in the 1988 Bush presidential campaign. Atwater's ascension and Marshner's descent left no doubt as to which faction in the Republican Party was more influential.

Reagan and his closest advisers had known even before the 1980 election what the White House policy priorities would be. Inflation ranked as the first, and most pressing, issue. Tax reform and economic recovery were, in Reagan's mind, a significant part of the battle against inflation. The next most important policy was crippling the Soviet Empire and rebuilding the United States' defense. Far down the list of policy priorities were social issues. The order of importance made sense. If inflation was not stemmed, and the Cold War not won peacefully, then, Reagan believed, there would likely be no United States. America could exist with abortion and gay rights; it probably could not survive either a massive economic collapse or a nuclear war with an expansionist Soviet Union.

Senator Goldwater shared the administration's priorities, though he had no interest in appearing to be friends with religious conservatives. As Goldwater argued, "I have seen many news items that referred to the Moral Majority, prolife, and other religious groups as 'the new right' and the 'new conservatism.' And I can say with conviction that the religious issues of these groups have little or nothing to do with conservative or liberal politics." Goldwater then offered a concluding recommendation that became memorialized on hundreds of thousands of political buttons: "Every good Christian ought to kick [Jerry] Falwell right in the ass."[22]

Vice President Bush rejected advice that he become friendlier with social conservatives in order to secure the 1988 presidential nomination: "I am not intimidated by those who suggest I better hew the line. Hell with them." An anonymous White House staffer assured the readers of the *Washington Post* that only a few social conservatives were in the administration. They were there, the staffer contended, not because they had any power but so that the White House could keep them under control. The staffer then harked back to Michael Corleone in *The Godfather: Part II*: "Hold your friends close, hold your enemies closer."[23]

Given the level of hostility religious conservatives faced within the Republican Party, as well as the limited political support Reagan gave them, they had no alternative but to mute their cries of betrayal. The Democratic Party was not a political alternative. It had fewer moral traditionalists in its ranks, and their influence waned as the socially conservative remnant shifted its loyalties to the Republican Party.

Religious conservatives also had to confront an unpleasant political fact: most voters did not support their social agenda. On the eve of the 1984 election, less than a quarter of Americans expressed support for a constitutional amendment to outlaw abortion. Public opinion surveys also revealed that fewer Americans regarded religion as being of any importance. In 1952, three-quarters of Americans regarded religious beliefs as relevant to their lives. By 1988, that proportion had fallen to 56 percent. While the ranks of conservative Protestant denominations expanded in the 1980s, it was a function of ideological reshuffling rather than the result of overall growth in the number of Christians. Socially liberal Protestant sects and the Catholic Church lost adherents to Southern Baptists and Pentecostals.

Though the majority of Americans in the 1980s, including the religiously observant, may have disapproved of abortion and same-sex marriage, they were uncomfortable addressing either matter politically. Most voters did not want to be put in a position of telling other people what they could and could not do, especially if it did not affect them directly. Increasing criminal penalties on drug dealers was acceptable because narcotics plainly affected public safety and the quality of life in the United States. But it was one thing to inflict punishment on a drug dealer and quite another to threaten someone with incarceration for terminating a pregnancy.

Reagan understood that a president had to bend to the contours of public opinion. At the same time, an effective leader had to attempt to shape public opinion, though success was not guaranteed. A good leader also had to be careful not to alienate those who offered support on other issues. As Reagan's Hollywood friend, Clint Eastwood, had observed in *Magnum Force* (1973): "A man's got to know his limitations." Reagan knew which goals were realistic and which were beyond a president's reach. Failing to know the difference had contributed to Jimmy Carter's downfall. Even Roosevelt, Reagan's idol, failed to persuade Americans that they had to fight in World War II. It took the Japanese attack on Pearl Harbor to move the American people fully in Roosevelt's position.

NOTES

1. Kenneth J. Heineman, *God Is a Conservative: Religion, Politics, and Morality in Contemporary America* (New York: New York University Press, 2005), 18–19.

2. Everett Carll Ladd Jr., *Where Have All the Voters Gone? The Fracturing of America's Political Parties* (New York: W. W. Norton, 1978), 39–42.

3. Heineman, *God Is a Conservative*, 113; Jerry Falwell, *Listen, America! The Conservative Blueprint for America's Moral Rebirth* (New York: Basic Books, 1981), 47, 62, 92.

4. Robert Freedman, "The Religious Right and the Carter Administration," *Historical Journal* 48 (March 2005): 231–60.

5. James Davison Hunter, *Culture Wars: The Struggle to Define America* (New York: Basic Books, 1991), 111.

6. Heineman, *God Is a Conservative*, 113.

7. Ronald Reagan, "Remarks to Participants in the March for Life Rally," January 22, 1988, Ronald Reagan Presidential Library and Museum.

8. Lewis L. Gould, *Grand Old Party: A History of Republicans* (New York: Random House, 2003), 425; Heineman, *God Is a Conservative*, 131.

9. Douglas Brinkley, ed., *The Reagan Diaries* (New York: HarperCollins, 2007), 217–18.

10. Heineman, *God Is a Conservative*, 143.

11. Ibid., 116.

12. Gregory L. Schneider, *The Conservative Century: From Reaction to Revolution* (Lanham, MD: Rowman and Littlefield, 2009), 85.

13. "Transcript of Ronald Reagan's 1980 Neshoba County Fair Speech," *Neshoba Democrat*, November 15, 2007.

14. Gould, *Grand Old Party*, 425.

15. Tim Naftali, "Ronald Reagan's Long-Hidden Racist Conversation with Richard Nixon," *The Atlantic*, July 30, 2019, https://www.theatlantic.com/ideas/archive/2019/07/ronald-reagans-racist-conversation-richard-nixon/595102.

16. Paul Kengor, "On Ronald Reagan's 'Racism,'" *American Spectator*, August 1, 2019, https://spectator.org/on-ronald-reagans-racism.

17. Heineman, *God Is a Conservative*, 114; Sheila Rule, "NAACP to Ask Reagan to Call Parley on the Plight of Minorities," *New York Times*, January 13, 1981.

18. Spencer Rich, "Dispelling Myths about Where America's Homeless People Come From," *Washington Post*, December 4, 1991.

19. "A Reagan Legacy: Amnesty for Illegal Immigrants," *NPR*, July 4, 2010.

20. Ibid.

21. Nicholas Confessore, "Quixotic '80 Campaign Gave Birth to Koch's' Powerful Network," *New York Times*, May 17, 2014.

22. Heineman, *God Is a Conservative*, 129.

23. Ibid., 131–32.

CHAPTER 5

"DO WE GET TO WIN THIS TIME?": POPULAR CULTURE AND PRESIDENTIAL PUBLIC RELATIONS IN THE EIGHTIES

During the 1930s, Americans would have found it nearly impossible to avoid images of, or references to, Franklin Roosevelt. The president could be seen in a 1933 Universal Pictures cartoon, *Confidence*, dancing in the Oval Office with Oswald Rabbit as the specter of the Great Depression retreated into the shadows. Even Roosevelt's bitter enemies, notably newspaper cartoonist Harold Gray, would invoke his name rather than ignore him. Whenever Gray's *Little Orphan Annie* confronted a union thug, an incompetent government bureaucrat, or a murderous communist, you could bet Roosevelt was working behind the scenes aiding America's enemies.

Roosevelt was highly conscious of the image he projected—which is why he largely avoided being photographed in a wheelchair or with his leg braces visible. He also understood the importance of shaping public opinion to achieve his policy goals. His "fireside chat" radio broadcasts enthralled millions of listeners, including Ronald Reagan, who hung on every word. Federally sponsored film documentaries such as *The Plow that Broke the Plains* (1936) touted Roosevelt's agricultural policies, among other initiatives. Once World War II broke out in Europe in 1939, Roosevelt called upon Hollywood to persuade Americans to prepare for possible military intervention.

Production companies, however, were often uncooperative. Although a number of studio heads were Jewish and had no love for Hitler, they were reluctant to make anti-Nazi, pro-British pictures. In part, they feared provoking an anti-Semitic backlash if the public saw them advocating for American military intervention. They also believed that antifascist films would be money losers. Moviegoers, the studio heads argued, wanted lighthearted comedies and fantasies, not screaming Hitlers and prancing Mussolinis.

In the face of studio resistance, Roosevelt countered with a threat. He warned the film studios that the federal government would pursue antitrust (monopoly) prosecution unless they made anti-Nazi movies. At that time, many studios not only produced films but also owned hundreds of theaters. By law, or at least by stretching the definition of antitrust law, the studios were vulnerable to federal prosecution for monopolizing the production *and distribution* of their films. In no time at all, Warner Brothers, Metro-Goldwyn-Mayer, and other studios began making anti-Nazi films.

Once the United States entered World War II, Hollywood fully mobilized. Reagan made a patriotic action picture, *Desperate Journey* (1942), along with military training films. Interspersed among the patriotic movies were a few films with pro-Soviet messages. Most moviegoers failed to notice that communist scriptwriters had insinuated leftist politics into their films. *The North Star* (1943), written by Communist Party stalwart Lillian Hellman, looked like a badly executed Western that replaced cowboys and Indians with Russians and Germans. Reagan's assurance to the House Committee on Un-American Activities in 1947 that Hollywood communists did not pose any great threat to the United States rested upon a professional insight: the pro-Soviet films produced during World War II were too badly written and acted to be effective propaganda.

Following the World War II, Hollywood and the television networks often made films and series with patriotic, anticommunist themes. In the television series *Mission Impossible* (CBS, 1966–1973), an elite group of

American spies outfoxed slow-witted Eastern European communists. Even Saturday morning cartoons evolved in the shadow of World War II and the Cold War. *Jonny Quest* (ABC, 1964–1965) battled Chinese communists alongside his father, a veteran of the Office of Strategic Services who went on to become a weapons developer for the Defense Department.

Hollywood in the 1940s and 1950s was largely made up of Cold War Democrats, with a fair sprinkling of conservatives (Jimmy Stewart, Charlton Heston) and Democrats who, like Reagan, became Republicans (Frank Sinatra). A new generation that came of age in the 1960s, however, often leaned to the Left and loathed anticommunist Democrats. Actress Jane Fonda, the daughter of actor Henry Fonda, won the nickname "Hanoi Jane" after going to North Vietnam and posing for photographs on a gun that purportedly had shot down U.S. planes. Hollywood, like the television networks and the recording industry, became more "message" oriented by the end of the 1960s. Most film, music, and network executives, though, tried to temper their younger colleagues' works, since they feared alienating customers.

Reagan, taking a retrospective look at the United States before the 1960s, lamented the sea change that had engulfed numerous cultural and civic institutions during his years as California governor:

> Those of us who are over thirty-five or so years of age grew up in a different America. We were taught, very directly, what it means to be an American. And we absorbed, almost in the air, a love of country and an appreciation of its institutions. If you didn't get these things from your family you got them from the neighborhood, from the father down the street who fought in Korea or the family who lost someone at Anzio. Or you could get a sense of patriotism from school. And if all else failed you could get a sense of patriotism from the popular culture. The movies celebrated democratic values and implicitly reinforced the idea that America was special. TV was like that, too, through the mid-sixties.[1]

The late 1960s cultural politics that Reagan abhorred was as overt as it was unimaginative. While the police officers in *Hawaii Five-0* (CBS, 1968–1980) continued to battle Chinese communist agents, they also contended with psychotic Vietnam veterans who went on killing sprees. Other television shows latched onto the crazed Vietnam veteran as a standard villain. Sometimes the Vietnam veteran was psychologically crippled because he had committed war crimes. On other occasions, the Vietnam veteran was a victim of a government that forced him to commit atrocities. In the latter scenario, there was usually a CIA operative lurking in the background, killing witnesses.

Even as television CIA operatives planned assassinations, network news reached the summit of its public influence. Offering commentary from South Vietnam in 1968, CBS News anchor Walter Cronkite proclaimed the North Vietnamese Tet Offensive to have been a disaster for the United States. In reality, the United States had crushed the communist insurgency, forcing North Vietnam to fight a conventional war that gave the United States a military advantage—though it came too late, given public exhaustion with the war. When President Lyndon Johnson saw Cronkite render his negative judgment on the war, he purportedly sighed that if he had lost Cronkite, then he had lost America. Subsequent presidents would never say that about other network and cable news hosts.

Cronkite's successors often lacked the invaluable journalistic experience he had acquired as a newspaper writer and war correspondent. Moreover, in Cronkite's day, there were three networks and public television. Given limited competition, Cronkite rose to the top of a small field. Within a generation there would be dozens, and then hundreds, of networks and channels, each competing for smaller slices of the viewing public.

The journalists who belonged to Cronkite's generation often had working-class backgrounds and had not gone to college. (Cronkite, who attended the University of Texas, was an exception.) While publishers were likely to be anti–New Deal Republicans, especially if they were part of the Hearst or Scripps-Howard chains, most journalists were Democrats. They strived for objectivity in their reporting, though when they went with American soldiers to Europe and the Pacific during World War II, they were cheering on the United States.

In contrast, the post-1960s generation of journalists was mainly college educated and, as a result of the divisive Vietnam War, looked upon the military with suspicion. For many of the journalists who had covered the civil rights protests in the South, their mission was not to be objective. They were in Mississippi as advocates for the oppressed. Objective reporting, such journalists believed, only served to keep racists in power. Their duty was to oppose the status quo.

After the Watergate affair and President Richard Nixon's resignation in 1974, investigative journalists Bob Woodward and Carl Bernstein became cultural icons. The 1976 film, *All the President's Men*, glamorized the two *Washington Post* reporters and inspired thousands of college students to major in journalism. It seemed as if nearly all baby boomer journalists wanted to uncover criminal misconduct in the federal government. Every subsequent presidential scandal, real, exaggerated, and imagined, would have "-gate" added to its end—though usually unsuccessfully, because it was clunky.

As journalism became advocacy oriented, the expanding, younger liberal arts professoriate became more radicalized. Like their counterparts in the news media and the entertainment industry, greater numbers of boomer humanities professors spoke out against what they saw as the agents of oppression. The United States' oppressors went by many names, but chief among them was Reagan. The California governor had waged rhetorical war against the liberal arts faculty and students at Berkeley, though he occasionally resorted to tear gas. Reagan berated activist professors in front of the television cameras, knowing that for every academic he angered, he gained more votes from taxpayers fed up with campus unrest.

Wealthy Reagan played tribune of the common people while conservatives depicted activist humanities professors, who often made less than high school–educated autoworkers, as snotty elitists. It was a brilliant political strategy that conservatives in the 1970s increasingly used against academics, journalists, screenwriters, actors, and directors. There were a few professors and actors who understood that if they overreacted to conservatives' gibes, they would look bad. Most, however, fell into the trap Reagan had set while serving as governor. The trick, Reagan knew, was to keep smiling while baiting critics with dismissive quips.

The entertainment industry was the first to discern that there was a disconnect between the "lessons" it wanted to impart to its less enlightened audience and what viewers took away. Television producers Norman Lear and Bud Yorkin found this to be true with one of their most popular television series, *All in the Family* (CBS, 1971–1979). Though Lear and Yorkin belonged to the mainstream Democratic World War II generation, their politics had moved to the Left as a result of the civil rights and anti–Vietnam War movements. Lear so despised, and feared, the New Right, that in 1980 he founded the liberal lobby group People for the American Way to counter the Moral Majority.

Drawing inspiration from British television and a 1970 film, *Joe*, which depicted conservative working-class whites as violent and moronic, Lear and Yorkin launched *All in the Family*. Their intention was to set up the lead character, patriarch Archie Bunker, as an ignorant, racist, working-class schmuck—the kind of person who voted for Nixon and Reagan. The voice of liberal, educated sanity was the son-in-law, Michael Stivic, whom Archie Bunker called "Meathead."[2]

Unfortunately for Lear and Yorkin, audiences fell in love with Bunker. Many working-class whites saw Bunker as a well-meaning, commonsensical man speaking forthrightly against affirmative action, the antiwar movement, and lawbreakers. In contrast, Stivic appeared to be a freeloading graduate student who lived off his hardworking father-in-law. Lear and Yorkin had not anticipated that millions of viewers found Bunker to be refreshing while concurring with Bunker that Stivic was an obnoxious, self-righteous meathead. It did not help Lear and Yorkin that actor Carroll O'Connor, while a liberal in real life, added depth to his characterization of Bunker. At the same time, actor Rob Reiner did not understand that the more he made Stivic the personification of virtue, the more repellent his character became.

Hollywood filmmakers experienced the same disconnect their television counterparts faced in the 1970s. There was no doubt in Hollywood that the Vietnam War was a compelling subject for film. Unlike World War II, however, most producers, and many boomer actors and actresses, wanted to make *antiwar* films using Vietnam as the backdrop. In 1978, *Coming Home*, with actress Jane Fonda, focused on the physically and psychologically wounded veterans of the Vietnam War. The Hollywood community bestowed upon *Coming Home* Oscars for Best Picture and Best Director and awarded Fonda with an Oscar as well. As a commercial enterprise, however, *Coming Home*'s gross domestic receipts of thirty-six million dollars paled in comparison to other Vietnam War films that were not as blatantly antiwar.

While most 1970s Vietnam War films outperformed *Coming Home* at the box office, two blockbusters stood out: *Apocalypse Now* (1979) and *The Deer Hunter* (1978). Director Francis Ford Coppola believed he was making an antiwar film with *Apocalypse Now*, much as he thought that

The Godfather (1972) was an anti-Mafia film. Coppola had not expected film audiences viewing *The Godfather* to cheer Michael Corleone as he wiped out the rival heads of New York's Five Families. He surprised himself again with *Apocalypse Now*. Moviegoers were thrilled when helicopter gunships, pulsating to the tune of Richard Wagner's *Ride of the Valkyries*, swept over a Vietnamese communist village. Coppola's message may have been antiwar, but his thrilling action scenes were what audiences remembered. *Apocalypse Now* had a domestic gross of seventy-eight million dollars. Even with a higher production budget than *Coming Home*, *Apocalypse Now* still generated greater income and larger audiences.

With *The Deer Hunter*, director Michael Cimino bestowed upon his working-class, white ethnic characters a dignity that others in Hollywood seldom emulated. Cimino showed his steelworkers-turned-soldiers as psychologically and physically scarred because of their experiences in Vietnam. His depiction of American and South Vietnamese soldiers being forced to play Russian roulette by their communist captors was as disturbing as it was graphic. At the end of the film, following the funeral of one of the veterans, the characters began singing *God Bless America* as they ate breakfast at a local tavern.

The Deer Hunter elicited a wide range of reaction—more so than any Vietnam War film before or since. Many in Hollywood and the news media denounced the film. Jane Fonda called it "a racist, Pentagon version of the war" for the film's negative depiction of North Vietnamese soldiers. Journalist Peter Arnett, who had won the Pulitzer Prize for his reporting on the Vietnam War, concurred with Fonda, condemning Cimino's film as "fascist trash."[3]

Leaving Fonda's and Arnett's criticisms aside, *The Deer Hunter* earned $49 million in domestic gross receipts and was so visually and dramatically compelling that the Hollywood community awarded it with Oscars for Best Picture and Best Director. (Adjusted for inflation, $49 million in 1978 would be equivalent to $173 million in 2019.) Most telling, movie audiences may have left the theater depressed, but when actress Meryl Streep began singing *God Bless America*, people stood up and sang with her. It was almost as if filmgoers were making a defiant statement that while the Vietnam War was awful, America stood proud and unapologetic. Cimino could not have predicted that his dirge would become a rally.

Reagan would not have been surprised by the pent-up patriotism *The Deer Hunter* had unleashed. As early as 1964, Reagan had warned that Johnson was backing the United States into a war in South Vietnam without a strategy for victory. Three years later, at his 1967 inaugural address as the newly elected governor of California, Reagan brought the Vietnam War and America's fading patriotism into stark relief:

> If, in glancing aloft, some of you were puzzled by the small size of our State Flag there is an explanation. That flag was carried into battle in Vietnam by young men of California. Many will not be coming home. One did, Sergeant Robert Howell, grievously wounded. He brought that flag back. I thought we would be proud to have it fly over the Capitol today. It might even serve to put our problems in better perspective. It might remind us of the need to give our sons and daughters a cause to believe in and banners to follow.[4]

Whether it was Reagan, a television producer, or a steelworker whose son had fought in Vietnam, there was a lesson each could draw by the end of the 1970s: Americans had become ideologically and culturally fragmented. Consequently, successful mass entertainment had become difficult, though not impossible. In response to cultural fragmentation, television, film, and the music industry turned increasingly toward niche marketing. With the rising sophistication of computer programing, demographic data could be more efficiently collected and analyzed. One key to success was to differentiate between overall viewing (or listening) numbers and, instead, look to the education and income characteristics of consumers. For many television producers this meant creating programs aimed at small but affluent audiences, as well as offering series to a broader, albeit frequently less affluent, audience. The expansion of cable, in competition with the three broadcast networks, accelerated what a later generation would call "market segmentation."

For the blue collars who wanted to watch conspicuous consumption but could not afford to do it in real life, a trio of television series emerged: *Dallas* (CBS, 1978–1991), *Falcon Crest* (CBS, 1981–1990), and *Dynasty* (ABC, 1981–1989). Critics considered the three shows to be the embodiment of "Reaganism," by which they meant crass celebrations of greed. Their producers agreed with the critics—material excess was the point of the shows. *Falcon Crest* shamelessly associated itself with "Reaganism" by casting the president's ex-wife, Jane Wyman, in a lead role. Stand-up comics tripped over themselves making off-color jokes about how Reagan might have felt watching his first wife (a glamorous grandmother) on television cavorting in designer gowns.

Dallas became the media's shorthand for referring to the Sunbelt and the kind of predatory oil executives who donated to Reagan's presidential campaigns. What many critics (and fans) did not realize was that *Dallas* was less a prime-time soap opera and more of a documentary. Actor Larry Hagman, a native of Texas, had found inspiration for his character of J. R. Ewing in a Lone Star legend: Clint Murchison Jr., a.k.a. "JR" or "Junior." The Murchisons were a clan of oil wildcatters who went from rags-to-riches-to-rags in two generations. JR Murchison founded the Dallas Cowboys football franchise, snorted a fortune in cocaine, and pursued future ex-wives with unbridled passion. His brother was a well-meaning art collector and philanthropist who stayed out of the family oil business, much like JR Ewing's brother Bobby Ewing. By the 1980s, JR Murchison had bankrupted his family and sold off the Dallas Cowboys. JR Ewing, in contrast, lived to cheat another day.

Cops and robbers had been a staple of television since the 1950s when Sgt. Joe Friday on *Dragnet* (NBC, 1951–1959) had lectured criminals into submission. (Network executives did a rebooted *Dragnet* series from 1967 to 1970 with many of the original actors.) In the 1980s, police shows fragmented along class, educational, and ideological lines. For the fans of the no-nonsense *Dirty Harry* film franchise, there was *Hunter* (NBC, 1984–1991). Lead actor Fred Dryer, a former National Football League player, physically resembled actor Clint Eastwood who had made *Dirty Harry* a byword in tough cops who crossed the line to get the job done. *Hunter* appealed to fans who despised government bureaucrats, criminal defense attorneys, and spineless liberal politicians. Sgt. Rick Hunter did his job in spite of "the system."

Critics who called Sgt. Hunter the television cop version of Reagan raised a valid point. Reagan had ridden a rising tide of public revulsion against urban crime all the way to the California governor's mansion. His law-and-order rhetoric predated San Francisco cop "Dirty" Harry Francis Callahan's first screen appearance in 1971. Reagan, like Dirty Harry (and Rick Hunter), was unrelenting. In one of his first presidential speeches

(From left) Lou Gossett Jr., Clint Eastwood, and Ronald Reagan. Like Eastwood's "Dirty Harry," Reagan had no tolerance for criminals or Soviet apologists. (Ronald Reagan Presidential Library and Museum)

on crime, Reagan took aim at liberals who blamed rising crime rates on poverty and societal injustice:

> At the very same time that crime rates have steadily risen, our nation has made unparalleled progress in raising the standard of living and improving the quality of life. It's obvious that prosperity doesn't decrease crime, just as it's obvious that deprivation and want don't necessarily increase crime. The truth is that today's criminals for the most part are not desperate people seeking bread for their families; crime is the way they've chosen to live....
>
> It's time, too, that we acknowledge the solution to the crime problem will not be found in the social worker's files, the psychiatrist's notes, or the bureaucrat's budgets. It's a problem of the human heart, and it's there we must look for the answer. We can begin by acknowledging some of those permanent things, those absolute truths I mentioned before. Two of those truths are that men are basically good but prone to evil, and society has a right to be protected from them.[5]

Dirty Harry could have spoken these same lines.

As if making a rebuttal to Reagan, NBC offered another cops-and-robbers show with a very different vibe from *Dirty Harry* and *Hunter*: *Hill Street Blues* (1981–1987). Writer Steven Bochco wanted a police show that emphasized poverty, despair, and injustice over car chases, gunplay, and clear-cut moral resolutions. *Hill Street Blues* never soared in the ratings, but network executives noticed two things. First, the critics showered praise on the show, and it received numerous Emmy nominations. Second, while the number of viewers paled in comparison with other police dramas, *Hill Street Blues* attracted a younger, college-educated, affluent audience. These were precisely the kinds of people advertisers hoped would buy their clients' expensive automobiles and beverages. Other network executives concluded that a great deal of money could be made by appealing to a small number of people in a narrow demographic range.

There was a third police show on NBC that made the Top Ten once during its run but typically had a low viewership—lower even than *Hill Street Blues*. As with *Hill Street Blues*, however, *Miami Vice* (1984–1990) attracted a highly desirable viewer demographic. Setting the series in a city that had become internationally famous as the home of "cocaine cowboys," guaranteed media attention out of proportion to its viewer numbers. Miami was also less expensive than New York City or Los Angeles to film in, with local officials eager to cooperate with a legitimate business enterprise. City leaders were fine whenever the NBC crew painted abandoned art deco buildings in various eye-catching pastels prior to filming. Unexpectedly, the painters inspired struggling Miami business owners to clean up their properties and sparked an urban revival movement.

Several factors beyond location set *Miami Vice* apart from other police shows in the 1980s. Producer Michael Mann had originally pitched the series to network executives as "MTV cops." (MTV, which launched in 1981, was a reference to the Music Television channel on cable that showed videos of rock performers.) *Miami Vice* often replaced dialogue with a music soundtrack that it paired with the screen action. While there were Top Forty rock songs featured, *Miami Vice* used a great deal of alternative, or "new wave" bands. Most mainstream rock radio stations would never play such cheerfully cynical groups as Depeche Mode, the Cure, New Order, or Talking Heads, but MTV and *Miami Vice* would.

Mann belonged to the new generation of network writers and producers. He had been on the fringes of the New Left at the University of

Wisconsin in the 1960s, but avoided violent extremism. Mann ensured that the show's heroes and villains reflected the ethnic and racial demographics of the filming locale—a practice only then being (slowly) adopted by other television series. Plots were fairly consistently left of center, with CIA and DEA operatives typically being little better than Colombian cocaine dealers.

Despite his political inclinations, Mann retained a Cold War sensibility. Two of his heroic characters had been in the Vietnam War; one of them could have given Sgt. Hunter lessons in getting the job done. When Lt. Martin Castillo (actor Edward James Olmos) confronted Russian KGB operatives armed with automatic weapons, he efficiently dispatched them with a Japanese samurai sword. By comparison, the precinct captain in *Hill Street Blues* only had to worry about paper cuts.

Miami Vice was not the first television series in the 1980s to feature Vietnam veterans and depict them in a positive light—though it was still rare. The chief characters in *Magnum, P.I.* (CBS, 1980–1988) were fun-loving, patriotic Vietnam veterans dedicated to helping others. (NBC launched a variation of *Magnum, P.I.* in 1983 with *The A-Team*, a show about fugitive, fun-loving Vietnam veterans who also helped those in need.) *Magnum, P.I.* producer Donald Bellisario came from a white ethnic Pennsylvania family, served in the marines, and made no secret of his admiration for Reagan. Series star Tom Selleck, who had helped with riot control in the 1960s while in the California National Guard, was equally vocal about his politics. He not only told interviewers that he read the conservative *National Review* but he later filmed television commercials for the magazine. Selleck delighted in attending Reagan's second inaugural festivities and enjoyed being a guest at several White House dinners.

Situation comedies, among them a few with overt political themes, intermixed with the legion of police shows. Producer Gary David Goldberg wanted to emulate *All in the Family* but without the abrasive edges. He turned *All in the Family* on its head by making the parents in *Family Ties* (NBC, 1982–1989) the wise liberals. Audiences, Goldberg believed, would likely respond better to liberal views if the voice of reason came from the adults rather than from a young "Meathead."

Family Ties was meant to be a vehicle for veteran actress Meredith Baxter (Birney) who played career woman and mother Elyse Keaton. Her husband, played by Michael Gross, was her ideological soulmate. A former

(From right) Nancy Reagan, Tom Selleck, and Steve Guttenberg. (Ronald Reagan Presidential Library and Museum)

hippie, Steven Keaton worked for an affiliate of the Public Broadcasting System. Largely unknown actor Michael J. Fox would be the Reaganite son. A highly opinionated teenager, Fox's Alex P. Keaton wore button-down collar shirts and was, to use a 1960s term, "square."

As had happened with *All in the Family,* an unexpected development occurred. Audiences, which steadily grew in size to the point where *Family Ties* became a Top Five television series, loved Alex P. Keaton—not his parents. Far from seeing Fox's character as a silly teenager filled with foolish ideas, viewers liked the idea of a polite boy who spoke in complete sentences and cleaned up after himself. Although Fox, like Carroll O'Connor, was liberal, his fine acting created an empathetic figure who, inadvertently, gave legitimacy to conservative ideas and insinuated them into a coveted prime-time viewing slot. Fox won three Emmys and launched a film career. The actors who played his parents, let alone the two women who portrayed his sisters, largely faded into the background. By 1984, the fictional Alex P. Keaton had become the popular-culture face of youthful conservatism.

The American film industry frequently found profits and liberal political conviction to be in conflict in the 1980s. Liberalism typically lost to the profit motive, though a writer-producer (Oliver Stone) and an actor-producer (Warren Beatty) waged a good fight. Stone, who had achieved great success writing nightmarish scripts such as *Midnight Express* (1978) and *Scarface* (1983), wanted to make the definitive anti–Vietnam War film. *Platoon* (1986) drew on some of his own combat experiences in Vietnam. Stone's climatic battle scene, however, was so riveting that audiences cheered as outnumbered American troops annihilated waves of Vietnamese communists with napalm, claymores, and guns. As Coppola had learned, and Stone rediscovered, antiwar action films were often a conceptional contradiction in terms.

In 1981 Beatty released *Reds*, the story of John Reed, Harvard graduate and grandfather of American communism. Beatty interspliced interviews with Reed's real-life radical contemporaries as they told the story of the 1917 Russian Revolution. *Reds* was a celebration of radicalism released just as Reagan was launching a second round of the Cold War. To Beatty's surprise, Reagan invited him to show *Reds* at a White House screening.

(From left) Nancy Reagan, Warren Beatty, and Diane Keaton at the White House screening of *Reds*. (Ronald Reagan Presidential Library and Museum)

As Reagan and Beatty discussed the film, and Hollywood anticommunist politics, the younger actor realized he shared common ground with the president. Beatty's depiction of John Reed showed an idealist who was beginning to see dangerous trends as Lenin rose to power. His Reed was also uncomfortable with sacrificing art in the name of politics. Reagan understood Beatty's portrayal of Reed all too well. He had seen radical actors he liked and respected, notably John Garfield, follow ideological hardliners—and meekly retreat any time Hollywood Stalinists berated them for expressing an interest in others' points of view. When asked about his experience with Reagan, Beatty simply replied, "I didn't agree with him, but I liked him very much."[6]

The two actors, while politically far apart, also shared a special interest: ensuring that legendary director Elia Kazan (1909–2003) received the honors worthy of one of Hollywood's greatest directors. Kazan's filmography was formidable: *Gentleman's Agreement* (1947), *A Streetcar Named Desire* (1951), *On the Waterfront* (1954), and *East of Eden* (1955), to list only a few. His unpardonable sin, in the eyes of many performers in Hollywood's younger generation, was his decision in 1952 to testify before the House Committee on Un-American Activities about his communist associates.

Beatty, who owed his stardom to Kazan's *Splendor in the Grass* (1961), believed that the director deserved an Academy Award for Lifetime Achievement. Reagan agreed, but every time someone put Kazan's name forward in Hollywood, a backlash erupted, and his nomination died. Disgusted, Reagan bypassed Hollywood and bestowed upon Kazan a Kennedy Center Award for Lifetime Achievement in 1982. Beatty kept lobbying and finally got Kazan recognized with a special Academy Award in 1999. Tellingly, at the 1999 Oscar awards show, television audiences saw Beatty, his wife (actress Annette Bening), and actor Karl Malden standing as they wildly cheered Kazan. Actor Tim Robbins and actress Susan Sarandon sat and scowled—as did numerous other performers.

The most popular films of the 1980s either avoided ideology or were unabashedly patriotic—and usually waving the flag with an intensity not seen since World War II. In the first category was writer-director John Hughes, who virtually trademarked apolitical upper-middle-class suburban Chicago teen comedies: *Sixteen Candles* (1984), *The Breakfast Club* (1985), *Pretty in Pink* (1986), and *Ferris Bueller's Day Off* (1986).

Hughes's characters, although often going through teenage angst, were still entertaining—much like the parts Mickey Rooney and Reagan had played in the 1930s and early 1940s.

Meanwhile, two Israeli cousins, Yorum Globus and Menahem Golan, fed Hollywood's appetite for profitable patriotic films. Globus's and Golan's production company, the Cannon Group, specialized in low-budget, moneymaking action films—what the Hollywood of the 1930s would have designated as B-list. Their new B-list action star, Chuck Norris, had acquired a near-cult following as a ninja warrior battling Asian drug triads. In the early 1980s, the Cannon Group substituted communists (and Arab terrorists) for drug dealers. Norris, who had lost a brother in the Vietnam War and who had been in the military himself, was eager to serve his country on the silver screen. He repeatedly praised Reagan for reviving America's patriotic spirit.

In *Missing in Action* (1984), Norris went on a secret mission to Vietnam to rescue American soldiers whom the communists still held prisoner. Norris sliced, strangled, and squashed Vietnamese communists, often using only his hands and feet. A year later, the Cannon Group released *Invasion USA* (1985). Russians, supplemented by hundreds of Cuban, Nicaraguan, and Vietnamese communists, staged terrorist attacks against unarmed Americans. Once again, Norris waded into combat, exterminating the communists. In 1986, Norris was back in *The Delta Force* (1986). This film drew on an Arab terrorist airplane hijacking a year earlier. In real life, the terrorists achieved their political objectives and got away. In the alternative reality *The Delta Force* created, Norris tore through the streets of Beirut on a motorcycle equipped with a lethal rocket launcher. No terrorist escaped American justice.

While critics ridiculed Norris, the film studios took the Cannon Group's bottom line seriously. *Missing in Action* had cost three million dollars to make and grossed twenty-six million dollars in domestic receipts. Though not as popular, *The Delta Force* had a 100 percent profit margin, compared to a 50 percent profit margin for *Invasion USA*. Most studios were fortunate to break even, and the majority of films lost money. In contrast, a Cannon Group–Chuck Norris commercial failure meant only having a 50 percent profit margin.

Major studios, notably United Artists, wanted to copy the Cannon Group's winning formula. Writer-director John Milius, an outspoken

Ronald Reagan and Arnold Schwarzenegger at the 1984 Republican Presidential National Convention. (Ronald Reagan Presidential Library and Museum)

conservative who had turned Austrian immigrant and bodybuilder Arnold Schwarzenegger (1947–) into a star with *Conan the Barbarian* (1982), decided to make a "communist invasion of America" film. *Red Dawn* (1984) had a B-list budget and cast. The premise was that communist Nicaraguans infiltrated American missile sites disguised as undocumented Mexican immigrants. Having crippled America's strategic defense system, the Soviet Union launched a few nuclear strikes on the United States. Most of Western Europe, with the exception of Britain, meekly surrendered to the Russians, as did Americans on the East and West Coasts.

Fortunately for the survival of American freedom, a plucky band of heartland teenagers launched a guerrilla insurgency against their Latin American and Russian oppressors. In a nod to gender equality, Milius cast two young women as insurgents who proved just as adept as men in killing communists with arrows, bombs, and heavy caliber machine guns. The insurgents faced overwhelming odds. To make matters worse, the community's liberal politicians collaborated with the communists and sent the youths' families to concentration camps prior to their execution. At the end, nearly all the insurgents died, though freedom ultimately prevailed.

Red Dawn was very profitable—it cost four million dollars to make and grossed thirty-eight million dollars domestically. (Western Europeans were less inclined than Americans to watch the film since Milius depicted them as cowardly ingrates.) The film not only brought some of its stars to the A-list (Patrick Swayze, Charlie Sheen, Jennifer Grey, and Lea Thompson) but also imprinted itself on American popular culture. "Wolverines," the name of the guerrilla band's high school mascot, became shorthand for resistance to liberal sellouts at home and radical enemies abroad.

Like Milius and Norris, A-list actor Sylvester Stallone admired Reagan and wanted to do his part. In 1982, Stallone had starred in *First Blood*. The film told the story of John Rambo, a misunderstood and persecuted Vietnam veteran who ended up waging war on a vicious small town. Rambo was neither a villain nor a victim. Made for $15 million, *First Blood* earned $125 million in ticket sales.

(From Left) Nancy and Ronald Reagan, Brigitte Nielsen, and Sylvester Stallone. (Ronald Reagan Presidential Library and Museum)

A sequel was inevitable. In 1985, Rambo went to Vietnam to rescue Americans still being held captive by Vietnamese communists. (The producers of *Rambo: First Blood Part 2* accused the Cannon Group of stealing their plot before they could get their own film into theaters.) In *Rambo: First Blood Part 2*, Stallone famously asked his commander, since Rambo was going back to Vietnam, "Do we get to win this time?" The answer was a resounding "Yes!" as Rambo developed inventive ways to kill Vietnamese and Russian communists—including shooting an arrow with an explosive attachment into the heart of a foul prison commander.

In the aftermath of the airplane hijacking that had inspired *The Delta Force*, an exasperated Reagan said that having seen *Rambo: First Blood Part 2*, he knew how he would prefer to deal with terrorists. While critics accused Reagan of confusing reality and fantasy, most Americans knew exactly what he meant and endorsed the sentiment. Reagan understood that it strengthened his political position with southerners and working-class whites to identify with strong popular-culture figures.

Rambo: First Blood Part 2 cost twenty-five million dollars to make and earned three hundred million dollars in gross domestic receipts. The film was so profitable that another sequel came along, *Rambo III* (1988). The third time around, Rambo went to Afghanistan and rescued his former commander from vicious Russians. In the final climatic battle scene, Rambo led an army of Pashtun Holy Warriors against the communists. Stallone earned points for originality by crashing a tank into a low-hovering Soviet helicopter gunship.

Stallone also enlisted his Philadelphia prizefighter character, Rocky Balboa, in the Cold War cause. In *Rocky IV* (1985), Stallone went to Russia to battle a steroid-enhanced, murderous communist. Rocky's tall, blond opponent, though representing Russian communism, could have been lovingly featured on a 1930s Nazi propaganda poster. At the end of the fight, Rocky urged his Russian audience to abandon their evil political system and work with the United States for peace. Produced on a budget of twenty-eight million dollars, *Rocky IV* grossed three hundred million dollars in the United States.

Paramount made the most financially lucrative, and visually compelling, Cold War film of the 1980s with *Top Gun* (1986). Featuring A-list actor Tom Cruise, *Top Gun* told the story of a group of naval aviators who shot down Russian MiGs. The film focused on swagger and aerial action, not geopolitics. Kenny Loggins recorded an iconic hit song, *Danger*

Zone, which made the film trailer look and sound like a high-priced MTV music video. (Indeed, it *became* an MTV video.) Some critics on the Left complained that *Top Gun* was little more than an extended recruiting ad for the U.S. Navy. They were right. Enlistments rose following the film's release. Produced at a cost of $15 million, *Top Gun* grossed $357 million globally. *Top Gun* performed well overseas partly because music and action reduced the English dialogue and partly because the enemy was not identified and, therefore, it did not seem like an anti-Russian film.

Even films that had no explicit ideological agenda or Cold War plot reflected the Reaganesque "spirit of the times" (or what the Germans called zeitgeist). In the comedy *Ghostbusters* (1984), the villain who unleashed the apocalypse on New York City was an arrogant Big Government bureaucrat from the Environmental Protection Agency. Across the country, in Los Angeles, Eurotrash leftist terrorists-turned-thieves crashed a Christmas office party at Nakatomi Plaza. Only a wisecracking New York cop, in over his head and making things up as he went, stood in their way. *Die Hard* made actor Bruce Willis an A-list action star, and the film enjoyed an enormous profit margin. Willis's John McClane epitomized the can-do attitude of an American hero confronted with arrogant foreigners. *Die Hard* also gave rise to a bit of folk wisdom that has endured to this day: It's not Christmas until John McClane drops Hans Gruber off the Nakatomi building.

One 1980s science fiction film comedy achieved political pop-culture immortality. *Back to the Future* (1985) has teenager Marty McFly (actor Michael J. Fox) go thirty years into the past thanks to a time machine built by Doc Brown (actor Christopher Lloyd). Stuck in 1955, McFly locates a younger Doc Brown and tries to convince him that in the future he will successfully build a time machine. A skeptical Brown asks McFly who the president is in 1985, and when the teenager replies, "Ronald Reagan," Brown snorts: "Ronald Reagan? The actor? Then who's vice president, Jerry Lewis? I suppose Jane Wyman is the First Lady! And Jack Benny is the Secretary of the Treasury!"

Reagan loved *Back to the Future* and appreciated how improbable it would have seemed in 1955 that he would be president in thirty years. Nancy Reagan, however, did not appreciate the notion that Jane Wyman would have ever been the First Lady. (Although Nancy Reagan held onto a grudge against Wyman, the *Falcon Crest* star had come to appreciate Reagan and boasted that she had voted for him in 1980 and 1984.) To thank the filmmakers for having given him a good laugh, and admiring Alex P. Keaton in any event, Reagan invited Fox and the other stars to the White House. More dramatically, he quoted Doc Brown in his 1986 State of the Union address: "Where we're going, we don't need roads!"[7]

The degree to which Reagan was tuned into popular culture, especially film and television, should not have been surprising. After all, he had taken his nickname and political tagline from a classic film, *Knute Rockne, All American* (1940). As the doomed football player George Gipp, Reagan had pleaded with legendary Notre Dame coach Knute Rockne to "win one for the Gipper." By the time Reagan entered electoral politics in the 1960s, growing numbers of voters were chanting at rallies, "Win one for the Gipper!" Nancy Reagan often led the Gipper chorus.

Ronald Reagan as the Gipper in, *Knute Rockne, All American*. This 1940 film gave Reagan his nickname and rallying cry: "Win one for the Gipper!" (Ronald Reagan Presidential Library and Museum)

Reagan responded to the events of his times and identified with the more traditionalist, patriotic aspects of American popular culture. Once he became president, though, Reagan began to influence the popular culture, as was apparent with the dialogue and premises underlying *Back to the Future* and even *Ghostbusters*. Reagan's cultural influence in the 1980s owed much to his charisma and charm. He disarmed numerous Hollywood liberals, among them Beatty and Fox, while inspiring other actors to join his cause. Charles Bronson, Clint Eastwood, Chuck Norris, Arnold Schwarzenegger, Tom Selleck, Sylvester Stallone, and Bruce Willis openly embraced Reagan. (Strangely enough, both Reagan and Eastwood had costarred with a primate.) Tim Matheson, who had voiced Jonny Quest and earned praise for his role as the oily Otter in *National Lampoon's Animal House* (1978), admired Reagan but largely kept his political opinions to himself for fear of angering Hollywood liberals and losing work.

There were, however, limits to Reagan's influence with Hollywood. Beyond actress Bo Derek, there were few Hollywood women in Reagan's political corner. Reagan also did poorly among African American actors, male and female. Laurence Tureaud, Mr. T from *The A-Team* and *Rocky III* (1982), however, worked with Nancy Reagan on her "Just Say No to Drugs" campaign. He even played Santa Claus in 1983 at a White House function. When the White House staffers' children seemed intimidated by the former professional wrestler, Nancy Reagan broke the ice by sitting on Mr. T's lap and giving him her Christmas wish list. She then kissed his mostly shaved head. It was the first time in American history that a First Lady sat on an African American's lap. The public loved it and the media, even Nancy Reagan's critics, widely distributed the photograph of Santa and his well-dressed helper.

Unfortunately for Reagan, he discovered early in his presidency that film and popular culture in general would never be dependable allies. John Hinckley Jr. had become obsessed with the 1976 film *Taxi Driver*. He identified with actor Robert De Niro's sociopath character and actress Jodie Foster, who played an abused prostitute. Wanting to earn Foster's attention, and hoping to protect her from her "enemies," Hinckley attempted to assassinate Reagan in 1981. Hinckley was the first presidential assassin to be inspired by a film. From Hinckley's perspective, if an actor could become president, then *Taxi Driver* could be just as real—and, therefore, Reagan was a threat to Foster.

"Do We Get to Win this Time?"

Nancy Reagan and Mr. T at a White House Christmas Party for staffers' children. Mr. T supported Nancy Reagan's "Just Say No to Drugs" campaign. (Ronald Reagan Presidential Library and Museum)

Outside of Hollywood, and male action stars, Reagan attracted sports figures to his side. In part, football players and coaches liked Reagan because he had played the game (in more ways than one). Reagan had also been in one of the greatest football films ever made. Moreover, he had done football commentary on radio and television. Most famously, and by pure coincidence, Reagan had ended up in a national television news box calling a game and explaining the rules to former Beatles member John Lennon. They got along well, though neither man was quite sure who the other was.

Reagan regularly welcomed football players and coaches to the White House. Tom Landry, the coach of the Dallas Cowboys, not only visited the White House but also campaigned for Reagan in 1984. The always humble Landry had proclaimed that the Cowboys were "America's Team" and Reagan was their commander in chief. Landry also filmed commercials for "the Gipper." His support for Reagan meant a great deal in Texas, which, in the 1980s, still elected Democrats to the governorship and kept the state legislature out of the hands of Republicans.

While Reagan drew considerable support from Hollywood and professional football, his success with the recording industry was less than stellar. Country music performers were often unabashedly conservative, while rock and roll, the dominant style of popular music since the 1960s, was nearly uniformly hostile to Reagan and the Cold War. Many rockers had embraced the 1960s counterculture and took great offense at Nancy Reagan's antidrug campaign. Some rockers regarded themselves as the voice of opposition to political tyrants—which they usually associated with Republicans.

There were a few Democrats, however, that rockers loathed. Tipper Gore, the wife of Democratic senator Al Gore Jr., of Tennessee, earned rockers' scorn in 1985 when she helped found the Parents' Music Resource Center. In a special hearing before Congress that Al Gore arranged, Tipper urged the federal government to place warning labels on record albums that contained "obscene lyrics." Rock performers denounced Tipper and her husband as right-wing reactionaries.

Rock critics regarded Bruce Springsteen and John Cougar Mellencamp as the musical political conscience of their generation. Springsteen wrote ballads about abandoned industrial towns and exploited working-class youths. He regarded *Born in the USA* (1984) as his battle cry against American aggression overseas and hopeless youths at home who often faced a choice between prison or military service—both of which were equally bad. Mellencamp decried Reaganomics' effects on farmers with *Rain on the Scarecrow* (1985). In 1983, with *Pink Houses*, Mellencamp had dismissed the "American dream" as an illusion if one was a poor minority.

To their surprise and despair, Springsteen and Mellencamp learned the same lesson Lear and Yorkin had with *All in the Family*. Springsteen may have written a diatribe, but listeners ignored his bitter lyrics and regarded the chorus as a cheer: "Born in the USA!" Mellencamp had a similar experience with *Pink Houses*. Generally, listeners did not notice his class and race arguments. Instead, as had happened with Springsteen, they latched on to the chorus: "Ain't that America, for you and me." The 1984 Reagan election campaign used both songs at campaign rallies. In response, Springsteen and Mellencamp threatened the White House with legal action for using their music without permission—a permission that they would have never given. Reagan supporters ignored both performers' complaints.

Other rock stars, in contrast to Springsteen and Mellencamp, were apolitical. David Bowie had successfully managed the transition from the androgynous persona of "Ziggy Stardust" in the 1970s to "Yuppie King" in the 1980s. He recorded dance music targeted to "young urban professionals" and college students who thought Lisa Birnbach's 1980 book, *The Official Preppy Handbook*, was a how-to-guide, not a satire. Top-Siders were the official "preppy" shoe, designed for wearing on yachts to avoid slipping but also great for any dance floor. Twenty-somethings just had to remember not to wear socks with their Top-Siders. Button-down shirt collars were required, although black T-shirts could be acceptable if worn with a jacket and tennis shoes. Clothing fibers should be cotton—never synthetic.

Preppies were prone to voting for Reagan when not dancing to Bowie, while boomer yuppies tended to be divided politically. The generation of youths who entered their twenties in the 1980s became the least Democratic-inclined cohort in sixty years. Forty percent were Republican, another 40 percent were independents who generally did not trust government or political parties, and just 20 percent voted Democratic.

During the 1984 campaign, Reagan rejoiced in the warm reception he received at college campuses such as Ohio State University. As he joyfully observed, "There certainly is a new generation on hand." Reagan further confided in his diary that he "was so in love with young Americans" that he became "choked up." The sixties generation of radical college students had, Reagan believed, been replaced by a much better group of youths.[8]

Reagan's level of support in the entertainment and political news fields (the two were becomingly increasingly intertwined in the 1980s), was less than what he received from the recording industry—and far smaller than what he got from college students. One of the few bright spots for Reagan was the entertainment/political satire show, *Saturday Night Live* (NBC, 1975–). *Saturday Night Live* had mercilessly mocked Nixon as a political vampire and Gerald Ford as a bumbling fool. Reagan, however, received a treatment that may have been gently mocking but one that also displayed a surprising level of respect, given the show's largely liberal writers and performers.

Ron Reagan Jr., the son of Nancy and Ronald Reagan, hosted an episode of *Saturday Night Live* in 1986. (No previous offspring of an incumbent president had ever hosted a major television network show.) In his opening sketch, the writers parodied the 1983 Tom Cruise film, *Risky Business*. The plot of *Risky Business* was that the parents left their son home alone for several days. He subsequently danced around the house in his underwear and opened a lucrative brothel. Ron Reagan, after conversing on the phone with his parents who had gone out of town, danced around the White House in his underwear—and danced quite well since that was his profession. The audience went wild and the Reagans loved the sketch. In another sketch, which parodied *Back to the Future*, Ron traveled to the 1950s, met his younger parents, and convinced his dad to become a conservative.

A subsequent 1986 episode of *Saturday Night Live* dealt with the Iran-Contra scandal. Show regular Phil Hartman, as President Reagan, appeared to be a glad-handing, vapid figure in front of photographers and news reporters. But secretly, Reagan was the mastermind behind funding the Nicaraguan Contras with the proceeds from illegal arms sales to Iran. Hartman's Reagan spoke fluent Arabic and German and could do advanced financial calculations and currency exchange rates off the top of his head. Much of the news media failed to understand what *Saturday Night Live* had discerned: Reagan might not have been a mastermind, but he was no idiot either.

Academic analyses of the news media coverage Reagan received showed that 64 percent of the reporting was negative. That negative proportion, though, was consistent with what Jimmy Carter had claimed in the 1970s and what Bill Clinton received in the 1990s. Most journalists, regardless of any liberal bias, were still hung over from Watergate. They tended to see their job as holding the president accountable and were certain that most politicians were untrustworthy.

Reagan was not much interested in the fact that the tone of his press coverage did not differ greatly from Carter's. In 1984, after receiving an enthusiastic response from many Jewish Democrats at a B'nai B'rith convention, Reagan privately fumed over the tepid coverage ABC, CBS, and NBC provided. Reagan summed his opinion up succinctly: the television network news divisions had done "a slick hatchet job" on him. This was just one reason out of many that the Reagan White House often bypassed the national news media to give "exclusive" interviews to local television and newspaper reporters. Those folks were grateful to have a chance to talk with a president and did not take a reflexive oppositional stance toward the White House. They also did not jump on Reagan every time he misspoke, which, when he became tired, predictably happened.[9]

Key to successful governance, Reagan knew, was promoting memorable spectacles—what the Romans had called "bread and circuses." Successful public relations initiatives had to tap into the popular culture while, at the same time, attempt to influence its tenor. The 1984 Summer Olympics, scheduled for Los Angeles, presented an enormous opportunity for Reagan to intertwine public relations with popular culture, while celebrating the United States' patriotic past. He called upon his own experiences as an athlete to underscore how the Olympics brought Americans of all backgrounds together:

> Well, you know, when I was a bit younger, being involved in athletics, I, like so many others, dreamed about the Olympics. I didn't get very close to them. The closest, I think, was at the University of Illinois. It was the State track and field championships for the high schools of Illinois. I was on the 880 relay, and I can remember handing off the baton to our anchorman. We didn't win, because there was a young fellow that was also anchorman on a high school team from Chicago: Ralph Metcalfe went on to win gold medals in '32 and in '36 in the Olympics.
>
> He and Jesse Owens were very, very special to my generation. I can remember what a great source of pride it was when they won that day in Berlin and Adolf Hitler, with his Aryan supremacy stupidity, had to stand up and swallow that stupidity when the gold medals were placed around the necks of some of our fine black athletes.
>
> Ralph Metcalfe and Jesse Owens were much more than great athletes; they were great Americans.[10]

Businessman and newly appointed Major League Baseball commissioner Peter Ueberroth coordinated the Los Angeles Olympics. A self-made millionaire, Ueberroth marketed the Olympic symbol to numerous corporations. The money generated from these transactions paid for related Olympics costs. In turn, American Olympics teams were inspired to pursue ever more corporate sponsors. Ueberroth's marketing strategy netted two hundred million dollars in profits for the Olympics. It had been fifty years since the Summer Olympics had made any money—usually they ended up in the red.

In retaliation for the United States boycotting the 1980 Summer Olympics, the Soviet Union and its Eastern European satellites stayed away from Los Angeles—though communist China participated for the first time since the Korean War. Without the Soviets, American athletes dominated most of the events. Overall, Americans won 174 medals, including 83 gold medals. Some 2.5 billion people around the world watched the 1984 Olympics on television—the largest audience up to that time.

Ueberroth made sure that there were forests of American flags on display and that television cameras took plenty of images of enthusiastic (largely American) spectators. The Soviet Union had been doing virtually the same thing at its national events for decades. In 1984, the United States closed the spectacle gap with the Russians. *Time* magazine reporter Lance Morrow likened the Olympics to "a Reagan campaign rally." Ueberroth, an economic conservative and social liberal, earned favorable media comparisons to Reagan. He rejected Republican calls to run for office in California, however, believing that cleaning cocaine out of baseball would consume most of his energy after the Olympics.[11]

The 1984 election year offered Reagan another major media event—the ceremonies surrounding the fortieth anniversary of the Allied D-Day landings at Normandy. Reagan was the first incumbent president to attend a D-Day commemoration. Even Dwight Eisenhower, who had planned the 1944 invasion, did not attend the tenth anniversary events. In 1984, thirty thousand D-Day veterans, along with seventy thousand of their relatives and friends, descended on Normandy. Many reporters and political pundits believed that the commemoration proved crucial to Reagan's re-election campaign. Certainly, Reagan's "Pointe du Hoc" speech memorializing the American Rangers, showed the president at his rhetorical best:

> The Rangers looked up and saw the enemy soldiers—the edge of the cliffs shooting down at them with machineguns and throwing grenades. And the American Rangers began to climb. They shot rope ladders over the face of these cliffs and began to pull themselves up. When one Ranger fell, another would take his place. When one rope was cut, a Ranger would grab another and begin his climb again. They climbed, shot back, and held their footing. Soon, one by one, the Rangers pulled themselves over the top, and

in seizing the firm land at the top of these cliffs, they began to seize back the continent of Europe. Two hundred and twenty-five came here. After two days of fighting, only ninety could still bear arms.

Behind me is a memorial that symbolizes the Ranger daggers that were thrust into the top of these cliffs. And before me are the men who put them there.

These are the boys of Pointe du Hoc. These are the men who took the cliffs. These are the champions who helped free a continent. These are the heroes who helped end a war.[12]

Reagan gave a heartfelt delivery of the words he and speechwriter Peggy Noonan had labored over before crossing the Atlantic. He was so stirring that any news coverage of subsequent D-Day anniversaries would centrally feature his performance. Not everyone, however, was impressed. The 1984 anniversary activities at Normandy upset two nations that were not invited: the Soviet Union and West Germany. The Soviet Union, though a World War II ally, had not participated in D-Day so it did not receive an invitation. There was also the fact that Reagan regarded Stalin as no better than Hitler. The U.S. alliance with the Soviet Union had been one of convenience, not conviction. As for the West Germans, arguing that they deserved to be there because they had also been victims of Nazism did not sit well with nearly everyone else in Europe and the United States.

As with the D-Day commemoration, the 1984 Republican National Convention benefited from expert staging. Choosing Dallas as the convention site was a stroke of genius. Historically Democratic Texas had never hosted a Republican national convention. Dallas served Reagan's interests on several levels. First, Republicans were hoping to sustain the political momentum moving Texas out of the Democratic column. Texas media saturated the Lone Star State with coverage of the convention. Second, in 1980 the Republicans had met in Detroit. Though wanting to keep Michigan in "Reagan Country," there was an important symbolism at play. Crime-ridden, deteriorating, *Democratic-run* Detroit was the past; economically dynamic Dallas, most especially its increasingly Republican suburbs, was the future.

Reagan was the star attraction of the 1984 convention—all others played well-choreographed supporting roles. UN Ambassador Jeane

Kirkpatrick announced her official break from the Democratic Party and proclaimed that at last there was a president who put "America first." Conservative stalwart Barry Goldwater appeared, though Reagan campaign managers made sure that the Arizona senator focused on economic and national defense policy and not on bashing the Moral Majority. Reagan set forth his vision succinctly: "We come together in a national crusade to make America great again, and to make a new beginning."[13]

The Republicans' public relations and advertising strategies in 1984 operated in tandem. On television, viewers could see happy images of Americans, bathed in sunshine, going to work. It was, as the announcer observed, "Morning in America." A young woman, with college diploma in hand standing next to her parents, vowed that she did not want to see the nation return to the "days of shame" that the Carter-Mondale team had inflicted upon the nation four years earlier.

On the public relations front, White House staffers kept repeating to the media that the Democratic National Convention was "the Temple of Doom." The reference was to the 1984 film, *Indiana Jones and the Temple of Doom*. In that film, cultists mindlessly practiced human sacrifice. The Temple of Doom riff seeped into late-night television comedy routines, while newspapers, even those with liberal politics, could not resist using the evocative popular-culture phrase.

Reagan's most striking fusion of popular culture and patriotic symbolism came with the restoration of the Statue of Liberty and Ellis Island. In 1982, Lee Iacocca, the charismatic chair of Chrysler, began working with the National Park Service to raise restoration funds from the private sector. Fixing the Statue of Liberty came with a price tag of $39 million, while transforming what was once an immigrant processing center into a museum cost an additional $128 million. By 1984, Iacocca had raised $100 million in donations, with more funds coming in daily.

The rededication ceremonies for the Statue of Liberty and Ellis Island were held just prior to Independence Day, 1986. Television producer David Wolper, who had put together the highly popular 1977 miniseries, *Roots*, coordinated "Liberty Weekend." There were four thousand guests in attendance, including the Reagans and French president François Mitterand—a gesture of appreciation to France for having given the Statue of Liberty to the United States a century earlier. Over the course of two and a half hours, millions of television viewers saw majestic, nineteenth-century wooden sailing ships in New York Harbor, musical entertainers, and fireworks set against the backdrop of "Lady Liberty."

Neil Diamond sang his evocative song, *Coming to America*, from his 1980 film, *The Jazz Singer*. While Diamond celebrated America as a haven of freedom, Frank Sinatra praised the United States for its ability to assimilate people of different backgrounds. Sinatra performed one of his early hits, *The House I Live In*, from his 1945 film by the same title. Reagan had always loved the song and movie, even if a Hollywood communist, Albert Maltz, had written the screenplay and another communist, Earl Robinson, had scored the music. Celebrating American cultural diversity and toleration were, Sinatra and Reagan believed, good things. Co-opting communists' creative work was just icing on the Statue of Liberty's centennial birthday cake.

Reagan's ability to set the media news agenda, and shape public perception, had limits—a few of which undercut his policy objectives and nearly derailed his presidency. The most important fact was that while Reagan could influence, and attempt to manipulate, news coverage, he had few media allies. William F. Buckley Jr., the founder of *National Review*, had hosted a conservative talk show, *Firing Line*, on PBS since 1966. *Firing Line* had a small viewership even in comparison to other public affairs/news shows. Buckley's repeated use of Latin phrases put off many conservatives who had not gone to Yale. His frequent criticism of Reagan on issues ranging from working with Mikhail Gorbachev to assessing Roosevelt's legacy also made him a difficult ally.

Through most of the 1980s, there was not much in the way of an alternative conservative media, though there was a more vibrant conservative counterculture thanks to a cadre of highly successful Hollywood action stars and football coaches. In 1987, Reagan appointees on the Federal Communications Commission (FCC) abandoned the "fairness doctrine." Created in 1949, the fairness doctrine required television and radio broadcasters to present both sides of a political issue. With the repeal of the fairness doctrine, conservatives had a chance to launch their own radio and television programs—without having to balance them with liberal points of view.

A few conservatives, notably a former disc jockey and sports announcer from Missouri, Rush Limbaugh, saw the largely neglected AM section on the radio dial as ripe territory for conservative talk shows. AM stations, long in the shadow of FM, were desperate for broadcast content, and talk shows were inexpensive to produce. Limbaugh launched his nationally syndicated talk radio program in 1988. While Limbaugh came on to the political scene too late to assist Reagan, he inspired a legion of conservatives to wade into radio and, eventually, television, broadcasting.

Even as Reagan scored well in both politics and popular culture, Democratic House members from the liberal wing of their party chafed under what they regarded as Tip O'Neill's ineffective leadership. They wanted a more "in your face" approach to Reagan. In an effort to mollify disaffected Democrats, O'Neill allowed liberal House members, and their allies in various prosecutors' offices, to launch a series of investigations into Reagan personnel. Their intention was to persuade the public that a "culture of corruption" existed in the Reagan White House. At least one hundred Reagan appointees were investigated, with a handful indicted but few convicted. (The standard of proof in a grand jury hearing is much lower than in a court of law for a criminal case.) Labor secretary Ray Donovan, who resigned his post when indicted, complained after a jury found him innocent of larceny charges, "Which office do I go to, to get my reputation back?"[14]

Reagan's political fortunes dipped when Democrats retook the Senate as a result of the 1986 midterm elections. Southern Democrats, in what proved to be their last hurrah, had convinced working-class white voters that they were moderates who would not reverse the Reagan Revolution. Controlling the Senate opened another front for Democrats to take on Reagan. If he could not be defeated at the ballot box, then perhaps he could be beaten in the court of public opinion.

The Iran Contra scandal was a self-inflicted Reagan White House wound that Senate Democrats hoped to worsen. Media figures covered the hearings extensively and tried to harken back to Watergate by calling the scandal "Iran-gate" and "Contra-gate." Neither formulation worked well, so the scandal just became known as Iran-Contra. The details of the scandal, as they emerged in Senate testimony and investigation by a special prosecutor, were damning. At best, Reagan could insist that he did not know what Oliver North and Robert McFarlane were planning. Reagan's stance elicited from media pundits a new twist on a 1970s Watergate investigative line: What didn't the president know and when didn't he know it? Iran-Contra drove Reagan's public approval down close to

20 percent, but he quickly recovered and scored a 65 percent approval rating within a year.

More damaging in the long term to Reagan than Iran-Contra was the unwillingness of the Democratic Senate to approve the nomination of Robert Bork to the U.S. Supreme Court in 1987. Norman Lear mobilized his lobby organization, People for the American Way, to launch a massive television and radio advertising attack on Bork. Distinguished actor Gregory Peck, evoking his lawyer character Atticus Finch from the 1962 film, *To Kill a Mockingbird,* warned that Bork was a threat to American freedom. Massachusetts senator Ted Kennedy, brother of president John F. Kennedy, went on television news shows warning that Bork, if placed on the Supreme Court, would overturn *Roe v. Wade* and force women to have dangerous back-alley abortions with coat hangers. Bork would also bring back racial segregation and electoral disenfranchisement.

Bork had any number of public relations issues and political liabilities. As a law professor at Yale, before entering the judiciary, Bork had written damning articles for the liberal *New Republic* magazine. Bork questioned the constitutionality of the 1964 Civil Rights Act, arguing that if African Americans wanted equality, then they should move out of Mississippi. Liberals found Bork's reasoning to be offensive; those who suffer discrimination should not have the burden placed upon them to move or remain and accept their situation. What was often missed in media and political discussions of Bork's earlier opinions was that he could not understand why anyone, Black or white, would want to continue living in such backward places.

Ultimately, Bork's public relations failure was not rooted in the fact that he was a conservative; his baggage came from being an Ivy League law professor. Few Americans had any firsthand experience with what law students experienced at elite schools. The 1973 film *The Paper Chase* had given audiences a taste of arrogant, belittling, condescending Ivy League law professors who flatly opined, "You come into here with skulls full of mush and leave thinking like a lawyer."

Bork had been a demanding professor, but he was also as influential as he was inspirational. With the exception of Clarence Thomas, most of his students became part of the Democratic Party Establishment: Bill Clinton, Gary Hart, Anita Hill, Robert Reich, and Hillary Rodham (Clinton), to list a few. Nearly all of Bork's students respected him, and some, such as Reich, were almost reverential. Bork made them think and demanded excellence.

Part of the problem for Bork was that what worked in a Yale classroom did not play well in front of a Senate hearing covered by the national news media. Bork had no toleration for people whom he considered to be slow witted, especially if they insisted that they were really smart. There was no doubt among viewers at home that Bork perceived Senate Judiciary Committee chair Joe Biden of Delaware to be an idiot. Bork's performance alternated between being condescending and intellectual—in other words, professorial. The Reagan administration had not been prepared for the intensity of opposition to Bork, let alone for the $2 million public-relations campaign Lear had organized (or $4.5 million when adjusted for inflation). Reagan had little choice but to find a less controversial alternative to Bork.

Frustrated conservatives coined a new term for what they believed they had witnessed at the judiciary hearings: "Borking." In their estimation, liberals, and their allies in Hollywood and the media, had engaged in vicious character assassination to defeat Bork's nomination. Ironically, liberals complained that conservatives had assassinated their character and misrepresented their views since the 1950s. They had called that "McCarthyism," named for Wisconsin senator Joseph McCarthy. As a political term, Borking did not achieve the same level of public acceptance as McCarthyism. In public-relations jargon, the "optics" in the Bork hearings were not favorable to making the Yale law professor look like a hapless victim.

If the Bork hearings proved anything, it was that there was a limit to how far a president, even a highly effective communicator such as Reagan, who was tuned into the popular culture, could shape the political agenda if the facts on the ground were damaging. Reagan did little to support Bork, and then he cut his losses. As for Bork, he had opinions on civil rights that were, outside Goldwater's circle, appalling. His public demeanor was just as off-putting, though in private conversation he could be charming and self-deprecating.

With Iran-Contra, there was no getting around the fact that Reagan officials, operating under the president's authority, illegally sold weapons to a terrorist state and, in defiance of Congress, used the proceeds to fund the Contras. Luckily for Reagan, Oliver North came across on television as someone who would have had no problem bypassing Congress and omitting critical information from his superiors.

Leaving Bork and Iran-Contra aside, Reagan was successful in shifting a significant portion of the popular culture toward a patriotic, more conservative, direction. Several factors contributed to that outcome. First, the twentysomethings who flocked to him in the eighties were reacting against the cultural and economic despair of their high school years in the seventies. They had no experience with, or memory of, what an effective political leader looked like. Reagan easily fit the bill. Second, Hollywood was not an ideological monolith in the 1980s. There were older and younger conservatives, as well as a remnant of Cold War Democrats, who championed anticommunism, law and order, and limited federal regulation of the economy. As for the Hollywood and musical entertainment figures not sympathetic to Reagan, they either chased profits over political principles or unintentionally delivered messages that were the exact opposite of what they had intended. Reagan, on average, was more effective at expressing himself than were Mellencamp, Springsteen, and Lear.

Perhaps what is most remarkable is how much Reagan succeeded in drawing on popular culture (even as he shaped it) to carry through his domestic and foreign policy agendas and win public approval. (His 1987 Brandenburg Gate speech in West Berlin was an evocative mixture of anti-Soviet rhetoric and stagecraft that served his foreign policy goals well.) No president since Roosevelt had been as successful. Even then, Roosevelt had four terms (really three), and party control of both branches of Congress, while Reagan had two terms and one branch of Congress—and, after 1986, neither branch. Reagan was not entirely joking when he confided to Warren Beatty, "I really don't understand how anyone could be president today *without* being an actor."[15]

NOTES

1. Ronald Reagan, "Farewell Address to the Nation," January 11, 1989, Ronald Reagan Presidential Library and Museum.

2. Christopher Lasch, "Critical View: Archie Bunker and the Liberal Mind," *Channels of Communication* 1 (October–November 1981): 34–35, 63; W. Curtis Miner, "Silent Majority TV: Programming the Lower Middle Class on

Network Television during the 1970s," paper presented to the Popular Culture Association, national conference, New Orleans, 2000.

3. Edward Martini, *Invisible Enemies: The American War in Vietnam, 1975–2000* (Amherst: University of Massachusetts Press, 2007), 53–68.

4. Ronald Reagan, "A Time for Choosing," October 27, 1964, Ronald Reagan Presidential Library and Museum; Ronald Reagan, "California Gubernatorial Address," January 5, 1967, Ronald Reagan Presidential Library and Museum.

5. Ronald Reagan, "Remarks at the Annual Meeting of the International Association of Chiefs of Police in New Orleans, Louisiana," September 28, 1981.

6. Chris Nashawaty, "Warren Beatty on his Unlikely Friendship with Ronald Reagan," *Entertainment*, November 11, 2016, https://ew.com/article/2016/11/11/warren-beatty-ronald-reagan-friendship-reds.

7. Mark Weinberg, "What I Learned Watching 'Back to the Future' with Ronald Reagan," *Politico*, February 27, 2018, https://www.politico.com/magazine/story/2018/02/27/ronald-reagan-press-aide-movie-nights-with-reagan-217095.

8. Douglas Brinkley, ed., *The Reagan Diaries* (New York: HarperCollins, 2007), 269, 274.

9. Ibid., 264.

10. Ronald Reagan, "Remarks at a Luncheon Meeting of the United States Olympic Committee in Los Angeles, California," March 3, 1983, Ronald Reagan Presidential Library and Museum.

11. Lance Morrow, "Feeling Proud Again: Olympic Organizer Peter Ueberroth," *Time* 125 (January 7, 1985): 20.

12. Ronald Reagan, "Remarks at a Ceremony Commemorating the 40th Anniversary of the Normandy Invasion, D-Day," June 6, 1984, Ronald Reagan Presidential Library and Museum.

13. Craig Hlavaty, "First Republican National Convention in Texas Led to Ronald Reagan Landslide," *Houston Chronicle*, August 19, 2016.

14. Selwyn Raab, "Donovan Cleared of Fraud Charges by Jury in Bronx," *New York Times*, May 26, 1987.

15. Nashawaty, "Warren Beatty on his Unlikely Friendship with Ronald Reagan."

Epilogue: Legacies of the Reagan Revolution

Political success and failure are often transient judgments, alternating with the flow of events across decades or generations. Among political pundits and scholars, there is a temptation to pronounce immediate judgment on who the winners and losers are, though it is a fool's errand. For instance, academics and pollsters ranked Harry Truman among America's least successful presidents when he left office in 1953. A few Democratic partisans in the early 1950s, notably Jeane Kirkpatrick and Ronald Reagan, appreciated what Truman had accomplished in the face of great domestic and international challenges, but they were a minority. By the 1970s, Truman had risen considerably in presidential rankings. Part of the explanation was that the passage of time allowed for a more dispassionate appraisal of Truman. It also helped Truman's reputation that by the time of Reagan's election in 1980, the failed presidencies of Richard Nixon, Gerald Ford, and Jimmy Carter made Truman's presidency seem all the more successful.

When Reagan left the White House in 1989, pundits and professors ranked him poorly, though his public-approval rating stood at a remarkable 65 percent. The perception gap between the experts and the people closed in Reagan's favor over the next twenty-five years. By 2016, political historians, regardless of partisan preferences, ranked Reagan as the ninth best president in American history—placing him in the company of Franklin Roosevelt, Abraham Lincoln, and Truman.

Like Truman, Reagan benefited from the frequent floundering of his successors. It also helped Reagan's reputation that his personal diary became available to researchers, providing a handwritten account of his day-to-day musings in the White House. The Reagan diary showed a pragmatic president with enormous self-composure and political skills. Reagan's reputation also benefited from the policy victories he racked up in the White House.

Reagan's presidency was, in some ways, a paradox. He spent much of his political career decrying government overreach and incompetency, and he advocated the devolution of many federal functions to the states. Despite that, Reagan did something unintended and what many people thought was impossible: he restored Americans' faith in (some aspects of) government. Public-opinion polls in the 1980s showed a steadily growing level of confidence in the executive branch and the military. Even Americans' approval of Congress and higher education marginally recovered from the political dysfunction of the 1960s and 1970s.

Although many conservatives complained that Sandra Day O'Connor was an undependable ally on the U.S. Supreme Court, they missed the larger picture: Reagan changed the ideological and intellectual complexion of the federal judiciary. O'Connor may have been a "swing voter," and Robert Bork may have been denied a seat on the nation's highest bench, but Reagan gave conservatives a more level playing field. Appointing Anton Scalia to the Supreme Court in 1986 threw an intellectually formidable conservative Catholic into the judicial mix. He may not have always been in the majority on decisions, but Scalia's thorough dissents laid the groundwork for subsequent legal challenges that appeared before the court.

In his two presidential terms, Reagan appointed, and the Senate confirmed, 402 federal judges. By way of comparison, Roosevelt, who was elected to four terms, named 207 federal judges. Truman, who served two terms, appointed 140 federal judges. To be sure the number of federal judgeships increased over time, but part of the reason for the disparity between Reagan and Roosevelt and Truman stemmed from the fact that conservative judges in the 1930s and 1940s often hung onto office until death. They did not want what they regarded as activist liberal presidents choosing their judicial successors.

Their slow walking to retirement (or otherwise) had other consequences beyond limiting the number of federal judges Roosevelt and Truman appointed. By the time federal judgeships became available, the young, liberal faithful had aged. It also meant that when the judicial logjam cleared, there would be a great cluster of liberal judges appointed around the same time—and all subsequently retiring or expiring at the same time. Reagan took advantage of the wave of judicial retirements in the 1980s. He also appointed judges so young that they would likely be in place for the next thirty years or more.

Reagan cited his economic policy, particularly his efforts toward tax-rate reductions, slow spending, and trimming federal regulations on business, as major accomplishments. Keynesian economic policy had failed to anticipate, let alone resolve, stagflation in the 1970s. Wages, as adjusted for inflation, declined during the 1970s. Federal social welfare programs and increased public-sector spending—the heart of Keynesian economics—did not bring wages up, let alone curb the inflation that was destroying the savings and incomes of millions of Americans. Many liberal Democrats and Republicans clung to the Keynesian faith largely because they could not imagine a viable alternative. As Republican presidential primary candidate George Herbert Walker Bush had sneeringly asserted in 1980, any economic policy that was not Keynesian was just "voodoo economics."

Arthur Laffer's "supply-side economics" offered a controversial alternative to Keynesian policy. Reagan was willing to take a leap of faith, as was Texas Democratic congressman Phil Gramm. Reducing tax rates and trimming federal regulations stabilized the U.S. economy. It also helped that Reagan embraced one Keynesian tenet: he kept Carter's hiked prime interest rates in place to squeeze inflation out of the economy. (Keynes himself regarded this tool as a last resort.) Thanks to falling inflation and an expanding economy, wages increased in the 1980s. The U.S. economy added millions of new jobs. Also, as Laffer had predicted, as tax rates declined, businesses invested and generated more revenue to the U.S. Treasury. Thereafter, tax cuts became a central part of the Republican Party's economic policy agenda.

The success of supply-side economics, however, was relative to its shortcomings. Greatly increasing military spending; slowing, but not reversing, federal entitlement outlays; and cutting taxes inevitably increased yearly deficits and the overall national debt. As a presidential candidate in 1980, Reagan had condemned Carter's $74 billion deficit and a national debt of $908 billion. The national debt in 1980 represented 32 percent of the United States' entire Gross Domestic Product (GDP). By the time Reagan left the White House eight years later, annual deficits ran $153 billion, and the national debt had climbed $2.8 *trillion*, or 50 percent of the GDP.

Reagan admitted his failure to reduce the national debt and balance the federal budget. He wanted to balance the federal budget, just as Roosevelt had pledged to do when he ran for president in 1932. Neither Reagan's nor Roosevelt's sincerity was in question, but their respective economic policies ensured that deficits and the national debt increased. Reagan was not going to reduce Roosevelt's legacy programs, no matter how much libertarians such as budget director David Stockman complained. Indeed, Reagan could be credited with helping to save, and extend the life of, New Deal–era programs, most especially Social Security.

Unintentionally, the debt and deficits of the 1980s opened the proverbial Pandora's Box. Once a president crossed the one-trillion-dollar debt threshold, there was apparently little desire to turn back. Democratic president Bill Clinton in the 1990s managed to balance the federal budget in the final years of his administration, but he, too, added to the national debt. By the early twenty-first century, trillions of dollars had become the new billions of dollars on the federal balance sheet. The national debt could be financed in part by the U.S. Treasury "buying up" notes or by selling the debt as an investment opportunity to foreign nations. Some American military leaders warned that giving potential foreign adversaries leverage over the U.S. economy through debt investment was a threat to national security. The only other option, since reducing federal outlays appeared to be politically impossible, was to default on the debt and collapse the international economic order.

The economic expansion of the 1980s was not uniformly spread across the United States. "Smokestack" industrial cities, especially in the Midwest and the Mid-Atlantic region, shed good-paying, unionized jobs. Decaying cities, among them, Akron, Buffalo, Cleveland, Detroit, and Pittsburgh, experienced population losses and rising crime and poverty rates throughout the 1980s and 1990s. Some communities managed, by the early twenty-first century, to reinvent themselves as postindustrial technology or "knowledge cities," but with fewer people. Most "knowledge city" residents were highly educated and compensated or had little education and were very poor—the middle class having largely been hollowed out.

Low-wage Sunbelt cities, as well as high-wage Silicon Valley settlements, prospered through the 1980s and into the twenty-first century. The Sunbelt even acquired industry, since the United States, no matter how wed to the knowledge-city model it had become, still needed homemade aircraft, automobiles, and appliances. Such Sunbelt businesses thrived in a region where labor unions were historically weak and state governments were reluctant to help enforce federal environmental, health, and safety regulations.

At the end of his second term, Reagan rejoiced in the fact that he had played a role in restoring Americans' sense of civic duty and patriotism. The U.S. military was better equipped, trained, and compensated than at any other time since World War II. Young Americans were lining up to join university ROTC units or seek admittance to the service academies, and all branches of the military made their enlistment quotas. On the other hand, the officer cadre and enlisted ranks continued to resemble the heavily working- and lower-middle-class, rural and small-town demographics of the Vietnam War era. The children of the upper-middle class largely continued to avoid military service just as they avoided living in working-class neighborhoods.

The U.S. military in the 1980s achieved a level of lethality that alarmed Leonid Brezhnev's successors. That alarm grew as the extent of the Soviet military's debacle in Afghanistan became obvious even to the most hawkish communist. It was clear that the U.S. military had recovered from its demoralizing, dysfunctional "Vietnam Syndrome." Reagan had argued since 1964 that muddled politicians (mostly Democrats), not American soldiers, were ensuring that the United States lost in Vietnam. From Reagan's perspective, if a president projected confidence in the military and a firm commitment to victory, then the United States could not lose a war. Whether or not that was true, Reagan believed it and, fretfully, so did Soviet leader Mikhail Gorbachev.

Reagan had succinctly summed up his endgame for the Cold War: we win, they lose. His remark seemed flip to both friend and foe alike, but Reagan was serious. He knew that the Soviet Union could not match American technology. That meant that the Strategic Defense Initiative, regardless of whether it was practical, would force his Soviet counterparts to reconsider their nuclear arms buildup. Additionally, Reagan was supplying Afghan rebels, who were exhausting Soviet financial and human resources. Gorbachev recognized that Afghanistan was a net loss.

There was also the considerable cost to the Soviet Union of maintaining the occupation of its Eastern European satellites and propping up its overseas dependencies. It was difficult for the Soviet Union to maintain order in a restless Poland and keep its Cuban ally financially afloat. Communist allies might be a good source of insurgents and troops (quality greatly varied), but overall they were a financial drain.

To the surprise of nearly everyone but Reagan, he and Gorbachev came up with a framework for a nuclear weapons drawdown and a cultural and economic opening to the West. It would have seemed incredible to Americans (and Russians) in 1981 that seven years later, Reagan would be able to talk freely with students and staff at Moscow State University—the alma mater of Mikhail and Raisa Gorbachev.

A few months after Reagan left the White House, the Soviet Empire cracked. The Berlin Wall ceased to be an obstacle to the free movement of people between East and West Germany. Gorbachev had informed Reagan that he would deprive the United States of an enemy. He had not imagined that, in the process of military de-escalation, Gorbachev would also deprive fellow communists of a major global power base. It took little time for the Russians to throw out the communist name Leningrad and, reaching into their history, restore czarist, Orthodox St. Petersburg. Although Gorbachev and a fledgling democracy survived a communist coup attempt, the last Soviet leader received little respect from his fellow citizens. Many forgot communist repression and longed for their superpower glory days. Desperate for income to support his family, Gorbachev filmed a commercial in 1997 for the Kansas-based restaurant chain, Pizza Hut.

In terms of domestic politics, while voters heartily approved of Reagan's bipartisanship, it was less than what it seemed. Nearly all of Reagan's Democratic allies in the House and Senate were southerners who were socially conservative and supportive of tax cuts and the military buildup. Democratic liberals were outraged by what they regarded as an ideological betrayal. Far from moving them toward bipartisanship, liberals wanted to purge the "Boll Weevils" from their party ranks. While that might make the ability of Democrats to control Congress and the White House more difficult, ideological purity trumped mundane political pragmatism. Purging conservative Democrats from Congress also meant casting out their voters, who were overwhelmingly working-class whites.

Meanwhile, Republicans faced their own internal reorganization. Some political analysts in the 1980s understood that there would be a point reached when working-class white southerners and northerners stopped

Epilogue: Legacies of the Reagan Revolution

voting Republican at the presidential level and supporting Democrats for Congress and state-level offices. Sooner than later, such voters would start embracing Republicans down ticket. That had been President Richard Nixon's dream in 1972, but Watergate had thwarted the "New Majority" he wanted to build.

The problem for conservatives in the 1980s was that as Republicans attracted more working-class white voters, they also acquired their economic and social issues. Reagan himself showed what happened when a product of the New Deal, and an admirer of Roosevelt and Truman, became the leader of the Republican Party. New Deal legacy programs remained untouched and some tariffs were imposed, or threatened to be imposed, to protect part of American industry and its workers. Unrepentant New Deal Reagan Democrats repelled free-market purists.

For their part, religiously conservative Democrats brought to the Republican Party a host of cultural issues. Socially liberal, upper-middle-class suburban Republicans were aghast that there were growing numbers in their midst who were opposed to abortion and gay rights. It would not be long before Republican liberals became Democrats.

Although Reagan did not initiate what would become known as the "great ideological sorting" of the two major parties and their voters, his outreach to Democratic conservatives and the legislative successes he achieved accelerated the process. Paradoxically, then, bipartisanship in the early 1980s led to a divisive, bitter partisanship afterward.

Ideological sorting paralleled the racial and ethnic sorting of Democrats and Republicans. In the 1980s, the two parties moved in opposite directions on such policies as affirmative action and law and order. Both issues had a major racial dimension. Democrats embraced affirmative action and greater federal oversight of business employment practices. They also complained about a racial bias in federal, state, and local anticrime laws and pointed to racially skewed incarceration rates. Republicans, in turn, criticized affirmative action and championed more aggressive anticrime measures.

As the 1984 Democratic presidential nominee, Walter Mondale recognized the growing racial divide between the two parties. He celebrated the "diversity" of the Democrats and derided the overwhelmingly white composition of the Republican Party. For his part, Reagan persisted in his rhetorical affirmation that there were Americans—not African Americans, not Mexican Americans, but just Americans. He may have referred to 1936 U.S. Olympian Jesse Owens as Black, but Reagan emphasized that the track star was first and always a great American hero. As with his 1986 dedication of the renovated Statue of Liberty, Reagan believed all people, regardless of race, ethnicity, or religion, went into the melting pot, from which they emerged as a single people. For their part, the Democrats needed racial identity politics to maintain their political competitiveness as much as Republicans benefited from the enormous influx of disaffected whites in the 1980s.

Beyond racial and moral politics, the Republicans experienced other fissures, most especially in the conservative movement, which had become central to the presidential nomination process. In part, Reagan, like his idol Roosevelt, helped hold the party together. Reagan instinctively knew how to cajole various factions. He was also an accomplished public speaker, mixing down-to-earth phrasing with soaring rhetoric. In his youth, Reagan had closely studied Roosevelt's speeches. A few conservative leaders complained that Reagan cited Roosevelt and proclaimed the virtues of Truman more often than he quoted Republicans. In response, Reagan challenged them to name a Republican president in the past fifty years who was worth quoting.

Reagan's absence from the national stage after the 1980s, however, did not tell the whole story about conservative fissures. The Cold War had bound conservatives together in what activists such as William F. Buckley Jr. called "fusionism." Libertarians, social conservatives, and anticommunist neoconservatives were united in their opposition to the Soviet Empire and its allies. Fear of international communism also made the isolationist wing of the Republican Party appear to be as dangerous as it was, to Cold Warriors, unpatriotic.

The end of the Cold War saw libertarians increasingly clash with religious conservatives. Neoconservatives searched for a new foreign enemy. Many looked to the Middle East. In reaction, isolationists reappeared in the 1990s. Overall, conservatives ran off in every direction, chasing different domestic and foreign policies that were frequently at odds with each other.

In 1988, George H. W. Bush argued that a vote for him would be the equivalent of a constitutionally prohibited third consecutive presidential term for Reagan. Then he pledged to build "a kinder, gentler America,"

Epilogue: Legacies of the Reagan Revolution

which many conservatives and liberals took as a rebuke to Reagan. Bush authorized his campaign manager, Lee Atwood, to attack Democratic presidential nominee and Massachusetts governor Michael Dukakis for allowing Black prisoners out on weekend passes to rape white women. Bush also proclaimed, "Read my lips, no new taxes," and, once elected, he raised taxes. When questioned about his change of heart on taxes, Bush replied, "Read my hips!"[1]

As with his rhetoric, tactics, and taxation policy, Bush's foreign policy represented a major departure from Reagan's. In the 1980s, Reagan had seen his military buildup as a shield, not a sword. The 1983 invasion of the Caribbean island of Grenada to rescue American students and oust Cuban troops had been a small-scale and quick operation. Most importantly, Grenada had been an exception, not the rule. Reagan preferred to arm anticommunist insurgencies and governments fighting Soviet-backed guerrillas. Most often, these were covert CIA operations.

Bush, in contrast, saw the U.S. military Reagan had enlarged and improved as a sword. In 1989, Bush sent troops to Panama to overthrow its leader and ensure a more friendly government. The Panama operation, which had some resemblance to Grenada, however, paled beside Bush's massive military intervention in the Middle East in 1990. The economic, military, and political fallout from Bush's Middle Eastern policy has continued into the present.

In 1990, with the end of the vicious war with Iran, Iraqi leader Saddam Hussein was looking for more oil resources. He asked Bush's ambassador to Iraq, April Glaspie, if the United States had any opinion as to whether he could invade neighboring Kuwait, which, historically, was culturally and economically intertwined with Iraq. Glaspie consulted with Bush and then responded that the United States had no position on the matter. Though the Soviets had armed and trained the Iraqi military, Hussein had been an American ally and he had done much in the 1980s to contain the spread of Iran's brand of revolutionary Islam. With that assurance, Hussein occupied Kuwait.

To Hussein's enormous surprise, Bush denounced the Iraqi invasion and neoconservatives in the administration and, through their media outlets, compared Hussein to Hitler. The United States sent hundreds of thousands of troops to Saudi Arabia in preparation for an attack on Kuwait and Iraq. There were other nations involved as part of the United

Nations' commitment to act against aggression, but, as with the Korea in 1950, the Persian Gulf War was overwhelmingly an American operation. In 1991, Bush launched an attack and decimated the Iraqi military. The results of Reagan's revamping of the American military were clear for the world to see.

Bush had badly miscalculated. His advisers, including Richard Cheney and Donald Rumsfeld, had assured him that there would be no need to race toward the Iraqi capital of Baghdad, as the people would rise up and overthrow Hussein. While there was a limited revolt, it proved ineffective. Hussein remained in power, deeply embittered against the United States. Meanwhile, Iraq's degraded military and political situation encouraged more Iranian terror attacks throughout the region.

Saudi national Osama Bin Laden, who had joined the Holy Warriors in Afghanistan in the 1980s to fight the Soviets, identified the United States as his new enemy. He resented the fact that Saudi Arabia had served as a host to U.S. troops, whom he regarded as infidels. With the Russians gone from Afghanistan, that crippled nation would make the perfect base of operations for Bin Laden to launch terror attacks against Americans.

Conservatives were divided over the wisdom of the Persian Gulf War. Reagan's former secretary of the navy, James Webb, denounced the war, as did Reagan's former communications director, Pat Buchanan. Libertarian activist Grover Norquist subsequently warned Republicans that Muslims abroad and in the United States were upset with U.S. military intervention in the Middle East. He urged the Republican Party to make a serious outreach effort to Arab Americans.

Norquist, Buchanan, and Webb, to varying degrees, also criticized the United States for favoring Israel over the Arab nations. As Buchanan had argued in the run-up to the Persian Gulf War, "There are only two groups that are beating the drums for war in the Middle East—the Israeli Defense Ministry and its amen corner in the United States." Neoconservatives condemned Buchanan for statements that they believed bordered on anti-Semitic. Norquist was more careful with his rhetoric than Buchanan was, but that did not stop neoconservatives from accusing him of being un-American and anti-Semitic—in no small part due to the fact that he was married to a Palestinian Muslim. Arab Americans, both Muslim and Christian, increasingly moved into the Democratic Party.[2]

Bush squandered the political capital Reagan had bequeathed him, which, along with a recession, helped former Arkansas governor Bill Clinton win the 1992 presidential election. It did not hurt Clinton's electoral prospects that billionaire Ross Perot ran as an independent presidential candidate and broke off a number of Republican voters who disliked Bush for raising taxes and waging war in the Middle East. Former Reagan adviser Pat Buchanan, citing those same issues, had earlier wounded Bush in the Republican presidential primaries.

In many ways, Democrat Clinton was a better ideological heir to Reagan than Republican Bush was. Clinton worked well with Republicans after they won control of the House and Senate in 1994. Among their legislative accomplishments were welfare entitlement reforms, the influx of federal funds to enable cities to hire more police officers nationwide, and tax cuts. Clinton believed that the Democratic Party, if it was to be competitive at the presidential election level, had to move to the Right and embrace much of Reagan's domestic policy agenda.

In foreign policy, however, Clinton stood between Reagan and Bush. Clinton greatly reduced the size and cost of the military, which helped him balance the federal budget—the so-called post–Cold War peace dividend. On the other hand, he maintained "no-fly zones" over Iraq to punish Hussein, which only further aggravated the Middle East. Clinton also militarily intervened in a genocidal Balkans civil war.

Although a 1960s anti–Vietnam War protestor, Clinton believed that the United States should intervene militarily if there was a compelling moral imperative and regardless of national security interests. Reagan, in contrast, was more of a pragmatist. He always balanced his anticommunist beliefs with an eye to U.S. security needs. The one time he failed to do so, in Lebanon, taught him a harsh lesson. The U.S. military, Reagan believed, should not and could not be an international social worker. Clinton disagreed.

One other foreign policy initiative Clinton took had long-term consequences: his decision to advocate for the expansion of the North Atlantic Treaty Organization (NATO) eastward toward Russia. As Truman's advisers had argued after World War II, NATO existed to keep the Russians out, the Americans in, and the Germans down. With the collapse of the Soviet Union and the reunification of Germany, NATO's purpose appeared to be over. Clinton, and his successors, however, allowed NATO to recruit former Soviet satellites and forge what looked like an anti-Russian military alliance. The goodwill built by Reagan and Gorbachev between their two nations evaporated over the course of the 1990s and early twenty-first century.

While conservative (and liberal) critics questioned the direction American foreign policy had taken under Bush and Clinton, moral traditionalists felt that their issues had taken a back seat. In 1988, Pat Robertson challenged Bush for the Republican presidential nomination. Robertson fell far short of his goal, but that did not deter him from electoral politics. In 1989, Robertson founded the Christian Coalition. He wanted to mobilize religiously conservative voters, especially at the congressional and state levels. Robertson also wanted to fill the void on the Religious Right when Jerry Falwell announced in 1989 that he was disbanding the Moral Majority. With great bravado, Falwell proclaimed that the Moral Majority had achieved its political agenda and was no longer needed.

The Christian Coalition mobilized about one-third of the total Republican presidential primary vote in the 1990s and perhaps accounted for one-quarter of the national electorate. By that measure, the Christian Coalition was more successful at getting out the vote in the 1990s than the Moral Majority had been in the 1980s, particularly for state and local elected offices. On the other hand, American culture in the 1990s was undergoing an enormous shift away from socially conservative policies. Moreover, the American people were becoming less religiously observant.

Regular weekly church attendance, which had plummeted to 40 percent of the U.S. population in 1970 (down from 49 percent in 1954), did not recover in the 1980s or afterward. Throughout the 1980s and on into the twenty-first century, membership across all religious denominations fell. The "mainline Protestant churches," notably the Episcopalian and Presbyterian Churches, typically lost up to a third of their members. In 1975, there had been 7.5 million ex-Catholics in the United States. That number rose to nearly 18 million by 2000 and to over 26 million in 2010. If not for the influx of Hispanic immigrants, the Roman Catholic Church in America would have been a shell of its former self.

While some conservative fundamentalist and evangelical sects grew in the 1980s and afterward, it was mainly because disenchanted Episcopalians and Catholics joined their ranks. Far more simply lost all faith. For those who drifted toward more conservative sects, often the feeling persisted that their home church had become too socially liberal. Others, especially Catholics, felt betrayed when it became apparent that numerous priests had sexually abused children for years while bishops covered up the problem. Even though Pope John II promised to reform the Catholic Church, the abuse—and the cover-ups—continued.

It was not only the Catholic and Episcopalian Churches that experienced troubled times. In 1987, Assemblies of God minister, television host, and Christian theme park operator Jim Bakker brought down his business empire with a sex scandal and embezzlement. Although Falwell and Robertson had nothing to do with Bakker, all conservative Christian organizations suffered a loss in reputation and funding. Donations to the Moral Majority fell, which is one of the real reasons Falwell disbanded his organization two years later. Robertson's *700 Club* television channel lost donors as well. Meanwhile, many business supporters of the Heritage Foundation stopped giving, voicing concern that the conservative think tank had become too entangled first with the Moral Majority and then with the Christian Coalition.

In the 1990s, there was a conservative legislative renaissance that House Republican strategist Newt Gingrich promoted. In 1994, Gingrich proposed a coordinated, nationwide congressional campaign with an aim to capturing the House and the Senate. His "Contract with America" had several elements that Reagan would have approved of, including welfare reform, tax cuts, and more federal resources to promote law and order across the United States. Gingrich frequently quoted "the Gipper" when not praising the example of vision and leadership Franklin Roosevelt had provided during the Great Depression and World War II. Not only did the Republicans capture the Senate and the House in 1994 and make Gingrich Speaker but they also held onto Congress for the next few election cycles. Conservatives, however, could not defeat Clinton who, in any event, proved to be a good partner with Gingrich when their egos did not get in the way.

One major difference between politics in the 1980s and 1990s was the emergence of a significant conservative news media. Talk radio pioneer Rush Limbaugh not only acquired an audience in the millions but also inspired other conservatives to launch their own shows. Some proved successful in building an audience, while many failed. Most of those who failed had little experience with broadcast media, and it showed. Limbaugh had

Republican House Speaker Newt Gingrich (on center left) and Democratic president Bill Clinton (front) alternated between feuding and partnering to advance a conservative economic agenda in the 1990s. (Library of Congress.)

begun his radio career as a sports announcer and disc jockey, not as a politician. Radio required a strong "voice" and the ability to fill airtime and hold peoples' attention. In those regards, Limbaugh shared some important traits with Reagan.

In 1996, wealthy Australian native Rupert Murdoch launched a conservative television news network: the Fox News channel. Conservative talk radio hosts often moved back and forth between various Fox News shows and their AM radio programs. Murdoch also started a neoconservative magazine, the *Weekly Standard*. Although the *Weekly Standard* routinely lost money, Murdoch used its columnists on his Fox News shows. He later acquired the *Wall Street Journal* and moved its columnists around his growing conservative media empire. While the conservative news media could not unseat Clinton, it promoted the "Contract with America" and gave congressional conservatives a valued public platform.

At the same time, however, liberal and radical voices on the Left acquired their own cable news networks and television talk shows. (They never successfully gained prominence in AM talk radio, in part because

Epilogue: Legacies of the Reagan Revolution

they did not understand the medium and in part because the demographics were too working- and lower-middle-class white.) The national television networks and their news programs, although inclined toward the Democratic Party, lost viewers who gravitated toward one of the liberal or conservative niche channels. As with entertainment, there was no longer any semblance of a mass news audience—just ideological and demographic fragments who tuned each other out.

The dawn of the twenty-first century brought profound changes to the United States that went far toward unwinding many of Reagan's domestic and foreign policy achievements. On September 11, 2001, terrorists affiliated with Bin Laden launched a coordinated attack against the United States. They crashed two airplanes into the World Trade Center twin towers, bringing both down. A third plane hit the Pentagon, and a fourth crashed in a Pennsylvania field after passengers stormed the cockpit and overpowered the terrorists. Three thousand died, either on September 11 or weeks or years later from illnesses acquired while cleaning up "Ground Zero" in New York City.

Terrorist attack, World Trade Center, September 11, 2001. Many of Ronald Reagan's economic and foreign-policy legacies vanished in the aftermath of the 9/11 attacks. (Library of Congress.)

President George W. Bush, the son of George H. W. Bush and a favorite of the *Weekly Standard* and of neoconservatives in general, wanted to strike at Bin Laden's training camps in Afghanistan. Congressional Democrats and Republicans, reeling from the 9/11 attacks, authorized military intervention in Afghanistan. After an initial military victory that subsequently proved to be an illusion, the United States became just as bogged down in Afghanistan as the Soviet Union had become in the 1980s.

Inexplicably, having failed to win in Afghanistan, Bush's advisers, especially his father's foreign policy architects, Cheney and Rumsfeld, began pushing in 2002 for military intervention against Iraq. They claimed—incorrectly, as it turned out—that Hussein was constructing "weapons of mass destruction" to be used against the United States and its allies. This time, Congress was divided, with many Democrats leery of starting another war before the first one was finished.

Democrats were not the only ones concerned about going to war in Iraq. Conservatives and libertarians were also leery. Buchanan, Norquist, and Webb, predictably, denounced military intervention in Iraq. The *Weekly Standard*'s columnists insisted that the war in Iraq would be short and victorious, as the Iraqi people would rise up against Hussein. They also questioned the patriotism of anti-interventionists. In 2003, Bush sent U.S. troops into Iraq and commenced an unending insurgency. By ultimately removing Hussein, Bush opened the door for Iran to further increase its influence in Iraq and across the region.

The wars that Bush launched in 2001 and 2003, which have continued into the present (2020), were not the only reason many conservatives turned against the Republican Party leadership and the neoconservatives. Immediately after the 9/11 attacks, Congress had adopted the Providing Appropriate Tools Required to Intercept and Obstruct Terrorism (PATRIOT) Act. The acronym was intended to place critics on the defensive, since it made them look unpatriotic. To the surprise of many conservatives, Phyllis Schlafly, along with Norquist, denounced the PATRIOT Act. Both were concerned about Congress giving the president the power to perform secret searches in citizens' homes, collect personal emails, launch covert wire taps, and collect the phone records of anyone deemed to have terrorist ties.

In the name of preserving Americans' security, George W. Bush had enormously expanded the role of the federal government in Americans' lives, most especially by placing them under surveillance. Additionally, his wars added trillions of dollars to the national debt and fueled increased deficit spending.

The Bush wars also did something else: as American casualties mounted in the futile effort to stabilize Afghanistan and Iraq, more youths stopped enlisting in the military. Many troops found that the Defense Department would not allow them to leave when their enlistments ended, while exhausted National Guard and Reserve troops were repeatedly deployed to the combat theaters. Bush had returned the American armed forces to 1970s levels of sinking morale and sagging recruitment. It was if Reagan's restoration of the U.S. military in the 1980s had not even had happened.

George H. W. Bush and George W. Bush nearly erased most of Reagan's political legacy. They were, however, virtually blameless for the conservatives' rout in social policy. While Reagan had mostly given social conservatives little more than rhetorical support on issues such as abortion, he was unequivocally a champion of the War on Drugs and law and order. By the early twenty-first century, large numbers of Americans saw the War on Drugs as futile and were repelled at the number of citizens who had been incarcerated for long periods of time for nonviolent offenses.

Ironically, the most dangerous narcotics to hit the United States in the 1990s were not illegal if prescribed by a doctor: pain killers, most often opioids. By the early twenty-first century, the United States had two million prescription pill addicts. Forty-two thousand died of overdoses just in 2016. The War on Drugs had focused on cocaine and narcotics smuggled into the United States. It had not occurred to federal authorities that a vast generation of addicts, supplied by major pharmaceutical companies and doctors, would become a major public health threat. Federal action was easier to take against Latin American cocaine suppliers than it was to confront a pharmaceutical industry that generously funded both major political parties.

Conservatives had long advocated a return of many governmental functions to the states, especially when it came to administering welfare programs. Liberals increasingly embraced their own style of federalism but with the intention of combating federal antidrug policies. Mostly Democratic-leaning states began to decriminalize marijuana possession and distribution. Such states did not regard marijuana as a "gateway" drug to cocaine. By 2019, nearly three dozen states had either fully legalized marijuana or allowed it for medical purposes with a doctor's prescription. Although marijuana possession and distribution remained a federal crime, state and local law enforcement followed their states' laws, not U.S. law. In a development that Reagan would likely have not imagined, organized crime syndicates did not operate the legal marijuana trade. Instead, pharmaceutical companies and brewers dominated the market. Many of the executives in these firms were Republican.

The growing public acceptance of marijuana paralleled calls to reconsider prison sentences for nonviolent offenders who may have been convicted of narcotics' charges. Many prisoners belonged to minority groups, suggesting that law enforcement may have been less than color-blind. Whether or not that was so, it still remained a fact that the penalties for crack, which was predominantly a drug of choice among the poor, were harsher than sentences passed on to middle-class users of higher-priced powder cocaine. Libertarians and growing numbers of Republicans called for revisiting the antidrug laws Congress had passed in the 1980s. The era of "Just Say No" essentially ended in the early twenty-first century.

Americans' attitudes toward gay rights and marriage also experienced a sea change at the beginning of the twenty-first century. Social conservatives, notably Falwell, Robertson, and Schlafly, had built their respective organizations and fundraising appeals around opposition to gay rights. (Reagan largely avoided the issue.) In 2004, their rout in what became known in the 1990s as the "culture war" began with the legalization of gay marriage in Massachusetts. Other states, mainly with strong liberal and libertarian populations, followed suit. Then, in 2015, the U.S. Supreme Court, in *Obergefell v. Hodges*, ruled that all states had to recognize the validity of gay marriage. The Court split five to four, with Reagan-appointed justice Anthony Kennedy joining the liberal majority and casting the deciding vote. (O'Connor had retired in 2006, leaving Kennedy to become the key swing voter on the Court.)

If the legacy of Reagan the policy maker and conservative champion had largely faded by 2019, the memory of Reagan the national leader remained vivid. Reagan, like Roosevelt, was the product of his times and came to power during a national and global crisis. Both were exhilarating and effective speakers. They had risen to the challenges of their times, and neither man let the perfect be the enemy of the good, as the saying went. Though both had a vision and stuck to general principles, Roosevelt and Reagan were always willing to negotiate. Neither had any use for uncompromising ideologues. As Reagan observed, "Die-hard conservatives thought that if I couldn't get everything I asked for, I should jump off the cliff with the flag flying—go down in flames."[3]

It was not just nostalgia that kept Reagan's memory alive and mainly revered. He spoke simply, yet eloquently, to Americans and encouraged them to move forward. Reagan may have, as his critics charged, celebrated an America that never existed, but at least his version of history was one worth aspiring to. His America was one where the people were united, were fair-minded, and aspired to greatness. Reagan's America defended democracy at home and abroad but was careful not to throw away the lives of soldiers and marines. Setbacks and disadvantages (whether of economic or social circumstance) were mere speed bumps on the road to a sunlit future.

There was nothing so tragic about Reagan than the fact that his Alzheimer's disease deprived him of the ability to enjoy retirement and to feel a satisfying sense of accomplishment. In 1994, in his final statement to the American people, Reagan delivered his own epitaph: "I now begin the journey that will lead me into the sunset of my life. I know that for America there will always be a bright dawn ahead."[4]

NOTES

1. Kenneth J. Heineman, *God Is a Conservative: Religion, Politics, and Morality in Contemporary America* (New York: New York University Press, 2005), 185.

2. Ibid., 190.

3. John Ehrman, *The Eighties: America in the Age of Reagan* (New Haven, CT: Yale University Press, 2005), 61.

4. Ronald Reagan, "Text of Letter Written by Ronald Reagan Announcing He Has Alzheimer's Disease," November 5, 1994, Ronald Reagan Presidential Library and Museum.

BIOGRAPHICAL ESSAYS

MENACHEM W. BEGIN (1913–1992)

The Israeli prime minister, from 1977 to 1983, Menachem Begin was an Eastern European Holocaust refugee who settled in Palestine. Determined to drive out British peacekeeping forces and establish an independent Zionist nation, Begin joined the terrorist group *Irgun*. In 1946, Begin took part in the bombing of the King David Hotel in Jerusalem, killing ninety-one people—most of them British and Palestinian. Begin subsequently rose in Israeli politics, becoming prime minister in 1977. Although an ideological hard-liner, Begin worked with Egyptian president Anwar Sadat and President Jimmy Carter to demilitarize Israel's border with Egypt, signing the Camp David Accords in 1978. Both Sadat and Begin subsequently shared a Nobel Peace Prize. Claiming the right of military preemption without a declaration of war, Begin bombed an Iraqi nuclear reactor in 1981 and invaded Lebanon in 1982. Begin placed President Ronald Reagan in an uncomfortable political position with much of the world, which condemned Israel's military actions.

LEONID I. BREZHNEV (1906–1982)

Leader of the Soviet Union from 1964 until his death in 1982. Leonid Brezhnev was part of a communist generation that acquired education and political opportunity under Soviet ruler Joseph Stalin. Convinced that his predecessor, Nikita Khrushchev, had backed down in the face of American military might during the 1962 Cuban Missile Crisis, Brezhnev was determined to expand the Soviet Union's nuclear arsenal and extend its support of communist insurgencies around the world. He also enunciated the "Brezhnev Doctrine," which stated that once a nation became a Soviet satellite, it could never leave. Brezhnev negotiated nuclear arms reductions with President Richard Nixon while increasing his nation's military capabilities. When communist China emerged as a Soviet rival and Islamic revolution took hold in Iran in the 1970s, Brezhnev became more fearful and aggressive. By the time of his death in 1982, Brezhnev had bequeathed to the Soviet Union a faltering economy and a military quagmire in Afghanistan.

EDMUND "PAT" BROWN (1905–1996)

A career politician who worked his way up the electoral ladder to governor of California (1959–1967), Pat Brown reorganized the public university system and greatly increased welfare spending. History, however, did not remember Brown for his reforms. The violent clashes between students and police at the Berkeley campus of the University of California, in 1964, and the Los Angeles Watts riot, in 1965, engendered an electoral backlash against California liberalism. Having handily beaten former Vice President Richard Nixon in the 1962 gubernatorial election, Brown regarded himself as a political dynamo. Brown also believed that he embodied virtue, while conservative critics were racist reactionaries. Ronald Reagan's victory against Brown in the 1966 California gubernatorial election encouraged the former actor to set his sights on the White House.

WILLIAM F. BUCKLEY JR. (1925–2008)

Heir to an oil fortune, William F. Buckley Jr. served in World War II, went to Yale, and joined the Central Intelligence Agency (CIA). In 1955, Buckley, disgusted with President Dwight Eisenhower's willingness to embrace, and even expand upon, New Deal programs, founded the *National Review* magazine. He built the *National Review* into the leading conservative intellectual magazine in the United States. Through the 1960s, Democratic liberals, confident of their ideas and political power, welcomed Buckley as a conservative gadfly—inviting him to appear on public affairs programs or to join them on the cocktail circuit. As the New Right emerged, however, and liberalism lost momentum, Buckley became less welcome in Democratic circles. President Ronald Reagan found Buckley to be a useful conduit to the conservative movement but differed sharply with him over a variety of domestic and foreign policy issues. To Buckley's dismay, Reagan never repudiated Franklin Roosevelt and the New Deal.

WILLIAM J. CASEY (1913–1987)

New York attorney, veteran of the Office of Strategic Services (OSS), and President Ronald Reagan's director of the Central Intelligence Agency from 1981 until his death in 1987, William J. Casey regarded himself as a devout Catholic and patriot, always prepared to set aside his legal practice to serve his country against Nazism and communism. As Reagan's CIA director, Casey took the lead in covert efforts to arm the Nicaraguan Contras and Afghan insurgents fighting Soviet troops and their allies. Political pundits suspected that Casey was deeply implicated in the Iran-Contra affair, but he died before he could testify before Congress.

JOHN TERRENCE "TERRY" DOLAN (1950–1986)

Cofounder of the National Conservative Political Action Committee (NCPAC) in 1975, Terry Dolan embraced anticommunism, opposed abortion, and wanted to decrease the cost and size of the federal government. In 1980, the NCPAC spent $2 million on behalf of Ronald Reagan's election and another $1.2 million to defeat several liberal Democratic senators. His brother, Anthony Dolan, served as a Reagan White House speechwriter. Although Terry Dolan had publicly defended gay rights in the early 1980s, most conservatives outside Washington were shocked to learn that he was gay—a fact that did not become widely known until he died of AIDS in 1986.

BARRY M. GOLDWATER (1909–1998)

A Phoenix, Arizona, department store heir, Arizona senator, ardent foe of Franklin Roosevelt and the New Deal, and a 1964 Republican presidential nominee, Goldwater entered politics to stop what he believed was the United States' drift toward socialism. With the support of Wisconsin senator Joseph McCarthy, Goldwater won a U.S. Senate seat in 1952 by defeating one of the authors of the Servicemen's Readjustment Act of 1944 (a.k.a. the "GI Bill of Rights"). An anticommunist libertarian, Goldwater opposed the 1964 Civil Rights Act and the 1965 Voting Rights Act on the grounds that the federal government had no constitutional right to interfere with state-level voting requirements and the rights of businesspeople to refuse service to whomever they wanted for any reason. As the 1964 Republican presidential nominee, Goldwater squarely attacked the New Deal's legacy programs, inspiring fear among millions of voters. Although Goldwater suffered a crushing landslide defeat, his campaign enlisted Ronald Reagan as a spokesperson, setting the actor on his road to the California governorship and the White House.

MIKHAIL S. GORBACHEV (1931–)

Although a product of the Soviet Union's political apparatus, Mikhail Gorbachev recognized that his country, as well as the Communist Party, had reached a breaking point. Leonid Brezhnev's foreign adventures had strained an already faltering Soviet economy by the time he invaded Afghanistan in 1979. The ensuing quagmire helped drag down the Soviet Union. Two of Brezhnev's successors only served briefly in the top leadership position before dying. Becoming the Soviet leader in 1985, Gorbachev understood that economic and political changes were necessary. He calculated, wrongly, that he could open up the economy and political system while keeping the Communist Party in power. He also wrongly thought that he could dissuade Ronald Reagan from pursuing the Strategic Defense Initiative (SDI), which the technologically inferior Soviet Union had no hope of emulating. Ultimately, Gorbachev and Reagan negotiated a reduction in nuclear weapons and laid the foundation for the end of the Cold War. In 1991, Gorbachev officially became the last leader of the (collapsing) Soviet Union.

WILLIAM PHILIP "PHIL" GRAMM (1942–)

A Texas A&M economics professor, Gramm won election to the U.S. House of Representatives in 1978 from the Fort Worth area. Gramm was a disciple of "supply-side" economist Arthur Laffer as well as an admirer of Ronald Reagan. When Reagan presented his economic and tax agenda to the House in 1981, Gramm lined up fellow Democrats, mostly southerners, to join Republicans in passing key legislation. Liberal critics branded Gramm and his Dixie allies as "Boll Weevils," referring to the parasite that had nearly destroyed the southern cotton industry decades earlier. House leader Thomas "Tip" O'Neill was outraged by what he perceived to be Gramm's political betrayal and attempted to defeat him in the Texas Democratic primaries. O'Neill failed, succeeding only in raising Gramm's profile across Texas and inadvertently aiding his election to the U.S. Senate as a Republican in 1984.

JEANE JORDAN KIRKPATRICK (1926–2006)

The daughter of a rambling Oklahoma wildcatter, Jeane Jordan demonstrated keen intelligence from an early age. She pursued an undergraduate degree in political science from Barnard and a master's degree from Columbia. It was rare for a woman to attend graduate school in the 1940s and nearly unheard of that one would obtain an analyst position with a federal national security organization: the Intelligence and Research Bureau of the U.S. State Department. While there she met and married Evron Kirkpatrick, a political scientist and veteran of the Office of Strategic Services (OSS) during World War II. In 1968, having completed a doctorate at Columbia, Jeane Kirkpatrick became a political science professor at Georgetown University. Like Ronald Reagan, Kirkpatrick was a Cold War Democrat who had grown disenchanted with the ideological direction of her party. Through the Committee on the Present Danger, Kirkpatrick became associated with neoconservatives. Like Kirkpatrick, most neoconservatives were disaffected Democrats looking for a new leader. Reagan appointed Kirkpatrick as his United Nations ambassador, but her influence in foreign policy in the 1980s was much greater than her title suggested. She became one of the most influential figures, female or male, in U.S. foreign policy circles.

DAVID H. KOCH (1940–2019)

A son of a Wichita, Kansas, oil pipeline construction contractor, David Koch helped build his father's millions into billions of dollars. Like his father, David Koch had strong libertarian sensibilities and a fear of federal overreach. Along with his brother Charles, David Koch helped found and fund the CATO Institute in 1977. The Koch brothers were convinced that the other Washington-based conservative think tanks, the American Enterprise Institute and the Heritage Foundation, were too liberal. In 1980, David Koch was the vice presidential candidate of the Libertarian Party. He called for eliminating most federal entitlement programs and most federal law enforcement agencies. Koch also warned that Ronald Reagan would prove to be little better than Franklin Roosevelt. Despite the electoral trouncing the Libertarian Party received in 1980, the Koch brothers continued to finance new libertarian initiatives and organizations, including the antitax Tea Party movement of the early twenty-first century.

ARTHUR B. LAFFER (1940–)

Born in Youngstown, Ohio, to a steel company executive, Arthur Laffer studied economics at Yale and earned an MBA and a doctorate from Stanford. Laffer taught economics at the University of Chicago and the University of Southern California after serving President Richard Nixon in the Office of Management and Budget. He became convinced that Keynesian economics were flawed in that higher taxes encouraged people to hide their assets rather than invest and expand economic opportunities. Subsequently, higher taxes resulted in lower amounts of money going into the federal treasury. Laffer contended that lowering tax rates would encourage greater investment and, consequently, lead to more money going into the federal treasury. This became known as "the Laffer Curve." Few could understand Laffer's views until *Wall Street Journal* reporter Jude Wanniski came along to explain them more simply and to rebrand them as "supply-side economics." Ronald Reagan embraced "the Laffer Curve," and it became the cornerstone of "Reaganomics" in the 1980s.

ANDREW W. MELLON (1855–1937)

Heir to a late-nineteenth-century Pittsburgh banking fortune, Andrew Mellon built an industrial empire (ALCOA, Gulf Oil, among other firms) and became a billionaire. He served three Republican presidents as secretary of the treasury: Warren Harding, Calvin Coolidge, and Herbert Hoover. His 1920s "Mellon Plan," a program of tax rate cuts, later inspired economist Arthur Laffer and Ronald Reagan. Mellon's tax reductions successfully encouraged greater business investment and an expansion of production. At the same time, however, the Mellon Plan did not address the lack of purchasing power of most Americans. Few Americans earned enough income to be required to pay federal taxes. By the 1970s, economic conditions had changed to the point where nearly all Americans paid taxes, meaning that a cut in tax rates would increase consumers' purchasing power.

WALTER F. MONDALE (1928–)

Walter Mondale was a product of Vice President Hubert Humphrey's Democratic-Farmer-Labor Party organization in Minnesota. As such, Mondale was a Cold Warrior and champion of union and civil rights. Elected to the U.S. Senate in the 1964 Democratic landslide victory, Mondale slowly turned against the United States' Cold War foreign policy. Democratic presidential candidate Jimmy Carter, in desperate need of a "Washington insider" to work with Congress, selected Mondale as his vice president. Defeated for reelection in 1980, Mondale captured the Democratic presidential nomination in 1984. Mondale pledged to raise taxes and reverse Ronald Reagan's Cold War foreign policy. In a humiliating electoral defeat, Mondale barely carried his home state, though he handily won the District of Columbia.

OLIVER L. NORTH (1943–)

A 1968 graduate of the U.S. Naval Academy, Oliver North served as a marine in Vietnam, where he earned a Silver Star and Bronze Star with V (Valor) for heroism in combat. North became convinced that congressional and news media liberals had undermined American resolve and morale in Vietnam. He joined Ronald Reagan's National Security Council in 1981 and took part in various operations, including the brief Grenada military intervention in 1983. Fearful that liberals would do to the anticommunist fighters in Nicaragua what he believed they had done to South Vietnamese troops, North took part in a scheme to circumvent congressional Democrats and arm the Contras with weapons purchased from the proceeds of illegal arms sales to Iran. North became a central figure in the "Iran-Contra" scandal of the late 1980s. Many in Democratic Party circles believed that Reagan knew more about North's schemes than he admitted, but they could not definitely prove it. North went on to become a Fox News Channel host and war correspondent in Iraq in the early twenty-first century.

SANDRA DAY O'CONNOR (1930–)

A graduate of the Stanford University School of Law in the early 1950s, Sandra Day O'Connor came from a western family of ranchers and politicians. She served in the Arizona legislature and was a judge on the superior court and the Arizona Court of Appeals. In 1981, Ronald Reagan appointed her as the first female member of the U.S. Supreme Court. As a justice, O'Connor upheld the fundamentals of the 1973 *Roe v. Wade* decision that had made abortion a right across the United States. Religious conservatives were appalled, but most conservatives, especially the business wing of the Republican Party, viewed her as an ally. In 2006, O'Connor retired from the Supreme Court.

THOMAS "TIP" O'NEILL (1912–1994)

An Irish Catholic son of Boston, Thomas "Tip" O'Neill served in the Massachusetts legislature until elected to the U.S. House of Representatives in 1952. O'Neill seamlessly made the transition from New Deal Democrat to Cold War Democrat to post-1960s liberal. O'Neill became Speaker of the House in 1977 and served in that position until 1987. A fierce critic and opponent of Ronald Reagan, O'Neill repeatedly found himself outflanked and stunned. His efforts to influence the selection of the 1984 Democratic presidential nomination led to one of the worst electoral defeats in American history. Reagan often invited O'Neill over to the White House for a drink and pleasant conversation. O'Neill went but complained to friends and staffers that Reagan was a dangerous man in the service of a vicious, right-wing agenda.

PHYLLIS STEWART SCHLAFLY (1924–2016)

Phyllis Schlafly earned a bachelor's and law degree from Washington University, in St. Louis. During World War II, she became a researcher for the conservative American Enterprise Association in New York City—which subsequently relocated to Washington, DC, and became known as the

American Enterprise Institute. Schlafly married a successful St. Louis attorney, who gave her the funds to privately publish a Barry Goldwater campaign book in 1964, *A Choice Not an Echo*. Her Goldwater book went on to sell three million copies and elevated Schlafly to the top rank of conservative activists. She founded the Eagle Forum in the 1970s to prevent ratification of the Equal Rights Amendment (ERA). Schlafly believed that the ERA would force women into combat if the draft were reinstated and that it would undermine the traditional family by promoting gay rights. She reached the zenith of her influence in conservative circles in 1980. As president, Reagan marginalized Schlafly—as he did with most social conservatives. In the early twenty-first century, Schlafly became a critic of Republican president George W. Bush and the surveillance regime he and Congress created after 9/11.

ARNOLD A. SCHWARZENEGGER (1947–)

As an Austrian who earned international renown as a bodybuilder, by the age of twenty Arnold Schwarzenegger had claimed the title of "Mr. Universe." At the age of twenty-one, Schwarzenegger immigrated to the United States, where he continued as a bodybuilder, part-time college student, construction worker, and aspiring actor. After watching President Richard Nixon on television, Schwarzenegger decided that he was a Republican since Nixon made more sense to him than the Democrats did. The 1982 film *Conan the Barbarian* made Schwarzenegger an action star. He went to the 1984 Republican National Convention in Dallas to meet his hero, Ronald Reagan. Although Schwarzenegger married a member of the Kennedy Democratic political dynasty, he considered himself to be a pragmatic conservative. Later, he served two terms as governor of California and attempted, but failed, to fix that state's fiscal issues.

ALAN K. SIMPSON (1931–)

Alan Simpson graduated from the University of Wyoming School of Law and subsequently served in the state legislature. Elected to the U.S. Senate as a Republican in 1978, Simpson embraced many of Ronald Reagan's economic policies. Simpson was instrumental in reforming the U.S. immigration system and assuring the rights of those who had come to the United States illegally with their parents. He supported abortion rights and was dismayed by the ballooning national debt. Simpson left the

Senate in 1996 and was one of the last members of Congress capable of forging a bipartisan consensus on numerous issues.

DAVID A. STOCKMAN (1946–)

David Stockman made the ideological journey from the religious Left to the libertarian Right in the 1960s as a student at Michigan State University. Elected as a Republican to the U.S. House of Representatives from western Michigan in 1976, Stockman was an anti–New Deal conservative. He opposed President Jimmy Carter's taxpayer-funded bailout of Chrysler and championed Ronald Reagan. He joined the Reagan administration in 1981 as director of the Office of Management and Budget (OMB). Leaking to a *Washington Post* reporter, Stockman attacked fellow Reagan staffers and complained that the president had failed to dismantle the New Deal's legacy programs and end deficit spending. Stockman's exposure as a leaker angered conservatives and thrilled liberal foes. Reagan kept Stockman in place at the OMB, where he became a marginalized, ineffective figurehead until he left the administration in 1985.

MARGARET H. THATCHER (1925–2013)

Margaret Thatcher graduated from Oxford with a degree in chemistry but was drawn to politics. She was elected to Parliament as a Conservative in 1959 and worked her way to the top of the party's leadership. As Britain's economy slid deeper into recession, and disruptive strikes swept the nation, Thatcher became the first female prime minister of Great Britain in 1979. Her strong personality and willingness to engage in debate with critics made her a near-mythic figure in Britain. Conservatives cheered her while those on the Left blamed her for nearly every social problem plaguing Britain. Thatcher stood loyally by Ronald Reagan as they confronted the Soviet Empire in the 1980s. She agreed with Reagan that Mikhail Gorbachev deserved to be treated as a relatively honest leader. Thatcher ended her political career in 1990, when restless Conservative Party members decided she had been in power long enough. Friends and foes called her the "Iron Lady," while her most famous political line became a veritable truism in the United States: "The problem with socialism is that you eventually run out of other peoples' money."

Primary Documents

1. "A Time for Choosing." Ronald Reagan Delivers His First National Political Speech, Championing Republican Presidential Candidate Barry Goldwater, 1964

A desperate Republican Party, watching its presidential nominee, Barry Goldwater, head toward a landslide defeat, faced financial disaster. Republican leaders needed to raise cash quickly and turned to Ronald Reagan. His nationally televised fundraising appeal brought millions of dollars into Republican coffers and raised Reagan's political profile. His speech, however, did little to prevent Goldwater's massive electoral defeat.

This is the issue of this election: Whether we believe in our capacity for self-government or whether we abandon the American Revolution and confess that a little intellectual elite in a far-distant capitol can plan our lives for us better than we can plan them ourselves. . . .

No government ever voluntarily reduces itself in size. So governments' programs, once launched, never disappear.

Actually, a government bureau is the nearest thing to eternal life we'll ever see on this earth.

Federal employees number two and a half million; and federal, state, and local, one out of six of the nation's work force employed by government. These proliferating bureaus with their thousands of regulations have cost us many of our constitutional safeguards. How many of us realize that today federal agents can invade a man's property without a warrant? They can impose a fine without a formal hearing, let alone a trial by jury? And they can seize and sell his property at auction to enforce the payment of that fine. . . .

Those who would trade our freedom for the soup kitchen of the welfare state have told us they have a utopian solution of peace without victory. They call their policy "accommodation." And they say if we'll only avoid any direct confrontation with the enemy, he'll forget his evil ways and learn to love us. All who oppose them are indicted as warmongers. They say we offer simple answers to complex problems. Well, perhaps there is a simple answer not an easy answer but simple: If you and I have the courage to tell our elected officials that we want our national policy based on what we know in our hearts is morally right.

We cannot buy our security, our freedom from the threat of the bomb by committing an immorality so great as saying to a billion human beings now enslaved behind the Iron Curtain, "Give up your dreams of freedom because to save our own skins, we're willing to make a deal with your slave masters. . . ."

You and I know and do not believe that life is so dear and peace so sweet as to be purchased at the price of chains and slavery. If nothing in life is worth dying for, when did this begin just in the face of this enemy? Or should Moses have told the children of Israel to live in slavery under the pharaohs? Should Christ have refused the cross? Should the patriots at Concord Bridge have thrown down their guns and refused to fire the shot heard 'round the world? The martyrs of history were not fools, and our honored dead who gave their lives to stop the advance of the Nazis didn't die in vain. Where, then, is the road to peace? Well it's a simple answer after all. . . .

You and I have a rendezvous with destiny.

We'll preserve for our children this, the last best hope of man on earth, or we'll sentence them to take the last step into a thousand years of darkness.

Source: Ronald Reagan, "A Time for Choosing," October 27, 1964. Ronald Reagan Presidential Library and Museum.

2. Ronald Reagan's First California Gubernatorial Inaugural Address, January 5, 1967

Having scored an electoral upset against Democratic incumbent Pat Brown, Reagan pledged to address the issues he had run on during the campaign. Reagan later carried many of these issues—notably crime, welfare, and the size and cost of government—into the 1980 presidential election. In a number of ways, Reagan's two terms as governor were a dress rehearsal for his presidency.

Government is the people's business, and every man, woman and child becomes a shareholder with the first penny of tax paid. . . . We are of the people, chosen by them to see that no permanent structure of government ever encroaches on freedom or assumes a power beyond that freely granted by the people. We stand between the taxpayer and the tax spender. . . .

The path we will chart is not an easy one. It demands much of those chosen to govern, but also from those who did the choosing. And let there be no mistake about this. We have come to a crossroad a time of decision and the path we follow turns away from any idea that government and those who serve it are omnipotent. It is a path impossible to follow unless we have faith in the collective wisdom and genius of the people. Along this path government will lead but not rule, listen but not lecture. It is the path of a Creative Society. . . .

When fiscally feasible, we hope to create a California crime technological foundation utilizing both public and private resources in a major effort to employ the most scientific techniques to control crime. At such a time, we should explore the idea of a state police academy to assure that police from even the smallest communities can have the most advanced training. We lead the nation in many things; we are going to stop leading in crime. Californians should be able to walk our streets safely day or night. The law abiding are entitled to at least as much protection as the lawbreakers. . . .

Welfare is another of our major problems. We are a humane and generous people and we accept without reservation our obligation to help the aged, disabled and those unfortunates who, through no fault of their own, must depend on their fellow man. But we are not going to perpetuate poverty by substituting a permanent dole for a paycheck. There is no humanity or charity in destroying self-reliance, dignity and self-respect the very substance of moral fiber. . . .

On the subject of education, hundreds of thousands of young men and women will receive an education in our state colleges and universities. We are proud of our ability to provide this opportunity for our youth and we believe it is no denial of academic freedom to provide this education within a framework of reasonable rules and regulations. Nor is it a violation of individual rights to require obedience to these rules and regulations or to insist that those unwilling to abide by them should get their education elsewhere. . . .

If, in glancing aloft, some of you were puzzled by the small size of our State Flag there is an explanation. That flag was carried into battle in Vietnam by young men of California. Many will not be coming home. One did, Sergeant Robert Howell, grievously wounded. He brought that flag back. I thought we would be proud to have it fly over the Capitol today. It might even serve to put our problems in better perspective. It might remind us of the need to give our sons and daughters a cause to believe in and banners to follow.

Source: "Ronald Reagan's First California Gubernatorial Inaugural Address, January 5, 1967." Ronald Reagan Presidential Library and Museum.

3. Ronald Reagan's First Presidential Inaugural Address, January 20, 1981

In his first presidential inaugural address, Ronald Reagan took a page from Franklin Roosevelt's 1933 playbook. Like Roosevelt, Reagan spelled out the economic difficulties confronting the nation. At the same time, Reagan reassured Americans that they could face those challenges and emerge triumphant. Both Reagan and Roosevelt understood that optimism could move a people onward, while pessimism could paralyze them.

These United States are confronted with an economic affliction of great proportions. We suffer from the longest and one of the worst sustained inflations in our national history. It distorts our economic decisions, penalizes thrift, and crushes the struggling young and the fixed-income elderly alike. It threatens to shatter the lives of millions of our people.

Idle industries have cast workers into unemployment, human misery, and personal indignity. Those who do work are denied a fair return for their labor by a tax system which penalizes successful achievement and keeps us from maintaining full productivity. . . .

The economic ills we suffer have come upon us over several decades. They will not go away in days, weeks, or months, but they will go away. They will go away because we as Americans have the capacity now, as we've had in the past, to do whatever needs to be done to preserve this last and greatest bastion of freedom.

In this present crisis, government is not the solution to our problem; government is the problem. From time to time we've been tempted to believe that society has become too complex to be managed by self-rule, that government by an elite group is superior to government for, by, and of the people. Well, if no one among us is capable of governing himself, then who among us has the capacity to govern someone else? All of us together, in and out of government, must bear the burden. The solutions we seek must be equitable, with no one group singled out to pay a higher price. . . .

Well, this administration's objective will be a healthy, vigorous, growing economy that provides equal opportunities for all Americans with no barriers born of bigotry or discrimination. Putting America back to work means putting all Americans back to work. Ending inflation means freeing all Americans from the terror of runaway living costs. All must share in the productive work of this "new beginning," and all must share in the bounty of a revived economy. With the idealism and fair play which are the core of our system and our strength, we can have a strong and prosperous America, at peace with itself and the world. . . .

It is no coincidence that our present troubles parallel and are proportionate to the intervention and intrusion in our lives that result from unnecessary and excessive growth of government. It is time for us to realize that we're too great a nation to limit ourselves to small dreams. We're not, as some would have us believe, doomed to an inevitable decline. I do not believe in a fate that will fall on us no matter what we do. I do believe in a fate that will fall on us if we do nothing. So, with all the creative energy at our command, let us begin an era of national renewal. Let us renew our determination, our courage, and our strength. And let us renew our faith and our hope.

Source: "Ronald Reagan's First Presidential Inaugural Address, January 20, 1981." Ronald Reagan Presidential Library and Museum.

4. Ronald Reagan Address before a Joint Session of the Congress on the Program for Economic Recovery, February 18, 1981

As part of Ronald Reagan's agenda of reducing taxes and the rate of growth in federal spending, he appeared before a joint session of Congress. Although speaking to hostile Democrats and skeptical Republicans, Reagan was actually directing his message to television viewers across the country. Quite simply, Reagan wanted to persuade Americans that he had worthy ideas and that they should place political pressure on their representatives and senators to support his agenda. Although House Speaker Tip O'Neill knew what Reagan was up to, he did not believe it appropriate, or politically wise, for him to prevent the president from using Congress as a stage prop.

All of us are aware of the punishing inflation which has for the first time in sixty years held to double-digit figures for two years in a row. Interest rates have reached absurd levels of more that 20 percent and over 15 percent for those who would borrow to buy a home. All across this land one can see newly built homes standing vacant, unsold because of mortgage interest rates....

Adding to our troubles is a mass of regulations imposed on the shopkeeper, the farmer, the craftsman, professionals, and major industry that is estimated to add $100 billion to the price of the things we buy, and it reduces our ability to produce. The rate of increase in American productivity, once one of the highest in the world, is among the lowest of all major industrial nations. Indeed, it has actually declined in the last three years.

Now, I've painted a pretty grim picture, but I think I've painted it accurately. It is within our power to change this picture, and we can act with hope. There's nothing wrong with our internal strengths. There has been no breakdown of the human, technological, and natural resources upon which the economy is built....

It's important to note that we're only reducing the rate of increase in taxing and spending. We're not attempting to cut either spending or taxing levels below that which we presently have. This plan will get our economy moving again, [create] productivity growth, and thus create the jobs that our people must have. . . .

We will continue to fulfill the obligations that spring from our national conscience. Those who, through no fault of their own, must depend on the rest of us—the poverty stricken, the disabled, the elderly, all those with true need—can rest assured that the social safety net of programs they depend on are exempt from any cuts. . . .

I believe that my duty as President requires that I recommend increases in defense spending over the coming years. I know that you're all aware—but I think it bears saying again—that since 1970 the Soviet Union has invested $300 billion more in its military forces than we have. As a result of its massive military buildup, the Soviets have made a significant numerical advantage in strategic nuclear delivery systems, tactical aircraft, submarines, artillery, and anti-aircraft defense. To allow this imbalance to continue is a threat to our national security. Notwithstanding our economic straits, making the financial changes beginning now is far less costly than waiting and having to attempt a crash program several years from now. . . .

Our proposal is for a 10-percent across-the-board cut every year for three years in the tax rates for all individual income taxpayers, making a total cut in the tax-cut rates of 30 percent. This three-year reduction will also apply to the tax on unearned income, leading toward an eventual elimination of the present differential between the tax on earned and unearned income. . . .

The taxing power of government must be used to provide revenues for legitimate government purposes. It must not be used to regulate the economy or bring about social change. We've tried that, and surely we must be able to see it doesn't work.

Source: "Ronald Reagan Address before a Joint Session of the Congress on the Program for Economic Recovery, February 18, 1981." Ronald Reagan Presidential Library and Museum.

5. Ronald Reagan Oval Office Address to the Nation on Federal Tax Reduction Legislation, July 27, 1981

To place pressure on uncooperative House Democrats to support his taxation policy, Ronald Reagan addressed the nation from the Oval Office. Reagan's presentation included easy-to-understand charts which he pointed to and explained their meaning. His style was conversational, not professorial. Moreover, though congenial, Reagan made it clear that Tip O'Neill's allies were, in his mind, political opportunists and obstructionists who had to be defeated if the United States was to recover economically.

Your voices have been heard—millions of you, Democrats, Republicans, and Independents, from every profession, trade and line of work, and from every part of this land. You sent a message that you wanted a new beginning. You wanted to change one little, two little word, two letter-word, I should say. It doesn't sound like much, but it sure can make a difference changing "by government," "control *by* government" to "control *of* government." . . .

If I could paraphrase a well-known statement by Will Rogers that he had never met a man he didn't like, I'm afraid we have some people around here who never met a tax they didn't hike. . . .

Our bipartisan tax bill targets three-quarters of its tax relief to middle-income wage earners who presently pay almost three-quarters of the total income tax. It also then indexes the tax brackets to ensure that you can keep that tax reduction in the years ahead. There also is, as I said, estate tax relief that will keep family farms and family-owned businesses in the family, and there are provisions for personal retirement plans and individual savings accounts.

Because our bipartisan bill is so clearly drawn and broadly based, it provides the kind of predictability and certainty that the financial segments of our society need to make investment decisions that stimulate productivity and make our economy grow. Even more important, if the tax cut goes to you, the American people, in the third year, that money returned to you won't be available to the Congress to spend, and that, in my view, is what this whole controversy comes down to. Are you entitled to the fruits of your own labor or does government have some presumptive right to spend and spend and spend? . . .

There's something else I want to tell you. Our bipartisan coalition worked out a tax bill we felt would provide incentive and stimulate productivity, thus reducing inflation and providing jobs for the unemployed. That was our only goal. Our opponents in the beginning didn't want a tax bill at all. So what is the purpose behind their change of heart? They've put a tax program together for one reason only: to provide themselves with a political victory. Never mind that it won't solve the economic problems confronting our country. Never mind that it won't get the wheels of industry turning again or eliminate the inflation which is eating us alive. . . .

During recent months many of you have asked what can you do to help make America strong again. I urge you again to contact your Senators and Congressmen. Tell them of your support for this bipartisan proposal. Tell them you believe this is an unequalled opportunity to help return America to prosperity and make government again the servant of the people. . . .

I've not taken your time this evening merely to ask you to trust me. Instead, I ask you to trust yourselves. That's what America is all about. Our struggle for nationhood, our unrelenting fight for freedom, our very existence—these have all rested on the assurance that you must be free to shape your life as you are best able to, that no one can stop you from reaching higher or take from you the creativity that has made America the envy of mankind

Source: "Ronald Reagan Oval Office Address to the Nation on Federal Tax Reduction Legislation, July 27, 1981." Ronald Reagan Presidential Library and Museum.

6. Ronald Reagan Remarks at the Annual Meeting of the International Association of Chiefs of Police in New Orleans, Louisiana, September 28, 1981

Early in his first presidential administration, Ronald Reagan made it clear that in terms of domestic policy, outside of economic reform, law and order constituted a major concern. As he informed law enforcement officials in 1981, criminals were morally deformed predators. To such people, crime was a choice—not a consequence of poverty and social environment. Reagan's subsequent antidrug and anticrime legislation emphasized these beliefs.

Crime has continued on the upswing. It has gone on regardless of the efforts that we make. Crime has increased in that thing that I mentioned, of the youthful offender, between eighteen and twenty-one. And that other problem I mentioned years ago, the incredible impact of drug addiction on the crime rate, continues. Studies of prison inmates have found that at least half admitted to using drugs in the month prior to their arrest. And it's still estimated that 50 to 60 percent of property crimes are drug-related.

From these statistics about youthful offenders and the impact of drug addiction on crime rates, a portrait emerges. The portrait is that of a stark, staring face, a face that belongs to a frightening reality of our time—the face of a human predator, the face of the habitual criminal. Nothing in nature is more cruel and more dangerous. . . .

At the very same time that crime rates have steadily risen, our nation has made unparalleled progress in raising the standard of living and improving the quality of life. It's obvious that prosperity doesn't decrease crime, just as it's obvious that deprivation and want don't necessarily increase crime. The truth is that today's criminals for the most part are not desperate people seeking bread for their families; crime is the way they've chosen to live. . . .

A tendency to downplay the permanent moral values has helped make crime the enormous problem that it is today, one that this administration has, as I've told you, made one of its top domestic priorities. But it has occurred to me that the root causes of our other major domestic problem, the growth of government and the decay of the economy, can be traced to many of the same sources of the crime problem. This is because the same utopian presumptions about human nature that hinder the swift administration of justice have also helped fuel the expansion of government.

Many of the social thinkers of the 1950s and '60s who discussed crime only in the context of disadvantaged childhoods and poverty-stricken neighborhoods were the same people who thought that massive government spending could wipe away our social ills. The underlying premise in both cases was a belief that there was nothing permanent or absolute about any man's nature, that he was a product of his material environment, and that by changing that environment—with government as the chief vehicle of change through educational, health, housing, and other programs—we could permanently change man and usher in a great new era.

Well, we've learned the price of too much government: runaway inflation, soaring unemployment, impossible interest rates. We've learned that Federal subsidies and government bureaucrats not only fail to solve social problems but frequently make them worse.

It's time, too, that we acknowledge the solution to the crime problem will not be found in the social worker's files, the psychiatrist's notes, or the bureaucrat's budgets. It's a problem of the human heart, and it's there we must look for the answer. We can begin by acknowledging some of those permanent things, those absolute truths I mentioned before. Two of those truths are that men are basically good but prone to evil, and society has a right to be protected from them.

Source: "Ronald Reagan Remarks at the Annual Meeting of the International Association of Chiefs of Police in New Orleans, Louisiana, September 28, 1981." Ronald Reagan Presidential Library and Museum.

7. National Security Decision Directive Number 17: National Security Directive on Cuba and Central America, January 4, 1982

Ronald Reagan waged a multi-front economic and political campaign against the Soviet Union. His anti-Soviet campaign included supporting military forces fighting Soviet troops or Soviet-backed insurgents. Given its proximity to the United States, Central America loomed large in Reagan's strategic thinking.

U.S. policy toward the Americas is characterized by strong support for those nations which embrace the principles of democracy and freedom for their people in a stable and peaceful environment. U.S. policy is therefore to assist in defeating the insurgency in El Salvador, and to oppose actions by Cuba, Nicaragua, or others to introduce into Central America heavy weapons, troops from outside the region, trained subversives, or arms and military supplies for insurgents. To adequately support U.S. policy, the following decisions have been made by the President based on discussion at the November 16, 1981, meeting of the National Security council:

1. Create a public information task force to inform the public and Congress of the critical situation in the area.

2. Economic support for a number of Central American and Caribbean countries (estimate $250 to $300 million FY [Fiscal Year] 1982 supplemental).

3. Agreement to use most of the $50 million Section 506 authority to increase military assistance to El Salvador and Honduras. Reprogram additional funds as necessary.

4. Provide military training for indigenous units and leaders both in and out of country.

5. Enhance U.S. and host country intelligence capabilities and sharing in the Caribbean Basin area.

6. Maintain trade and credit to Nicaragua as long as the government permits the private sector to operate effectively.

7. Expedite measures to tighten the economic sanctions against Cuba.

8. Encourage cooperative efforts to defeat externally supported insurgency by pursuing a multilateral step-by-step approach.

9. Support democratic forces in Nicaragua.

10. Prepare appropriate military contingency plans for action against Cuban forces should they be introduced into Central America.

11. Improve military preparedness against Cuba and develop contingency plans for action against Cuba.

[Signed] Ronald Reagan

Source: "National Security Decision Directive Number 17: National Security Decision Directive on Cuba and Central America." Ronald Reagan Presidential Library and Museum.

8. Ronald Reagan Remarks at the Conservative Political Action Conference Dinner, Washington, DC, February 18, 1983

Ronald Reagan's speech to the Conservative Political Action Conference annual meeting in Washington, DC, was directed toward the "true believers" among his supporters: the American Conservative Union, the Young Americans for Freedom, and the magazine staffers of the conservative National Review and Human Events. He emphasized his conservative beliefs and successes, dwelling not on his frequent, and often successful, efforts to compromise when necessary to score a legislative policy win. Many conservative activists were not happy with Reagan's apparent lack of ideological purity, dismissing the notion that the perfect was the enemy of the good.

For the first time in half a century, we've developed a whole new cadre of young conservatives in government. We've shown that conservatives can do more than criticize; we've shown that we can govern and move our legislation through the Congress. . . .

Let's confess, let's admit that we've turned the corner on the economy. And we're especially proud of one thing: When we hit heavy weather, we didn't panic, we didn't go for fast bromides and quick fixes, the huge tax increases or wage and price controls recommended by so many. And our stubbornness, if you want to call it that, will quite literally pay off for every American in the years ahead.

So, let me pledge to you tonight: Carefully, we have set out on the road to recovery. We will not be deterred. We will not be turned back. I reject the policies of the past, the policies of tax and tax, spend and spend, elect and elect. The lesson of these failed policies is clear; I've said this before: You can't drink yourself sober or spend yourself rich, and you can't prime the pump without pumping the prime—as somebody did, like to 21 and a half percent in 1980.

And a word is in order here on the most historic of all the legislative reforms we've achieved in the last two years—that of tax indexing. You can understand the terror that strikes in the heart of those whose principal constituency is big government. Bracket creep is government's hidden incentive to inflate the currency and bring on inflation, and indexing will end that. It will end those huge, hidden subsidies for bigger and bigger government. In the future, if we get indexing planted firmly as a law of the land, the advocates of big government who want money, more money for their social spending, their social engineering schemes, will have to go to the people and say right out loud: We want more money from your weekly paycheck, so we're raising your taxes. Do that instead of sneaking it out by way of inflation, which they have helped bring on. . . .

But I think you can see how even this debate shows things are changing for the better. It highlights the essential differences between two philosophies now contending for power in American political life. One is the philosophy of the past—a philosophy that has as its constituents an ill-assorted mix of elitists and special-interest groups who see government as the principal vehicle of social change, who believe that the only thing we have to fear is the people, who must be watched and regulated and superintended from Washington.

On the other hand, our political philosophy is at the heart of the new political consensus that emerged in America at the beginning of this decade, one that I believe all—well, I believe it will dominate American politics for many decades. The economic disasters brought about by too much government were the catalysts for this consensus. During the seventies, the American people began to see misdirected, overgrown government as the source of many of our social problems—not the solution.

Source: "Ronald Reagan Remarks at the Conservative Political Action Conference Dinner," Washington, DC, February 18, 1983. Ronald Reagan Presidential Library and Museum.

9. Ronald Reagan Remarks at the Annual Convention of the National Association of Evangelicals, Orlando, Florida, March 8, 1983

Ronald Reagan's address to the National Association of Evangelicals in 1983 went down in history as his "Evil Empire" speech. While Reagan cautioned evangelicals against joining the nuclear freeze movement, he also urged them to avoid the temptations of religious and racial hatred. To Reagan, communism, racism, and anti-Semitism were intertwined sins of people who turned their back on God. The American and international news media focused on "evil empire" and largely ignored, or failed to understand, Reagan's larger philosophical point concerning the nature of sin.

I want you to know that this administration is motivated by a political philosophy that sees the greatness of America in you, her people, and in your families, churches, neighborhoods, communities—the institutions that foster and nourish values like concern for others and respect for the rule of law under God.

Now, I don't have to tell you that this puts us in opposition to, or at least out of step with, a prevailing attitude of many who have turned to a modern-day secularism, discarding the tried and time-tested values upon which our very civilization is based. No matter how well intentioned, their value system is radically different from that of most Americans. And while they proclaim that they're freeing us from superstitions of the past, they've taken upon themselves the job of superintending us by government rule and regulation. Sometimes their voices are louder than ours, but they are not yet a majority. . . .

We know that living in this world means dealing with what philosophers would call the phenomenology of evil or, as theologians would put it, the doctrine of sin.

There is sin and evil in the world, and we're enjoined by Scripture and the Lord Jesus to oppose it with all our might. Our nation, too, has a legacy of evil with which it must deal. The glory of this land has been its capacity for transcending the moral evils of our past. For example, the long struggle of minority citizens for equal rights, once a source of disunity and civil war, is now a point of pride for all Americans. We must never go back. There is no room for racism, anti-Semitism, or other forms of ethnic and racial hatred in this country. . . .

And this brings me to my final point today. During my first press conference as President, in answer to a direct question, I pointed out that, as good Marxist-Leninists, the Soviet leaders have openly and publicly declared that the only morality they recognize is that which will further their cause, which is world revolution. I think I should point out I was only quoting Lenin, their guiding spirit, who said in 1920 that they repudiate all morality that proceeds from supernatural ideas—that's their name for religion—or ideas that are outside class conceptions. Morality is entirely subordinate to the interests of class war. . . .

Well, I think the refusal of many influential people to accept this elementary fact of Soviet doctrine illustrates an historical reluctance to see totalitarian powers for what they are. We saw this phenomenon in the 1930s. We see it too often today. . . .

So, in your discussions of the nuclear freeze proposals, I urge you to beware the temptation of pride—the temptation of blithely declaring yourselves above it all and label both sides equally at fault, to ignore the facts of history and the aggressive impulses of an evil empire, to simply call the arms race a giant misunderstanding and thereby remove yourself from the struggle between right and wrong and good and evil.

Source: "Ronald Reagan Remarks at the Annual Convention of the National Association of Evangelicals, Orlando, Florida, March 8, 1983." Ronald Reagan Presidential Library and Museum.

10. Ronald Reagan Proclamation 5147: National Sanctity of Human Life Day, January 13, 1984

Ronald Reagan gave opponents of abortion a great deal of rhetorical support. However, he taped his remarks to the foes of abortion who turned out for protest marches in Washington, rather than appear in person. Reagan expended no political capital pushing for legislation to ban abortion. Issuing proclamations critical of abortion had no legal force or action behind it. Although personally opposed to abortion, Reagan recognized that the mother also had constitutional rights and that somehow all interests had to be weighed into consideration. Abortion was one of the few issues where Reagan largely failed to satisfy either side. Those opposed to abortion criticized Reagan for doing too little while those who supported abortion believed Reagan was doing too much.

The values and freedoms we cherish as Americans rest on our fundamental commitment to the sanctity of human life. The first of the "unalienable rights" affirmed by our Declaration of Independence is the right to life itself, a right the Declaration states has been endowed by our Creator on all human beings—whether young or old, weak or strong, healthy or handicapped.

Since 1973, however, more than 15 million unborn children have died in legalized abortions—a tragedy of stunning dimensions that stands in sad contrast to our belief that each life is sacred. These children, over tenfold the number of Americans lost in all our Nation's wars, will never laugh, never sing, never experience the joy of human love; nor will they strive to heal the sick, or feed the poor, or make peace among nations. Abortion has denied them the first and most basic of human rights, and we are infinitely poorer for their loss.

We are poorer not simply for lives not led and for contributions not made, but also for the erosion of our sense of the worth and dignity of every individual. To diminish the value of one category of human life is to diminish us all. Slavery, which treated blacks as something less than human, to be bought and sold if convenient, cheapened human life and mocked our dedication to the freedom and equality of all men and women. Can we say that abortion—which treats the unborn as something less than human, to be destroyed if convenient—will be less corrosive to the values we hold dear?

We have been given the precious gift of human life, made more precious still by our births in or pilgrimages to a land of freedom. It is fitting, then, on the anniversary of the Supreme Court decision in *Roe v. Wade* that struck down State anti-abortion laws, that we reflect anew on these blessings, and on our corresponding responsibility to guard with care the lives and freedoms of even the weakest of our fellow human beings.

Now, therefore, I, Ronald Reagan, President of the United States of America, do hereby proclaim Sunday, January 22, 1984, as National Sanctity of Human Life Day. I call upon the citizens of this blessed land to gather on that day in homes and places of worship to give thanks for the gift of life, and to reaffirm our commitment to the dignity of every human being and the sanctity of each human life.

Source: "Ronald Reagan Proclamation 5147: National Sanctity of Human Life Day, January 13, 1984." Ronald Reagan Presidential Library and Museum.

11. Ronald Reagan Address to the Nation on United States Policy in Central America, May 9, 1984

> *In an effort to place political pressure on House Democrats opposed to aiding anticommunist forces in Central America, Ronald Reagan made frequent appeals to the public. As he observed, states such as Texas were closer to the Central American combat theater than Washington, DC, was. What happened in El Salvador and Nicaragua, Reagan warned, could spill over into the United States. Therefore, it was in U.S. security interests to stabilize the region and squash violent communist insurgencies and their sponsors.*

Our diplomatic objectives will not be attained by good will and noble aspirations alone. In the last fifteen years, the growth of Soviet military power has meant a radical change in the nature of the world we live in.

Now, this does not mean, as some would have us believe, that we're in imminent danger of nuclear war. We're not. As long as we maintain the strategic balance and make it more stable by reducing the level of weapons on both sides, then we can count on the basic prudence of the Soviet leaders to avoid that kind of challenge to us.

They are presently challenging us with a different kind of weapon: subversion and the use of surrogate forces, Cubans, for example. We've seen it intensifying during the last ten years, as the Soviet Union and its surrogates move to establish control over Vietnam, Laos, Cambodia, Angola, Ethiopia, South Yemen, Afghanistan, and recently, closer to home, in Nicaragua and now El Salvador. It's the fate of this region, Central America, that I want to talk to you about tonight.

The issue is our effort to promote democracy and economic well-being in the face of Cuban and Nicaraguan aggression, aided and abetted by the Soviet Union. It is definitely not about plans to send American troops into combat in Central America. Each year, the Soviet Union provides Cuba with $4 billion in assistance, and it sends tons of weapons to foment revolution here in our hemisphere.

The defense policy of the United States is based on a simple premise: We do not start wars. We will never be the aggressor. We maintain our strength in order to deter and defend against aggression, to preserve freedom and peace. We help our friends defend themselves.

Central America is a region of great importance to the United States. And it is so close: San Salvador is closer to Houston, Texas, than Houston is to Washington, DC. Central America is America. It's at our doorstep, and it's become the stage for a bold attempt by the Soviet Union, Cuba, and Nicaragua to install communism by force throughout the hemisphere. . . .

By aiding the Communist guerrillas in El Salvador, Nicaragua's unelected government is trying to overthrow the duly elected government of a neighboring country. Like Nicaragua, the Government of El Salvador was born of revolution, but unlike Nicaragua it has held three elections, the most recent a Presidential election last Sunday. It has made great progress toward democracy. In this last election, 80 percent of the people of El Salvador braved Communist threats and guerrilla violence to vote for peace and freedom. . . .

There are those in this country who would yield to the temptation to do nothing. They are the new isolationists, very much like the isolationists of the late 1930's who knew what was happening in Europe, but chose not to face the terrible challenge history had given them. They preferred a policy of wishful thinking, that if they only gave up one more country, allowed just one more international transgression, and surely sooner or later the aggressor's appetite would be satisfied. Well, they didn't stop the aggressors; they emboldened them. They didn't prevent war; they assured it.

Source: "Ronald Reagan Address to the Nation on United States Policy in Central America," May 9, 1984. Ronald Reagan Presidential Library and Museum.

12. Ronald Reagan Remarks Accepting the Presidential Nomination at the Republican National Convention in Dallas, Texas, August 23, 1984

Ronald Reagan's address to the 1984 Republican National Convention gave enthusiastic party representatives, and the viewing audience, numerous reasons to reject the Democrats' presidential nominee. Although avoiding mentioning Walter Mondale specifically, Reagan associated him with Jimmy Carter's failed presidency. Reagan also highlighted the dark depiction of the U.S. Democrats had painted at their convention. New York governor Mario Cuomo's eloquent denunciation of Reagan's domestic and foreign policies became, in Reagan's hands, a damning indictment of the Democrats' pessimism and inability to see the bright future ahead.

The choices this year are not just between two different personalities or between two political parties. They're between two different visions of the future, two fundamentally different ways of governing—their government of pessimism, fear, and limits, or ours of hope, confidence, and growth.

Their government sees people only as members of groups; ours serves all the people of America as individuals. Theirs lives in the past, seeking to apply the old and failed policies to an era that has passed them by. Ours learns from the past and strives to change by boldly charting a new course for the future. Theirs lives by promises, the bigger, the better. We offer proven, workable answers.

Our opponents began this campaign hoping that America has a poor memory. Well, let's take them on a little stroll down memory lane. Let's remind them of how a 4.8-percent inflation rate in 1976 became back-to-back years of double-digit inflation—the worst since World War I—punishing the poor and the elderly, young couples striving to start their new lives, and working people struggling to make ends meet.

Inflation was not some plague borne on the wind; it was a deliberate part of their official economic policy, needed, they said, to maintain prosperity. They didn't tell us that with it would come the highest interest rates since the Civil War. As average monthly mortgage payments more than doubled, home building nearly ground to a halt; tens of thousands of carpenters and others were thrown out of work. And who controlled both Houses of the Congress and the executive branch at that time? Not us, not us. . . .

In 1980 the people decided with us that the economic crisis was not caused by the fact that they lived too well. Government lived too well. It was time for tax increases to be an act of last resort, not of first resort. . . .

Our government was also in serious trouble abroad. We had aircraft that couldn't fly and ships that couldn't leave port. Many of our military were on food stamps because of meager earnings, and reenlistments were down. Ammunition was low, and spare parts were in short supply. . . .

We can all be proud that pessimism is ended. America is coming back and is more confident than ever about the future. Tonight, we thank the citizens of the United States whose faith and unwillingness to give up on themselves or this country saved us all. . . .

Today our troops have newer and better equipment; their morale is higher. The better armed they are, the less likely it is they will have to use that equipment. But if, heaven forbid, they're ever called upon to defend this nation, nothing would be more immoral than asking them to do so with weapons inferior to those of any possible opponent. . . .

Isn't our choice really not one of left or right, but of up or down? Down through the welfare state to statism, to more and more government largesse accompanied always by more government authority, less individual liberty and, ultimately, totalitarianism, always advanced as for our own good. The alternative is the dream conceived by our Founding Fathers, up to the ultimate in individual freedom consistent with an orderly society.

Source: "Ronald Reagan Remarks Accepting the Presidential Nomination at the Republican National Convention in Dallas, Texas," August 23, 1984. Ronald Reagan Presidential Library and Museum.

13. Ronald Reagan Remarks at an Ecumenical Prayer Breakfast in Dallas, Texas, August 23, 1984

Although not a regular churchgoer, Ronald Reagan was religious, though not sectarian. Given his upbringing in an interfaith family, this was not surprising. He truly believed that morality sprang from religious belief and that morality, in turn, helped produce a just political order. Logically, then, it followed that a secularized society would find it difficult to build a just moral order. At the same time, however, Reagan did not advocate for federal action to combat secularization in the public square. Reagan believed that religious and secular values should be debated, with neither side imposing their agenda on the other. In the end, this meant that Reagan would never be a partisan of the Moral Majority any more than he would consider an alliance with the secular Left.

I believe that faith and religion play a critical role in the political life of our nation—and always has—and that the church—and by that I mean all churches, all denominations—has had a strong influence on the state. And this has worked to our benefit as a nation. . . .

Religion played not only a strong role in our national life; it played a positive role. The abolitionist movement was at heart a moral and religious movement; so was the modern civil rights struggle. And throughout this time, the state was tolerant of religious belief, expression, and practice. Society, too, was tolerant.

But in the 1960s this began to change. We began to make great steps toward secularizing our nation and removing religion from its honored place. . . .

When John Kennedy was running for President in 1960, he said that his church would not dictate his Presidency any more than he would speak for his church. Just so, and proper. But John Kennedy was speaking in an America in which the role of religion—and by that I mean the role of all churches—was secure. Abortion was not a political issue. Prayer was not a political issue. The right of church schools to operate was not a political issue. And it was broadly acknowledged that religious leaders had a right and a duty to speak out on the issues of the day. They held a place of respect, and a politician who spoke to or of them with a lack of respect would not long survive in the political arena.

It was acknowledged then that religion held a special place, occupied a special territory in the hearts of the citizenry. The climate has changed greatly since then. And since it has, it logically follows that religion needs defenders against those who care only for the interests of the state....

The truth is, politics and morality are inseparable. And as morality's foundation is religion, religion and politics are necessarily related. We need religion as a guide. We need it because we are imperfect, and our government needs the church, because only those humble enough to admit they're sinners can bring to democracy the tolerance it requires in order to survive....

I submit to you that the tolerant society is open to and encouraging of all religions. And this does not weaken us; it strengthens us, it makes us strong. You know, if we look back through history to all those great civilizations, those great nations that rose up to even world dominance and then deteriorated, declined, and fell, we find they all had one thing in common. One of the significant forerunners of their fall was their turning away from their God or gods.

Without God, there is no virtue, because there's no prompting of the conscience. Without God, we're mired in the material, that flat world that tells us only what the senses perceive. Without God, there is a coarsening of the society. And without God, democracy will not and cannot long endure. If we ever forget that we're one nation under God, then we will be a nation gone under.

Source: "Ronald Reagan Remarks at an Ecumenical Prayer Breakfast in Dallas, Texas," August 23, 1984. Ronald Reagan Presidential Library and Museum.

14. Ronald Reagan Foreword Written for a Report on the Strategic Defense Initiative, January 3, 1985

Ronald Reagan found the prospect of a nuclear third world war to be a terrifying, likely end-of-the-world event. He found the policy of Mutually Assured Destruction (MAD) to be morally unacceptable. Reagan became convinced that a shield

> to block Soviet missiles from hitting the United States and its allies was as desirable as it was feasible. This shield became known as the Strategic Defense Initiative (SDI). Detractors mockingly called SDI "Star Wars." Soviet leader Mikhail Gorbachev, however, took SDI very seriously as he knew his country had little chance of developing similar technology.

Since the advent of nuclear weapons, every President has sought to minimize the risk of nuclear destruction by maintaining effective forces to deter aggression and by pursuing complementary arms control agreements. This approach has worked. We and our allies have succeeded in preventing nuclear war while protecting Western security for nearly four decades.

Originally, we relied on balanced defensive and offensive forces to deter. But over the last twenty years, the United States has nearly abandoned efforts to develop and deploy defenses against nuclear weapons, relying instead almost exclusively on the threat of nuclear retaliation. We accepted the notion that if both we and the Soviet Union were able to retaliate with devastating power even after absorbing a first strike, that stable deterrence would endure. That rather novel concept seemed at the time to be sensible for two reasons. First, the Soviets stated that they believed that both sides should have roughly equal forces and neither side should seek to alter the balance to gain unilateral advantage. Second, there did not seem to be any alternative. The state of the art in defensive systems did not permit an effective defensive system.

Today both of these basic assumptions are being called into question. The pace of the Soviet offensive and defensive buildup has upset the balance in the areas of greatest importance during crises. Furthermore, new technologies are now at hand which may make possible a truly effective non-nuclear defense.

For these reasons and because of the awesome destructive potential of nuclear weapons, we must seek another means of deterring war. It is both militarily and morally necessary. Certainly, there should be a better way to strengthen peace and stability, a way to move away from a future that relies so heavily on the prospect of rapid and massive nuclear retaliation and toward greater reliance on defensive systems which threaten no one.

On March 23, 1983, I announced my decision to take an important first step toward this goal by directing the establishment of a comprehensive and intensive research program, the Strategic Defense Initiative, aimed at eventually eliminating the threat posed by nuclear armed ballistic missiles.

The Strategic Defense Initiative (SDI) is a program of vigorous research focused on advanced defensive technologies with the aim of finding ways to provide a better basis for deterring aggression, strengthening stability, and increasing the security of the United States and our allies. The SDI research program will provide to a future President and a future Congress the technical knowledge required to support a decision on whether to develop and later deploy advanced defensive system.

At the same time, the United States is committed to the negotiation of equal and verifiable agreements which bring real reductions in the power of the nuclear arsenals of both sides. To this end, my Administration has proposed to the Soviet Union a comprehensive set of arms control proposals. We are working tirelessly for the success of these efforts, but we can and must go further in trying to strengthen the peace.

Source: "Ronald Reagan Foreword Written for a Report on the Strategic Defense Initiative," January 3, 1985. Ronald Reagan Presidential Library and Museum.

15. Ronald Reagan Remarks at the Opening Ceremonies of the Statue of Liberty Centennial Celebration in New York, New York, July 3, 1986

Ronald Reagan considered the restoration of the Statue of Liberty and Ellis Island to be among his most important symbolic undertakings as president. To Reagan, the Statue of Liberty was a reminder that though the nation contained every ethnic, religious, and racial group from around the world, united they were Americans. The Statue of Liberty, "the mother of exiles," welcomed all in search of freedom. On the Right, some conservatives groused that not all immigrants should be welcomed, while on the Left, voices complained that most of the forebears of African Americans had come bound in chains. Reagan ignored the critics and forged ahead to celebrate the United States he wanted citizens to see and love as he did.

We celebrate something more than the restoration of this statue's physical grandeur. Another worker here, Scott Aronsen, a marble restorer, has put it well: "I grew up in Brooklyn and never went to the Statue of Liberty. But when I first walked in there to work, I thought about my grandfather's coming through here." And which of us does not think of other grandfathers and grandmothers, from so many places around the globe, for whom this statue was the first glimpse of America?

"She was silhouetted very clear," one of them wrote about standing on deck as their ship entered New York Harbor. "We passed her very slowly. Of course we had to look up. She was beautiful." Another talked of how all the passengers rushed to one side of the boat for a fast look at their new home and at her. "Everybody was crying. The whole boat bent toward her. She was beautiful with the early morning light." To millions returning home, especially from foreign wars, she was also special. A young World War I captain of artillery described how, on a troopship returning from France, even the most hard-bitten veteran had trouble blinking back the tears. "I've never seen anything that looked so good," that doughboy, Harry Truman, wrote to his fiancé, Bess, back in Independence, Missouri, "as the Liberty Lady in New York Harbor."

And that is why tonight we celebrate this mother of exiles who lifts her light beside the golden door. Many of us have seen the picture of another worker here, a tool belt around his waist, balanced on a narrow metal rod of scaffolding, leaning over to place a kiss on the forehead of Miss Liberty. Tony Soraci, the grandson of immigrant Italians, said it was something he was proud to do, "something to tell my grandchildren." . . .

We sometimes forget that even those who came here first to settle the new land were also strangers. I've spoken before of the tiny *Arabella*, a ship at anchor just off the Massachusetts coast. A little group of Puritans huddled on the deck. And then John Winthrop, who would later become the first Governor of Massachusetts, reminded his fellow Puritans there on that tiny deck that they must keep faith with their God, that the eyes of all the world were upon them, and that they must not forsake the mission that God had sent them on, and they must be a light unto the nations of all the world—a shining city upon a hill.

Call it mysticism if you will, I have always believed there was some divine providence that placed this great land here between the two great oceans, to be found by a special kind of people from every corner of the world, who had a special love for freedom and a special courage that enabled them to leave their own land, leave their friends and their countrymen, and come to this new and strange land to build a New World of peace and freedom and hope.

Source: "Ronald Reagan Remarks at the Opening Ceremonies of the Statue of Liberty Centennial Celebration in New York, New York," July 3, 1986. Ronald Reagan Presidential Library and Museum.

16. Ronald Reagan Remarks on East-West Relations at the Brandenburg Gate in West Berlin, June 12, 1987

Ronald Reagan was eager to work with Soviet leader Mikhail Gorbachev toward building peaceful relations, but not so eager as to reduce the United States' economic, military, and political pressure on the Soviet Union. In West Berlin in 1987, standing close to the Brandenburg Gate, which divided democratic West Berlin from communist East Berlin, Reagan challenged Gorbachev to tear down the Berlin Wall. Both Reagan and Gorbachev understood that if the Berlin Wall came down, it would likely set off a chain reaction across Soviet-occupied Eastern Europe, culminating in the dismantling of the Soviet Empire.

Behind me stands a wall that encircles the free sectors of this city, part of a vast system of barriers that divides the entire continent of Europe. From the Baltic, south, those barriers cut across Germany in a gash of barbed wire, concrete, dog runs, and guard towers. Farther south, there may be no visible, no obvious wall. But there remain armed guards and checkpoints all the same—still a restriction on the right to travel, still an instrument to impose upon ordinary men and women the will of a totalitarian state. Yet it is here in Berlin where the wall emerges most clearly; here, cutting across your city, where the news photo and the television screen have imprinted this brutal division of a continent upon the mind of the world. Standing before the Brandenburg Gate, every man is a German, separated from his fellow men. Every man is a Berliner, forced to look upon a scar. . . .

Yet I do not come here to lament. For I find in Berlin a message of hope, even in the shadow of this wall, a message of triumph. In this season of spring in 1945, the people of Berlin emerged from their air raid shelters to find devastation. Thousands of miles away, the people of the United States reached out to help. And in 1947 Secretary of State—as you've been told—George Marshall announced the creation of what would become known as the Marshall plan. Speaking precisely forty years ago this month, he said: "Our policy is directed not against any country or doctrine, but against hunger, poverty, desperation, and chaos." . . .

In the Communist world, we see failure, technological backwardness, declining standards of health, even want of the most basic kind-too little food. Even today, the Soviet Union still cannot feed itself. After these four decades, then, there stands before the entire world one great and inescapable conclusion: Freedom leads to prosperity. Freedom replaces the ancient hatreds among the nations with comity and peace. Freedom is the victor.

And now the Soviets themselves may, in a limited way, be coming to understand the importance of freedom. We hear much from Moscow about a new policy of reform and openness. Some political prisoners have been released. Certain foreign news broadcasts are no longer being jammed. Some economic enterprises have been permitted to operate with greater freedom from state control. Are these the beginnings of profound changes in the Soviet state? Or are they token gestures, intended to raise false hopes in the West, or to strengthen the Soviet system without changing it? We welcome change and openness; for we believe that freedom and security go together, that the advance of human liberty can only strengthen the cause of world peace.

There is one sign the Soviets can make that would be unmistakable, that would advance dramatically the cause of freedom and peace. General Secretary Gorbachev, if you seek peace, if you seek prosperity for the Soviet Union and Eastern Europe, if you seek liberalization: Come here to this gate! Mr. Gorbachev, open this gate! Mr. Gorbachev, tear down this wall!

Source: "Ronald Reagan Remarks on East-West Relations at the Brandenburg Gate in West Berlin," June 12, 1987. Ronald Reagan Presidential Library and Museum.

17. Remarks and a Question-and-Answer Session with the Students and Faculty at Moscow State University, May 31, 1988

In an extraordinary moment toward what would be the end of the Cold War, Ronald Reagan spoke to a group of students at Moscow State University. He was not censored. The students were clearly excited to listen to an American president and then ask him questions. Reagan informed them that "information technology" was in the process of bringing down global communication barriers. Subtly, he told them that the Soviet Union, if opened to the free exchange of information and ideas, could not long persist. It would be up to them to create a new political order, one that was, hopefully, democratic.

Standing here before a mural of your revolution, I want to talk about a very different revolution that is taking place right now, quietly sweeping the globe without bloodshed or conflict. Its effects are peaceful, but they will fundamentally alter our world, shatter old assumptions, and reshape our lives. It's easy to underestimate because it's not accompanied by banners or fanfare. It's been called the technological or information revolution, and as its emblem, one might take the tiny silicon chip, no bigger than a fingerprint. One of these chips has more computing power than a roomful of old-style computers. . . .

Like a chrysalis, we're emerging from the economy of the Industrial Revolution—an economy confined to and limited by the Earth's physical resources—into, as one economist titled his book, *The Economy in Mind*, in which there are no bounds on human imagination and the freedom to create is the most precious natural resource. Think of that little computer chip. Its value isn't in the sand from which it is made but in the microscopic architecture designed into it by ingenious human minds. Or take the example of the satellite relaying this broadcast around the world, which replaces thousands of tons of copper mined from the Earth and molded into wire. In the new economy, human invention increasingly makes physical resources obsolete. We're breaking through the material conditions of existence to a world where man creates his own destiny. Even as we explore the most advanced reaches of science, we're returning to the age-old wisdom of our culture, a wisdom contained in the book of Genesis in the Bible: In the beginning was the spirit, and it was from this spirit that the material abundance of creation issued forth. . . .

We are seeing the power of economic freedom spreading around the world. Places such as the Republic of Korea, Singapore, Taiwan have vaulted into the technological era, barely pausing in the industrial age along the way. . . . At the same time, the growth of democracy has become one of the most powerful political movements of our age. In Latin America in the 1970s, only a third of the population lived under democratic government; today over 90 percent does. In the Philippines, in the Republic of Korea, free, contested, democratic elections are the order of the day. Throughout the world, free markets are the model for growth. Democracy is the standard by which governments are measured. . . .

Freedom is the right to question and change the established way of doing things. It is the continuing revolution of the marketplace. It is the understanding that allows us to recognize shortcomings and seek solutions. It is the right to put forth an idea, scoffed at by the experts, and watch it catch fire among the people. It is the right to dream—to follow your dream or stick to your conscience, even if you're the only one in a sea of doubters. Freedom is the recognition that no single person, no single authority or government has a monopoly on the truth, but that every individual life is infinitely precious, that every one of us put on this world has been put there for a reason and has something to offer.

Source: "Remarks and a Question-and-Answer Session with the Students and Faculty at Moscow State University," May 31, 1988. Ronald Reagan Presidential Library and Museum.

18. Ronald Reagan Remarks at the Veterans' Day Ceremony at the Vietnam Veterans Memorial, Washington, DC, November 11, 1988

Ronald Reagan's views on the divisive Vietnam War remained unchanging from 1964 when he filmed a campaign commercial for Barry Goldwater to 1988 at the end of his presidency. He blamed Lyndon Johnson for fighting half-heartedly and ineffectively and criticized those Americans who took their frustrations with the war out on Vietnam veterans by branding them as "baby killers." Reagan had no doubt that the Vietnam War was "a noble cause."

We're gathered today, just as we have gathered before, to remember those who served, those who fought, those still missing, and those who gave their last full measure of devotion for our country. We're gathered at a monument on which the names of our fallen friends and loved ones are engraved, and with crosses instead of diamonds beside them, the names of those whose fate we do not yet know. One of those who fell wrote, shortly before his death, these words: "Take what they have left and what they have taught you with their dying and keep it with your own. And take one moment to embrace those gentle heroes you left behind."

Well, today, Veterans Day, as we do every year, we take that moment to embrace the gentle heroes of Vietnam and of all our wars. We remember those who were called upon to give all a person can give, and we remember those who were prepared to make that sacrifice if it were demanded of them in the line of duty, though it never was. Most of all, we remember the devotion and gallantry with which all of them ennobled their nation as they became champions of a noble cause.

I'm not speaking provocatively here. Unlike the other wars of this century, of course, there were deep divisions about the wisdom and rightness of the Vietnam war. Both sides spoke with honesty and fervor. And what more can we ask in our democracy? And yet after more than a decade of desperate boat people, after the killing fields of Cambodia, after all that has happened in that unhappy part of the world, who can doubt that the cause for which our men fought was just? It was, after all, however imperfectly pursued, the cause of freedom; and they showed uncommon courage in its service. Perhaps at this late date we can all agree that we've learned one lesson: that young Americans must never again be sent to fight and die unless we are prepared to let them win.

But beyond that, we remember today that all our gentle heroes of Vietnam have given us a lesson in something more: a lesson in living love. Yes, for all of them, those who came back and those who did not, their love for their families lives. Their love for their buddies on the battlefields and friends back home lives. Their love of their country lives. . . .

For too long a time, they stood in a chill wind, as if on a winter night's watch. And in that night, their deeds spoke to us, but we knew them not. And their voices called to us, but we heard them not. Yet in this land that

God has blessed, the dawn always at last follows the dark, and now morning has come. The night is over. We see these men and know them once again—and know how much we owe them, how much they have given us, and how much we can never fully repay. And not just as individuals but as a nation, we say we love you.

Source: "Ronald Reagan Remarks at the Veterans' Day Ceremony at the Vietnam Veterans Memorial, Washington, DC," November 11, 1988. Ronald Reagan Presidential Library and Museum.

19. Ronald Reagan Farewell Address to the Nation, January 11, 1989

In Ronald Reagan's Farewell Address, he summarized the successes and the failures of his presidency, being sure to credit the American people with his successes. He also advised Americans to cherish their freedoms and learn the values that made the nation great.

The way I see it, there were two great triumphs, two things that I'm proudest of. One is the economic recovery, in which the people of America created—and filled—19 million new jobs. The other is the recovery of our morale. America is respected again in the world and looked to for leadership. . . .

Some pundits said our programs would result in catastrophe. Our views on foreign affairs would cause war. Our plans for the economy would cause inflation to soar and bring about economic collapse. I even remember one highly respected economist saying, back in 1982, that "[t]he engines of economic growth have shut down here, and they're likely to stay that way for years to come." Well, he and the other opinion leaders were wrong. The fact is, what they called "radical" was really "right." What they called "dangerous" was just "desperately needed."

And in all of that time I won a nickname, "The Great Communicator." But I never thought it was my style or the words I used that made a difference: it was the content. I wasn't a great communicator, but I communicated great things, and they didn't spring full bloom from my brow, they came from the heart of a great nation—from our experience, our wisdom, and our belief in the principles that have guided us for two centuries.

They called it the Reagan revolution. Well, I'll accept that, but for me it always seemed more like the great rediscovery, a rediscovery of our values and our common sense. . . .

The lesson of all this was, of course, that because we're a great nation, our challenges seem complex. It will always be this way. But as long as we remember our first principles and believe in ourselves, the future will always be ours. And something else we learned: Once you begin a great movement, there's no telling where it will end. We meant to change a nation, and instead, we changed a world. . . .

I think we have stopped a lot of what needed stopping. And I hope we have once again reminded people that man is not free unless government is limited. There's a clear cause and effect here that is as neat and predictable as a law of physics: As government expands, liberty contracts. . . .

I've been asked if I have any regrets. Well, I do. The deficit is one. I've been talking a great deal about that lately, but tonight isn't for arguments, and I'm going to hold my tongue. But an observation: I've had my share of victories in the Congress, but what few people noticed is that I never won anything you didn't win for me. They never saw my troops, they never saw Reagan's regiments, the American people. You won every battle with every call you made and letter you wrote demanding action. . . .

Finally, there is a great tradition of warnings in Presidential farewells, and I've got one that's been on my mind for some time. But oddly enough it starts with one of the things I'm proudest of in the past eight years: the resurgence of national pride that I called the new patriotism. This national feeling is good, but it won't count for much, and it won't last unless it's grounded in thoughtfulness and knowledge.

Source: "Ronald Reagan Farewell Address to the Nation," January 11, 1989. Ronald Reagan Presidential Library and Museum.

ANNOTATED
BIBLIOGRAPHY

Historians of American politics paid little attention to the post–World War II Right, except to issue condemnations of ideological extremists. The classic example of this tendency is Daniel Bell, *The Radical Right* (Piscataway, NJ: Transaction, 1964). For many of the scholars who came of age during World War II, the United States' future belonged to Franklin Roosevelt and his heirs. And for many in the generation who went to graduate school during the turbulent 1960s, the emerging New Right was not to be taken seriously. Their enemy was Cold War Democrats. Neither baby boomer graduate students nor their professors could imagine that conservatism would ever come to national power. Even after Ronald Reagan's election in 1980, academics were slow to study a political and social movement that they regarded as out of step with social progress and, for some, deplorable. Historian Leo P. Ribuffo observed, in "The Discovery and Rediscovery of American Conservatism Broadly Conceived," *OAH Magazine of History* 17 (January 2003): 5–10, that the situation slowly changed in the 1990s.

Today American conservatism is a major field of academic inquiry, and numerous scholarly and popular articles and books have appeared. Many of these works avoid "cause pleading." Others are less so, with their authors convinced that Reagan was either a great leader or the embodiment of a cruel America that was almost beyond redemption. At the very least, conservative policies and politics are regular topics of study and conversation.

The study of American conservatism has grown to embrace such areas as economic and foreign policy, mass media, electoral coalitions, religious movements, and race relations. This is all to the good. Variety makes, or should make, for good and necessary reading. Complexity also has its cherished place. As noted below, scholars are studying conservative think tanks, the evolution of a conservative media, and the social consequences of 1980s anticrime policies.

GENERAL HISTORIES OF AMERICAN CONSERVATISM SINCE 1932

Gregory L. Schneider has written two useful histories of twentieth-century American conservatism, the first a document reader and the second an overview: *Conservatism in America Since 1930: A Reader* (New York: New York University Press, 2003); and *The Conservative Century: From Reaction to Revolution* (Lanham, MD: Rowman and Littlefield, 2009). An overview of conservatism that includes primary documents is Kenneth J. Heineman, *The Rise of Contemporary Conservatism in the United States* (New York: Routledge, 2019). Readers should also consult Jonathan M. Schoenwald, *A Time for Choosing: The Rise of Modern American Conservatism* (New York: Oxford University Press, 2001).

Other general histories include David T. Courtright, *No Right Turn: Conservative Politics in a Liberal America* (Cambridge, MA: Harvard University Press, 2010); Donald T. Critchlow, *The Conservative Ascendancy: How the Republican Right Rose to Power in Modern America* (Lawrence: University Press of Kansas, 2011); Michael Bowen, *The Roots of Modern Conservatism: Dewey, Taft, and the Battle for the Soul of the Republican Party* (Chapel Hill: University of North Carolina Press, 2011); and Jerome T. Himmelstein, *To the Right: The Transformation of American Conservatism* (Berkeley: University of California Press, 1990).

A fine intellectual history of American conservatism is Patrick Allitt, *The Conservatives: Ideas and Personalities through American History* (New Haven, CT: Yale University Press, 2014). Lisa McGirr has emphasized the John Birch–extremist tendencies of conservatism with, *Suburban Warriors: The Origins of the New American Right* (Princeton, NJ: Princeton University Press, 2001). Other scholars have looked to the Sunbelt as an incubator of modern conservatism, among them, Michelle Nickerson and Darren Dochuk, eds., *Sunbelt Rising: The Politics of Space, Place, and Region* (Philadelphia: University of Pennsylvania Press, 2011).

RONALD REAGAN

The most comprehensive, and deeply analytical, treatments of Ronald Reagan are H. W. Brands, *Reagan: The Life* (New York: Doubleday, 2015) and William E. Pemberton, *Exit with Honor: The Life and Presidency of Ronald Reagan* (Armonk, NY: M. E. Sharpe, 1988). An insightful survey of presidents from Franklin Roosevelt to the early twenty-first century is William E. Leuchtenburg, *In the Shadow of FDR: From Harry Truman to Barack Obama* (Ithaca, NY: Cornell University Press, 2009).

Intriguing treatments of Reagan include John P. Diggins, *Ronald Reagan: Fate, Freedom, and the Making of History* (New York: W. W. Norton, 2007); Matthew Dallek, *The Right Moment: Ronald Reagan's First Victory and the Decisive Turning Point in American Politics* (New York: Free Press, 2000); Robert Mann, *Becoming Ronald Reagan: The Rise of a Conservative Icon* (Lincoln: University of Nebraska Press, 2019); Henry Olsen, *The Working-Class Republican: Ronald Reagan and the Return of Blue-Collar Conservatism* (New York: Broadside Books, 2017); and Lou Cannon, *President Reagan: The Role of a Lifetime* (New York: Public Affairs Press, 2000).

For the best insights into Reagan's view of policy and politics, see Douglas Brinkley, ed., *The Reagan Diaries* (New York: HarperCollins, 2007) as well as Kiron K. Skinner, Annelise Anderson, and Martin Anderson, eds., *Reagan, In His Own Hand: The Writings of Ronald Reagan that Reveal His Revolutionary Vision for America* (New York: Touchstone Books, 2001).

Among the Reagan historiography there are works that have sought to emulate Arthur Schlesinger Jr.'s multivolume opus, *The Age of Roosevelt*. (In 2003, Mariner Books in Boston republished the three-volume classic: *The Crisis of the Old Order, 1919–1933*; *The Coming of the New Deal, 1933–1935*; and *The Politics of Upheaval, 1935–1936*.) On the critical side is Sean Wilentz, *The Age of Reagan: A History, 1974–2008* (New York: HarperCollins, 2008). For a more celebratory interpretation of Reagan, see Steven F. Hayward, *The Age of Reagan: The Fall of the Old Liberal Order, 1964–1980* (New York: Prima Lifestyles, 2001); and *The Age of Reagan: The Conservative Counterrevolution, 1980–1989* (New York: Crown Forum, 2009). The most evenhanded account is John Ehrman, *The Eighties: America in the Age of Reagan* (New Haven, CT: Yale University Press, 2005).

Conservative activist and political analyst Craig Shirley has authored several books on Reagan. Although generally glowing in their treatment of Reagan, each one is well written and provides insights. Readers should begin with *Reagan Rising: The Decisive Years, 1976–1980* (New York: Broadside Books, 2017).

MEMOIRS OF THE REAGAN ADMINISTRATION

Reagan White House staffers wrote numerous memoirs, some of which are self-serving. It was no different with Franklin Roosevelt, though in an earlier age, many White House figures waited years, if not decades, before airing their views, but this was not the case with Reagan. Read all with caution.

Two of the most self-serving and defensive memoirs by Reagan White House personnel are Donald T. Regan, *For the Record: From Wall Street to Washington* (New York: Harcourt Brace Jovanovich, 1988); and David A. Stockman, *The Triumph of Politics: Why the Reagan Revolution Failed* (New York: Harper & Row, 1986). The tone of both memoirs is that if only Reagan had listened to their economic and political advice, his administration would have been successful.

For insights into the Reagan White House press operation, see Peggy Noonan, *What I Saw at the Revolution: A Political Life in the Reagan Era* (New York: Random House, 1990); and Patrick J. Buchanan, *Right from the Beginning* (Boston: Little, Brown, 1988). Both books are well written and entertaining, though Buchanan has a better sense of humor.

BIOGRAPHIES OF PROMINENT REAGAN-ERA CONSERVATIVES

Arizona senator and conservative torch carrier Barry Goldwater has gained academic interest in the past three decades. The two best biographies are Robert Alan Goldberg, *Barry Goldwater* (New Haven, CT: Yale University Press, 1995); and Rick Perlstein, *Before the Storm: Barry Goldwater and the Unmaking of the American Consensus* (New York: Nation Books, 2009). Of historical interest is Barry Goldwater's ghostwritten campaign autobiography, *The Conscience of a Conservative* (Washington, DC: Regnery Publishers, 1960).

The best biography of conservative editor and intellectual William F. Buckley Jr. is John B. Judis, *William F. Buckley, Jr.: Patron Saint of the Conservatives* (New York: Simon and Schuster, 1988).

Eagle Forum and STOP-ERA leader Phyllis Schlafly is studied in Donald T. Critchlow, *Phyllis Schlafly and Grassroots Conservatism: A Woman's Crusade* (Princeton, NJ: Princeton University Press, 2008). An earlier study of Schlafly is Carol Felsenthal, *Phyllis Schlafly: The Sweetheart of the Silent Majority* (Washington, DC: Regnery Gateway, 1982). For an insight into Schlafly's beliefs, see her campaign biography (of sorts) for Goldwater, *A Choice Not an Echo: The Inside Story of How American Presidents Are Chosen* (Washington, DC: Regnery Publishers, reprint edition, 2014).

ECONOMIC POLICY IN THE AGE OF REAGAN

There is little consensus on the impact of Reaganomics on the United States. For instance, Richard S. Williamson, "A New Federalism: Proposals and Achievements of President Reagan's First Three Years," *Publius* 16 (Winter 1986): 11–28, celebrated Reaganomics as a policy success. In contrast, Michael Moffitt, "Shocks, Deadlocks, and Scorched Earth: Reaganomics and the Decline of U.S. Hegemony," *World Policy Journal* 4 (Fall 1987): 553–82, believed that Reaganomics had led to mounting national debt and weakened America's position in the world. The truth is that both writers were as much wrong as they were right.

Other insightful assessments of Reaganomics include Michael Comiskey, "The Promise and Performance of Reaganomics," *Polity* 20 (Winter 1987): 316–31; and Jon C. Teaford, *Cities of the Heartland: The Rise and Fall of the Industrial Midwest* (Bloomington: Indiana University Press, 1994).

Readers are also urged to consult Jude Wanniski, "Taxes, Revenues, and the 'Laffer Curve,'" *Public Interest* 33 (Fall 1978): 3–16.

RACE AND AMERICAN CONSERVATISM

The subject of race and American conservatism has been covered well in Allan J. Lichtman, *White Protestant Nation: The Rise of the American Conservative Movement* (New York: Atlantic Monthly Press, 2008); Joseph Crespino, *Strom Thurmond's America* (New York: Hill and Wang, 2012); and Dan Carter, *The Politics of Rage: George Wallace, the Origins of the New Conservatism, and the Transformation of American Politics* (Baton Rouge: Louisiana State University Press, 2000).

For the early years of race and reaction in the post–World War II era, see Kari Frederickson, *The Dixiecrat Revolt and the End of the Solid South, 1932–1968* (Chapel Hill: University of North Carolina Press, 2001).

SOCIAL CONSERVATISM AND THE RELIGIOUS RIGHT

A good starting point for the Religious Right is Jerry Falwell's "manifesto" for the Moral Majority, *Listen, America! The Conservative Blueprint for America's Moral Rebirth* (New York: Doubleday, 1981). For a classic account of religious conservatism before the 1980s, see Leo Ribuffo, *The Old Christian Right: The Protestant Far Right from the Great Depression to the Cold War* (Philadelphia: Temple University Press, 1983).

Balanced scholarly accounts of religious conservatism since the 1960s include Kenneth J. Heineman, *God Is a Conservative: Religion, Politics, and Morality in Contemporary America* (New York: New York University Press, 2005); James Davison Hunter, *Culture Wars: The Struggle to Define America* (New York: Basic Books, 1991); William Martin, *With God on Our Side: The Rise of the Religious Right in America* (New York: Broadway Books, 1996); and Daniel K. Williams, *God's Own Party: The Making of the Christian Right* (New York: Oxford University Press, 2010). Readers would also be well advised to consult David John Marley, "Ronald Reagan and the Splintering of the Christian Right," *Journal of Church and State* 48 (October 2006): 851–68.

For a fine micro study of social traditionalism and the evangelical Protestant estrangement from President Jimmy Carter, see Robert Freedman, "The Religious Right and the Carter Administration," *Historical Journal* 48 (March 2005): 231–60.

The relationship between corporations and the Religious Right has recently been studied in Darren E. Grem, *The Blessings of Business: How Corporations Shaped Conservative Christianity* (New York: Oxford University Press, 2016).

LAW AND ORDER

Ronald Reagan's path to power, first to the California governorship and then to the U.S. presidency, owed much to rising urban crime rates and campus violence in the 1960s. While campus violence de-escalated in the 1970s, American cities became more crime ridden and violent.

For an excellent discussion of California politics, Reagan, and campus protest at Berkeley, see W. J. Rorabaugh, *Berkeley at War: The 1960s* (New York: Oxford University Press, 1989).

The public reaction against urban crime is discussed eloquently in such works as Kenneth D. Durr, *Behind the Backlash: White Working-Class Politics in Baltimore, 1940–1980* (Chapel Hill: University of North Carolina Press, 2003); Michael D. Flamm, *Law and Order: Street Crime, Civil Unrest, and the Crisis of Liberalism in the 1960s* (New York: Columbia University Press, 2007); and Thomas J. Sugrue, *The Origins of the Urban Crisis: Race and Inequality in Postwar Detroit* (Princeton, NJ: Princeton University Press, 1996).

THINK TANKS AND CONSERVATIVE MEDIA

Conservative think tanks, notably the Washington, DC–based trinity of the American Enterprise Institute, CATO, and the Heritage Foundation, have received some attention. An earlier, hostile discussion of conservative donors and their efforts to influence federal economic policy is Michael W. Miles, *The Odyssey of the American Right* (New York: Oxford University Press, 1980). More recently, Kim Fein-Phillips updated Miles with *Invisible Hands: The Making of the Conservative Movement from the New Deal to Reagan* (New York: W. W. Norton, 2009). Of particular value is John Stahl, *Right Moves: The Conservative Think Tank in American Political Culture since 1945* (Chapel Hill: University of North Carolina Press, 2016).

For an excellent account of the emergence and evolution of conservative media, see Nicole Hemmer, *Messengers of the Right: Conservative Media and the Transformation of American Politics* (Philadelphia: University of Pennsylvania Press, 2016).

U.S. COLD WAR FOREIGN POLICY

Political divisions over the Vietnam War that led to a breakdown in the Cold War foreign policy consensus are treated in Robert Timberg, *The Nightingale's Song* (New York: Free Press, 1996); and Tom Wells, *The War Within: America's Battle over Vietnam* (Berkeley: University of California Press, 1994). Timberg is especially recommended, as the Vietnam

War–era naval and marine figures he discusses went on to play roles in the Iran-Contra scandal of the 1980s.

John Ehrman does an excellent job of discussing the origins of neoconservative foreign policy in *The Rise of Neoconservatism: Intellectuals and Foreign Affairs, 1945–1994* (New Haven, CT: Yale University Press, 1995).

Ronald Reagan and the Cold War receives excellent treatment in James Mann, *The Rebellion of Ronald Reagan: A History of the End of the Cold War* (New York: Viking, 2009); Bartholomew Sparrow, *The Strategist: Brent Scowcroft and the Call of National Security* (New York: PublicAffairs, 2015); and Andrew E. Busch, "Ronald Reagan and the Defeat of the Soviet Empire," *Presidential Studies Quarterly* 27 (Summer 1997): 451–66.

No discussion of Reagan-era foreign policy would be complete without reading this critical primary document: Jeane Kirkpatrick, "Dictatorships and Double Standards," *Commentary* 68 (November 1979): 34–54. Another classic work, by historian George C. Herring, is useful in establishing the context of U.S. foreign relations over more than two hundred years. See George C. Herring, *From Colony to Superpower: U.S. Foreign Relations since 1775* (New York: Oxford University Press, 2008).

For an insightful analysis of post-Reagan foreign policy, Michael Mandelbaum's book, *Mission Failure: America and the World in the Post–Cold War Era* (New York: Oxford University Press, 2016), is indispensable.

POPULAR CULTURE

For the classic, extremely hostile, critique of Ronald Reagan and popular culture in the 1980s, see Michael Paul Rogin, *Ronald Reagan, The Movie and Other Episodes in Political Demonology* (Berkeley: University of California Press, 1988). A more balanced approach is Philip Jenkins, *Decade of Nightmares: The End of the Sixties and the Making of Eighties America* (New York: Oxford University Press, 2006). Another useful work is Gil Troy, *Morning in America: How Ronald Reagan Invented the 1980s* (Princeton, NJ: Princeton University Press, 2005).

DEMOCRATS

The Democratic Party's rout in the 1970s and 1980s is well analyzed in Steve Fraser and Gary Gerstle, eds., *The Rise and Fall of the New Deal Order, 1930–1980* (Princeton, NJ: Princeton University Press, 1989); Ronald Radosh, *Divided They Fell: The Demise of the Democratic Party, 1964–1996* (New York: Free Press, 1996); and Steve Gillon, *The Democrats' Dilemma: Walter F. Mondale and the Liberal Legacy* (New York: Columbia University Press, 1992). For an insider's account of the Democratic Party's failures, see Tip O'Neill, *Man of the House: The Life and Political Memoirs of Speaker Tip O'Neill* (New York: Random House, 1987).

No discussion of Democrats would be complete without reading Michael Barone's magisterial book, *Our Country: The Shaping of America from Roosevelt to Reagan* (New York: Free Press, 1990).

REPUBLICANS

The definitive history of the Republican Party is Lewis L. Gould, *Grand Old Party: A History of Republicans* (New York: Random House, 2003). Much of the post-1930 story of the Republican Party is intertwined with the rise and evolution of conservatism and is noted above.

CONSERVATIVE YOUTH

Conservative youths in the 1960s, a number of whom went on to positions in the Reagan administration, have received thorough treatment in Rebecca E. Klatch, *A Generation Divided: The New Left, the New Right, and the 1960s* (Berkeley: University of California Press, 1999); and Gregory L. Schneider, *Cadres for Conservatism: Young Americans for Freedom and the Rise of the Contemporary Right* (New York: New York University Press, 1999).

WEBSITES

The following websites are useful to students and scholars interested in presidential politics and U.S. domestic and foreign policy, most especially since the 1960s. Included are think tanks, which run the ideological spectrum, as well as presidential libraries, independent research sites, and federal and university-affiliated websites.

Federal Sites

Library of Congress, https://www.loc.gov.

U.S. Department of Justice, Federal Bureau of Investigation (FBI), Uniform Crime Reporting Statistics, https://ucr.fbi.gov.

Independent Research Sites

Center for Responsive Politics, Washington, DC, https://www.opensecrets.org.

Pew Research Center, https://www.pewresearch.org.

Presidential Libraries

Gerald Ford Presidential Library and Museum, https://www.fordlibrarymuseum.gov.

Jimmy Carter Presidential Library and Museum, https://www.jimmycarterlibrary.gov.

Lyndon Johnson Presidential Library, http://www.lbjlibrary.org.

Ronald Reagan Presidential Library and Museum, https://www.reaganlibrary.gov.

Think Tanks

American Enterprise Institute (AEI), Washington, DC, http://www.aei.org.

The American Presidency Project, University of California, Santa Barbara, http://www.presidency.ucsb.edu/index.php.

Brookings, https://www.brookings.edu.

CATO Institute, Washington, DC, https://www.cato.org.

Heritage Foundation, Washington, DC, http://www.heritage.org.

University Site

Miller Center (University of Virginia), https://millercenter.org.

INDEX

Note: Page numbers in *italics* indicate photos.

Abortion issues, xxxiii, 108, *109*, 116–118, 171, 202, 221
Afghanistan
   deployment of U.S. Stinger missiles to, xxxviii, 58
   Soviet invasion of, xxxv, 49, 57–58, 179, 184, 196, 198
   U.S. military intervention in, 190, 191
AFL-CIO, 132. *See also* Congress of Industrial Organizations (CIO)
Agnew, Spiro, 31
AIDS, 119, 197
Air traffic controllers' strike, xxxvi, 98
All in the Family (television series), 143–144, 150, 151
All the President's Men (film), 143
Allen, Richard, 42, 50
American Enterprise Institute (AEI), 81, 114, 134, 200, 203
Americans for Democratic Action (ADA), xxviii–xxix, 12
Andropov, Yuri, xxxvi, xxxviii, 58, 59, 60
Angola, 30, 222
Apocalypse Now (film), 144–145

Arafat, Yasser, 53
Arkin, William, 63
A-Team, The (television series), 150
Atwood, Lee, 183

Baby boom generation, 24, 86, 143
Back to the Future (film), 158, 160, 164
Baker, Howard, 46–47, 81
Beatty, Warren, 152–153, 160, 173
Begin, Menachem W., *54*, 195
   bombing of nuclear reactor in Iraq, xxxv, 195
   Camp David Accords, 47, 195
   invasion of Lebanon, 54, 195
Bergsten, C. Fred, 85
Berlin Wall, xxx, xl, 68–69, 180, 230–231
Bernstein, Carl, 143
Biden, Joe, 172
Bin Laden, Osama, xl, 57, 184, 189–190
Blacklisting, 14
Bloom County (comic strip), 50
"Boll Weevils" (pro-Reagan southern Democrats), xxxvi, 89–92, 180, 199

Bork, Robert, 171–173, 176
Boulware, Lemuel, 15–16
Brady, James, 87
Brandenburg Gate, Reagan's
    remarks, xxxix, 68–69, 173
  call for Gorbachev to bring down
    Berlin Wall, 231
  on legacy of Berlin Wall, 230
  on reasons for hope, 231
  text (primary document), 230–231
Brezhnev, Leonid I., 195–196
  Afghanistan policy, 49, 57, 58,
    196
  Arms Limitations Talks (SALT),
    44–45
  arms sales, 33
  death of, xxxvi, 58, 195
  legacy of, 64–65, 196
Brezhnev Doctrine, xxxii, 195–196
Brown, Edmund "Pat," 196
  California gubernatorial election
    (1966), xxxii, 19, 26–27
  response to student unrest and
    protests, 25
  response to Watts riot, 25–26
Brown v. Board of Education, xxx
Bryan, Williams Jennings, 95
Buchanan, Patrick J., 56, 184–185,
    190
Buckley, William F., Jr., 196
  founder of *National Review*, xxx,
    121, 196
  founder of Young Americans for
    Freedom, 133–134
  on "fusionism," 182
  host of *Firing Line*, 169
  on Panama Canal, 46
Bush, George H. W.
  CIA director, 45
  foreign policy, 183–184, 186
  Persian Gulf War, xl, 183–184
  presidential election of 1988, xl,
    135–136, 182–183
  presidential election of 1992, xl,
    185
  presidential primaries of 1980, 81
  vice president, xxxv, 81
  on "voodoo economics," 81, 177
Bush, George W.
  legacy of, 190–191
  military interventions in
    Afghanistan and Iraq, xli,
    190–191
  neoconservatives and, xli, 190
  PATRIOT Act, xli, 190
  War on Terror, xli
Bush, Prescott, 19

California gubernatorial inaugural
    address, Reagan's first
  on crime, 207
  on education, 208
  text (primary document),
    207–208
  on welfare, 207–208
Camp David Accords, 47, 195
Carter, Jimmy, 42
  Camp David Accords, 47, 195
  domestic policy, 34–35
  foreign policy, 33–34
  Iranian hostage crisis, 34
  Moral Majority and, xxxv, 34–35
  Panama Canal negotiations, 44,
    46–47, 48
  presidential election of 1980,
    xxxv, 34–35
  presidential election of 1976,
    xxxiv, 32–33
  repudiation of Truman Doctrine,
    xxxiv, 33

Index

Casey, William J., 197
  covert operations role, *51*, 52, 197
  director of CIA, 50, 197
  member of Committee on the Present Danger, 42
CATO Institute, 134, 199–200
Central America, Reagan's address on United States policy in
  on Cuba, 222
  on El Salvador, 222
  on isolationism, 223
  on Nicaragua, 222
  on Soviet influence, 222–223
  text (primary document), 221–223
Central Intelligence Agency (CIA)
  Ford administration and, 45
  history of, 40
  Office of Strategic Services, 40, 44, 50, 141, 197, 199
  Reagan administration and, xxxviii, 50, 51, 52–53, 58, 183, 197
  television depictions of, 142, 150
Cheney, Richard, 31, 184, 190
Chernenko, Konstantin, xxxviii, 65
Chernobyl nuclear accident, xxxix, 66
Christian Coalition, xl, 186–187
Churchill, Winston, 64
Civil Rights Act of 1964, xxxi, 20, 22, 27, 122, 124, 171, 198
Clifford, Clark, 35
Clinton, Bill, xl, 164, 171, 178, 185–186, 187, 188
Cold War Democrats, 43, 55, 68, 94, 141, 173, 199, 202
Coming Home (film), 144
Commentary (magazine), 48, 55
Committee on the Present Danger, xxxiv, 42–43, 45–46, 50, 82, 199

Comprehensive Crime Control Act of 1984, xxxviii, 127
Congress of Industrial Organizations (CIO), 8, 11, 19. *See also* AFL-CIO
Conservative Political Action Conference Dinner, Reagan's remarks
  on government spending, 217
  on tax indexing, 217
  text (primary document), 216–218
  on young conservatives, 217
Cronkite, Walter, 142
Cuba and Central America, Reagan's National Security Directive on (primary document)
  on creation of public information task force, 215
  on Cuba, 216
  on economic support, 216
  on El Salvador, 216
  on Honduras, 216
  on intelligence, 216
  on Nicaragua, 216
  on trade, 216
Cuomo, Mario, 95–97, 99, 223

Dallas (television series), 146–147
Davis, Nancy. *See* Reagan, Nancy Davis
Davis, Patti Reagan, xxix
D-Day, fortieth anniversary ceremonies, 166–167
Deer Hunter, The (film), xxxiv, 144–146
Democratic National Convention of 1948, 12
Democratic National Convention of 1984, 95, 168

Democratic National Convention of 1968, xxxii, 41, 125
Desperate Journey (film), 8, 140
Dewey, Thomas, 40
Diamond, Neil, 169
Dirty Harry film franchise, 147–149
Dixiecrats, 12
Dolan, Anthony, 119, 197
Dolan, John Terrence "Terry," 197
  cofounder and chair of National Conservative Political Action Committee, 119, 197
  death of, 119, 197
Donovan, Ray, 170
Dukakis, Michael, 52, 183
Dynasty (television series), 146–147

Eastwood, Clint, 136, 147, *148*, 160
Economic Recovery Tax Act of 1981, 82–83
Ecumenical prayer breakfast, Reagan's remarks
  on inseparability of politics and morality, 226
  on Kennedy, 225
  on role of faith, 225
  text (primary document), 225–226
  on tolerance, 226
Eisenhower, Dwight D.
  domestic policy, 17–18, 94
  foreign policy, 19
  Little Rock school integration crisis, xxx
  presidential election of 1952, xxix, 19
  Republican Party and, 19, 31, 74, 121–122
El Salvador, 30, 33, 48, 51–52, 215, 216, 222

Equal Rights Amendment (ERA), 30, 31, 32, 114–116, 118, 203
"Evil Empire" speech, xxxvii, 62–63, 218–220. *See also* National Association of Evangelicals, Reagan's remarks

Fairness doctrine, 169
Falcon Crest (television series), 146–147
Falwell, Jerry, xxxv, xl, 34, 107–111, *111*, 113–114, 116–117, 119–121, 133–135, 186–187, 192
Family Ties (television series), 150–151
"Farewell Address to the Nation" (Reagan)
  on economic recovery, 235
  on nickname "The Great Communicator," 235
  on Reagan Revolution, 236
  on recovery of morale, 235
  on regrets, 236
  text (primary document), 235–236
Federal tax reduction legislation, Reagan's Oval Office address
  on bipartisan nature of bill, 212–213
  in inflation, 213
  on role of government, 212
  text (primary document), 212–213
  on unemployment, 213
Film. *See* Hollywood; Popular culture
Fonda, Jane, 141, 144, 145
Ford, Betty, 30, 31, 32
Ford, Gerald
  appointed vice president, xxxiii, 31
  domestic policy, 30, 116
  foreign policy, 30–31, 45–46, 63
  Panama Canal deal, 46–47

Index

presidential election of 1976, xxxiv, 32
presidential primaries of 1976, xxxiv, 31–32
Saturday Night Live on, 163
"Whip Inflation Now" ("WIN") logo, 31
Fowler, Henry, 42
Fox, Michael J., 151, 158, 159, 160
Fox News, 188, 202

Gay rights, 34, 119–120, 134–135, 136, 181, 192, 197, 203
Gender gap, 118–119
General Electric (GE), xxx, 14–17
Ghostbusters (film), 158, 160
Gilder, George, 80–81
Gingrich, Newt, xl, 187, *188*
Glaspie, April, 183
Gold standard, 75–76
Goldwater, Barry M., *21*, 197
   domestic policy positions, 19–20, 122, 197, 198
   elected to U.S. Senate, xxx, 197–198
   foreign policy positions, 20
   libertarianism and, 133, 198
   presidential election of 1964, 19–22, 82, 94, 96, 198
   Reagan's "A Time for Choosing" speech in support of, xxxi–xxxii, 20–21, 32, 198
   religious conservatives and, 135, 168
   Republican presidential nominee, xxxi, 19–20
   Schlafly's *A Choice, Not an Echo* in support of, xxxi, 114
   See also "Time for Choosing, A" (Reagan)

Gorbachev, Mikhail S., 66, 198
   Afghanistan policy, 179
   Chernobyl nuclear accident, xxxix, 66
   glasnost, 65–66
   Intermediate-Range Nuclear Forces Treaty, xxxix, 68, 180
   legacy of, 180, 198
   perestroika, 65
   Reagan and, xxxix, 66–70, 125, 180, 186, 198
   Reagan's Brandenburg Gate speech, xxxix
   succeeds Chernenko as Soviet leader, xxxviii, 65
   See also Brandenburg Gate, Reagan's remarks
Gorbachev, Raisa, 65, *67*, 180
Gore, Al, 162
Gore, Tipper, 162
Gramm, William Philip "Phil," 198–199
   elected to Senate as Republican, 99, 199
   pro-Reagan southern Democrats, xxxvi, 89, 90, 92, 177, 199
   supply-side economics supporter, 177, 198
"Great Communicator," Reagan as, 235
Great Depression, 4, 6, 14–15, 19, 73, 75, 78, 88, 91, 139, 187
Great Society programs, 18, 21–24
Greider, William, 85–87
Grenada, xxxvii, 51, 183, 201
Guatemala, 30, 34, 48, 51

Hawaii Five-0 (television series), 141–142
Helms, Jesse, 32, 116, *116*, 123

Heritage Foundation, 57–58, 81–82, 83, 133–134, 187, 200
Hesburgh, Theodore, 132
Hezbollah, xxxvii, 55, 56
Hill Street Blues (television series), 149–150
Hinckley, John, Jr., 87, 160
Hitler, Adolf, xxviii, 9–10, 140
HIV/AIDS, 119, 197
Holden, Bill, 10–11, 13–14
Hollywood. *See* Popular culture
Hollywood Hearings, xxviii, 10–12
Holmes, Oliver Wendell, 5
Homelessness, xxxiv, 129–131
Hooks, Benjamin, 125
House Committee on Un-American Activities, xxviii, 10–12, 140, 153
Hudson, Rock, 119
Humphrey, Hubert, xxxiii, 12–13, 29, 201
Huntington, Samuel, 133
Hussein, Saddam, xl, xli, 53, 183–184, 185, 190

Immigration and Reform Control Act of 1986, 132
Immigration reform, 131–132
Inflation, 83, 90–91, 97, 100–101, 135
  Keynesian economics and, 74, 77
  OPEC oil embargo and, xxxiii, 31
  Reagan on, 208, 209, 210, 213, 215, 217, 224, 235
  stagflation, xxxiv, 34, 77, 177
Intermediate-Range Nuclear Forces Treaty of 1987, xxxix, 68
International Association of Chiefs of Police in New Orleans, Reagan's remarks
  on crime, 214
  on impact of drug addiction, 214
  on role of government, 214–215
  text (primary document), 213–215
Iran-Contra scandal, xxxix, 57, 164, 170–173, 197, 201
Iranian hostage crisis, 34
Iranian Islamic Revolution, xxxv, 49
Iran-Iraq War, xxxv, 53
Iraq
  Israel's bombing of nuclear reactor in, xxxv, 195
  Persian Gulf War, xl, 183–184
  U.S. military intervention in, xli, 190–191
Israel, xxxv, xxxvii, 31, 47, 53–57, 77, 120, 184, 195

Jackson, Henry, 46
John Paul II, Pope, xxxv, 58–59, 59, 63
Johnny Quest (television series), 141
Johnson, Lyndon
  "Daisy Girl ad," 20
  foreign policy, 20
  Great Society programs, 18, 21–24
  presidential election of 1964, 20–23
  succeeds Kennedy as president, xxxi, 18
  Vietnam War, xxxii, 18, 20–21, 23–25
  War on Poverty, 18, 22–23

Kazan, Elia, 153
Kennan, George, 46
Kennedy, Anthony, xli, 192
Kennedy, John F., xxx, xxxi, 18, 19, 45, 63, 69, 225
Kennedy, Ted, 61, 171
Kerry, John, 52

Keynes, George Maynard, 73
Keynesian economics, 73–78, 81, 88, 94, 177, 200
Khrushchev, Nikita, 195
King, Martin Luther, Jr., xxxii, 108, 123
Kirkpatrick, Evron, 40, 199
Kirkpatrick, Jeane Jordan, 41, 199
  academic career, 40–41, 199
  casts first presidential vote for Truman, xxix, 40
  Cold War Democrat, 43, 55, 68, 199
  "Dictatorships and Double Standards" (Commentary), 48
  early years and education, 39–40, 199
  on Gorbachev, 68
  legacy of, 199
  member of Committee on the Present Danger, 42, 199
  neoconservatism and, 48, 55, 199
  on Reagan's "Evil Empire" speech, 63
  on Soviet's invasion of Afghanistan, 49
  U.S. ambassador to the UN, *41*, 50, 52, 53, 54, 199
Kissinger, Henry, 30, 46, 66–68
Knowledge economy, 76
Knute Rockne, All American (film), xxviii, 159, *159*
Koch, Charles, 134, 199–200
Koch, David H., 199–200
  CATO Institute and, 199–200
  vice presidential candidate of Libertarian Party, 200
Korean War, xxix, xxx, 24, 112, 166, 184
Krauthammer, Charles, 67

Laffer, Arthur B., 200
  education and career, 78, 200
  "Laffer Curve," 78–79, 200
  supply-side economics theory, 78–81, 83, 85, 89, 100, 102, 177, 198, 200
  Wanniski, Jude, and, xxxiv, 78–81
Lear, Norman, 143–144, 162, 171, 172, 173
Lebanon, xxxvii, 53–57, 185, 195
Lehman, John, 42, 50, 60
Lenin, Vladimir, 65, 153, 219
Lewis, John L., 8
Limbaugh, Rush, 169–170, 187–188
Lincoln, Abraham, 21, 27, 96

Magnum, P.I. (television series), 150
Mao Tse-Tung, xxix
Marshner, Connie, 134–135
McCarthy, Joseph, 172, 197–198
McFarlane, Robert, xxxviii, xxxix, 56–57, 170
McGovern, George, xxxiii, 41–42, 44, 46, 48, 52
McNamara, Robert, 24–25
Medicaid, 23
Medicare, 23
Mellencamp, John Cougar, 162–163, 173
Mellon, Andrew W., 200
  tax policy and "supply-side" economics, xxvii, 3–4, 78, 79, 80, 200–201
  U.S. Treasury secretary, xxvii, 78, 79, 200
Miami Vice (television series), 149–150
Milius, John, 154–156
Mission Impossible (television series), 140–141

Mondale, Walter F., 96, 201
  Clinton administration and, xl
  Cold Warrior, 201
  elected to U.S. Senate, 201
  presidential campaign of 1984, xxxviii, 95–96, 97–100, 132, 181, 201
  vice president, 95, 168, 201
Moral Majority, xxxv, xl, 110–111, 113, 121, 135, 144, 168, 187–188
"Morning in America" campaign ad, 168
Moscow State University, Reagan's remarks and question-and-answer session
  on democracy, 233
  on freedom, 233
  on information revolution, 232
  text (primary document), 232–233
Murdoch, Rupert, 183
Murray, Philip, 8, 11, 12
Mutual assured destruction (MAD) doctrine, 45, 61, 68, 226–227

NAACP (National Association for the Advancement of Colored Peoples), 121, 125
National Association of Evangelicals, xxxvii, 62
National Association of Evangelicals, Reagan's remarks
  on secularism, 218–219
  on sin and phenomenology of evil, 219
  on Soviet Union, 219–220
  text (primary document), 218–220
National Review (magazine), xxx, 46, 49, 67, 80, 121, 150, 169, 196
Neoconservatives ("neocons")
  American Enterprise Institute, 81, 134
  anticommunist, 182
  Bush (41) administration and, 183
  Bush (43) administration and, 190
  Cold War Democrats and, 43, 48, 55, 199
  Commentary (magazine), 48, 55
  Committee on the Present Danger and, xxxiv, 42–43, 199
  definition of, xxxiv, 43
  Ford administration and, 45
  history of, xxxiv, 43
  isolationist, 182
  Israel and, 55, 120, 184
  Persian Gulf War and, 183–184
  Reagan administration and, 55–56
  Weekly Standard (magazine), 188, 190
Neshoba County speech (Reagan), 122–123
New Deal, 5
  Americans for Democratic Action and, 12
  anti-New Deal conservatives, 19, 114, 142, 196–198, 204
  Reagan and, 5–6, 10, 17–18, 87, 178, 181
  Reagan Democrats and, 32
  Republican Party and, 19
Nicaragua
  Boland Amendment and, xxxvii, xxxix, 52, 56
  communist insurgency, xxxv, 30, 34, 47–48
  Contras, 56, 197
  Iran-Contra scandal, xxxix, 57, 164, 170–173, 197, 201
  National Security Directive on Cuba and Central America, 215, 216
  Reagan administration and, 47–48, 50–52, 197, 201, 215, 216

Reagan's address on U.S. Policy in Central America, 222
Soviet Union and, 30, 34
in television and film, 154, 155, 164
Nixon, Richard, 18
   appointment of Gerald Ford as vice president, 31
   California gubernatorial election of 1962, 19, 27, 196
   creation of Drug Enforcement Administration, 29
   creation of Environmental Protection Agency, xxxiii, 29, 83
   creation of Occupational Safety and Health Administration, xxxiii, 29, 83
   domestic policy, 29
   Eisenhower and, 19
   foreign policy, 46, 63, 67–68, 196
   on Gorbachev, 67
   influence on Arnold Schwarzenegger, 203
   on Keynesian economics, 74
   presidential election of 1972, xxxiii, 30, 42
   presidential election of 1960, xxx, 19
   presidential election of 1968, xxxiii, 28–29
   recording of conversation with Reagan, 124
   resignation of, xxxiii, 30, 143
   Selective Service lottery, xxxiii, 29
   Vietnam War, 29
   Watergate affair, 30, 143
Noonan, Peggy, 167
Norquist, Grover, 184, 190
Norris, Chuck, 154, 156
North, Oliver L., 201
   Iran-Contra scandal, xxxviii, xxxix, 56–57, 170, 172–173, 201–202
   military service, 201
   on National Security Council, 56, 201
North Star, The (film), 140
Nuclear freeze movement, 61–63, 218, 219–220

Obergefell v. Hodges, xli, 192
O'Connor, Carroll, 144, 151
O'Connor, Sandra Day, 202
   legacy of, 176, 202
   nominated to U.S. Supreme Court, 117, 202
   retirement of, 192, 202
O'Connor v. Donaldson, xxxiii, 130
Office of Strategic Services (OSS), 40, 44, 50, 141, 197, 199. *See also* Central Intelligence Agency (CIA)
Olympics, Summer (Los Angeles, 1984), xxxviii, 165–166
Omnibus Budget Reconciliation Act of 1981, xxxvi, 82
O'Neill, Thomas "Tip," 202
   on "Boll Weevil" Democrats, xxxvi
   Clinton administration and, xl
   divided Democrats and, 84, 87, 89, 91, 132, 170, 199
   influence on 1984 presidential election, 95, 202
   Iran-Contra scandal and, 52
   midterm elections of 1982, xxxvii, 92
   Reagan and, xxxv, xxxviii, 84, 92–93, 94, 202
   warns Reagan he will pass no legislation, xxxv, 84

Organization of Petroleum Exporting Countries (OPEC), xxxiii, 31
Owens, Jesse, 165, 182

Palestinian Liberation Organization (PLO), xxxvii, 53–56
Panama Canal, 44, 46–48, 183
PATRIOT Act, xli, 190
Patriotism, xxxviii, 60, 140–141, 146, 150, 153–154, 160, 168, 173, 179, 190, 236
Pearl Harbor attack, xxviii, 8, 137
Peck, Gregory, 171
Pentecostal movement, 112–113, 120
Perot, Ross, 185
Persian Gulf War, xl, 183–184
Phillips, Howard, 67
Pipes, Richard, 45–46, 50
Planned Parenthood, 118
Platoon (film), 152
Poland, xxviii, xxxv, 58–60, 180
Popular culture
  All in the Family (television series), 143–144, 150, 151
  All the President's Men (film), 143
  Apocalypse Now (film), 144–145
  The A-Team (television series), 150
  Back to the Future (film), 158, 160, 164
  CIA in, 142, 150
  Cold War films, 157–158
  Coming Home (film), 144
  Dallas (television series), 146–147
  Deer Hunter, The (film), xxxiv, 144–146
  Desperate Journey (film), 8, 140
  Dirty Harry film franchise, 147–149
  Dynasty (television series), 146–147
  Falcon Crest (television series), 146–147
  Family Ties (television series), 150–151
  film industry and Franklin Roosevelt, 139–140
  Ghostbusters (film), 158, 160
  Hawaii Five-0 (television series), 141–142
  Hill Street Blues (television series), 149–150
  Johnny Quest (television series), 141
  Knute Rockne, All American (film), xxviii, 159, *159*
  Magnum, P.I. (television series), 150
  Miami Vice (television series), 149–150
  Mission Impossible (television series), 140–141
  Nicaragua in, 154, 155, 164
  The North Star (film), 140
  patriotic films, 154–157
  Platoon (film), 152
  police and detective programs, 147–150
  political and apolitical rock stars, 162–163
  Rambo film franchise, 156–157
  Reagan's legacy, 159–160, 168–169, 173
  rededication ceremonies for the Statue of Liberty and Ellis Island, 168–169
  Reds (film), 152–153
  Risky Business (film), 164
  situation comedies, 150–151
  Splendor in the Grass (film), 153
  sports figures, 161–162

Taxi Driver (film), 160
Top Gun (film), xxxix, 157–158
war and antiwar films, 144–145
Presidential inaugural address, Reagan's first
  on economic difficulties, 208–209
  on role of government, 209
  text (primary document), 208–209
  on unemployment, 209
Presidential nomination, Reagan's acceptance remarks
  on inflation, 224
  on military readiness, 224
  text (primary document), 223–225
  on two visions of government, 223
  on welfare, 224
"Proclamation 5147: National Sanctity of Human Life Day"
  on abortion statistics, 220
  on comparison of abortion to slavery, 220–221
  on right to life, 220
  on *Roe v. Wade*, 221
  text (primary document), 220–223
Program for Economic Recovery, Reagan's address before joint session of Congress
  on inflation, 210
  on military spending, 211
  on regulations, 210
  on taxes, 211
  text (primary document), 210–212

Reagan, Jack (Reagan's father), 2, 3, 4–5, 6, 13, 14, 131
Reagan, Maureen, xxviii
Reagan, Michael, xxviii
Reagan, Nancy Davis, 67
  acting career, 14
  death of, xli
  family of, 14, 16–17
  Hollywood and, *151, 152,* 156, 158, 159, 160, *161*
  "Just Say No to Drugs" campaign, 128–129, *129,* 160, 162
  marriage to Ronald Reagan, xxix, 14, *15*
  political influence on Ronald Reagan, 16–17
Reagan, Neil (Reagan's brother), 2, 3
Reagan, Nelle Wilson (Reagan's mother), 2, 3, 9, 131
Reagan, Ron, Jr., xxix, 164
Reagan, Ronald
  acting career, 7–9
  Alzheimer's diagnosis, xl, 193
  assassination attempt on, xxxv, 87, 160
  birth of, xxvii, 2
  California gubernatorial election (1966), xxxii, 19, 26–27, *26*
  contract with Warner Brothers Studios, 6–7
  death of, xli
  Desperate Journey (film), 8, 140
  divorce from Jane Wyman, xxix, 13–14
  early years, 2–6
  education, xxvii, 2–3, 4, 6
  enlists in U.S. Army Reserve, xxvii, 7, 9
  governor of California, 27–31
  Hollywood and, xxvii, 7–12, 17, 50, 119
  host of *General Electric Theater*, 14, *16*
  joins Screen Actors Guild, xxvii, 8
  Knute Rockne, All American (film), xxviii, 159, *159*
  marriage to Jane Wyman, xxviii, 8

Reagan, Ronald (*Continued*)
  marriage to Nancy Davis, xxix, 14, *15*
  move to Los Angeles, 7
  parents of, 2
  president of Screen Actors Guild, xxviii, 11–13, 18
  presidential election of 1980, xxxv, 34–35
  presidential election of 1984, xxxviii, 60, 96–100
  presidential primaries of 1976, xxxiv, 31–32
  radio sports announcer, 6–7, *7*
  registers as a Republican, 18
  Republican National Convention address (1976), 32
  Roosevelt's influence on, 5–6, *7*, 8, 16, 18, 21, 94, 97, 102, 178, 181, 182
  spokesman for General Electric, xxx, 14–17
  vote for Roosevelt, xxvii, 5
  World War II, 8–10, 17
Reagan Democrats, 31–32, 99, 181
Reagan Doctrine, 63
Reaganomics, 81, 86, 90, 94–95, 99–100, 129–130, 162, 200. *See also* Supply-side economics
Reds (film), 152–153
Republican National Convention of 1984, 117, *155*, 167–168, 203. *See also* Presidential nomination, Reagan's acceptance remarks
Republican National Convention of 1976, 32, 115–116
Reserve Officers' Training Corps (ROTC), 25, 44, 60–61, 179
Risky Business (film), 164

Robertson, Marion "Pat," xl, 34, 111–114, *112*, 116, 134, 186–187, 192
Roe v. Wade, xxxiii, 108, *109*, 116–117, 171, 202, 221
Romney, George, 85
Roosevelt, Franklin Delano
  Cold War Democrats and, 43
  death of, xxviii, 10
  Eisenhower's "Modern Republicanism" and, xxix
  film industry and, 139–140
  influence on Reagan, 5–6, *7*, 8, 16, 18, 21, 94, 97, 102, 178, 181, 182
  Keynesian economics and, 73, 74, 75
  legacy of, 173, 176
  lend-lease program, xxviii
  opposition to Federal Deposit Insurance Corporation, 102
  presidential election of 1936, xxvii, 6
  presidential election of 1932, 5
  public image of, 139–140
  Reagan's first presidential vote for, xxvii, 5
  World War II and, 137
  See also New Deal
Rumsfeld, Donald, 184, 190

Sadat, Anwar, 47, 195
Saturday Night Live (television program), 163–164
Savings and loan institutions (S&Ls) crisis, 102
Schlafly, Phyllis Stewart, *115*, 202
  A Choice Not an Echo, xxxi, 114, 203
  denunciation of PATRIOT Act, 190

Index

founder of Eagle Forum, 67, 115, 203
legacy of, 114–115, 203
Reagan and, 67, 116, 133
religious conservatives and, 114–116, 133, 192
Republican National Convention of 1976, 32
Schwarzenegger, Arnold A., 203
  bodybuilding career, 203
  Conan the Barbarian (film), 155, 203
  political career, 203
  Reagan and, *155*, 160, 203
Screen Actors Guild (SAG)
  Reagan as president of, 11–13, 18
  Reagan joins, 8
  strike of 1960, 13
September 11, 2001, terrorist attacks, 189, *189*
Shultz, George, 62–63, 68
Simpson, Alan K., 203–204
  elected to U.S. Senate, 203
  on immigration, 131, 132, 203–204
  Reagan and, 131, 203
Social Security, xxxviii, 6, 17, 20, 22, 75, 92–94, 101, 122, 134, 178
South Korea, 33, 44, 99, 100
Southern Baptists, 34, 89, 108–109, 112–113, 120–121, 136
Southern Manifesto, xxx, 111
Soviet Union
  arms treaties and negotiations, xxxix, 44–45, 61, 68
  Carter administration and, 33–34, 44–45, 49
  Ford administration and, 30–31, 45–46

  invasion of Afghanistan, xxxv, 49, 57–58, 179, 184, 196, 198
  Johnson administration and, 20
  Kennedy administration and, 18
  Nixon administration and, 29
  Reagan administration and, 50, 52, 57–70
  Reagan's "evil empire" speech, xxxvii, 62–63, 218–220
  See also individual leaders
Splendor in the Grass (film), 153
Springsteen, Bruce, 162–163, 173
Stalin, Joseph, xxx, 10, 59–60, 64–65, 167, 195
Stallone, Sylvester, *156*, 156–157
"Star Wars." *See* Strategic Defense Initiative (SDI)
Statue of Liberty centennial celebration, xxxix, 168–169, 182
Statue of Liberty centennial celebration, Reagan's remarks
  on immigrants' impressions of Statue of Liberty, 228–229
  on providence, 229–230
  on Puritans, 229
  on shining city upon a hill, 229
  text (primary document), 228–230
Stockman, David A., *87*, 204
  leaks to news media, xxxvi, 86, 204
  Office of Management and Budget director, xxxvi, 86, 204
  Reagan and, 86–87, 204
Strategic Arms Limitations Talks (SALT), 44
Strategic Defense Initiative (SDI), xxxvii, 61–64, 198

Strategic Defense Initiative (SDI), Reagan's foreword written for report on
   on changing assumptions of defensive strategy, 227
   on creation of SDI, 227–228
   on purpose of SDI, 228
   on Soviet arms buildup, 227
   text (primary document), 226–228
Supply-side economics, xxvii, 4, 78–81, 85, 177, 198–199, 200
Swope, Gerard, 14–15

Taft, Robert A., 10, 19
Tax Equity and Fiscal Responsibility Act, 93
Taxi Driver (film), 160
Television. *See* Popular culture
Thatcher, Margaret H., 63, 204
   foreign policy of, 63–64, 204
   as "Iron Lady," 204
   prime minister, 204
   Reagan and, 63–64, 204
Thomas, John Parnell, 10–12
Thomas Road Baptist Church, 34, 108
Thurmond, Strom, xxix, 12, 40
Thurow, Lester, 94
"Time for Choosing, A" (Reagan), xxxi–xxxii, 20, 32
   on freedom, 206
   on government bureaus, 205–206
   on Iron Curtain, 206
   text (primary document), 205–207
Top Gun (film), xxxix, 157–158
Trickle-down economics, 95
Trudeau, Pierre, 63
Truman, Harry
   Cold War Democrats and, 43
   domestic policy, 17
   federal judge appointments, 176
   foreign policy, xxviii, xxix, 10, 12, 25, 33, 42, 46, 63
   Goldwater on, 19
   legacy of, 175
   neoconservatives and, 43
   presidential election of 1948, xxix, 12–13, 40
   Reagan's campaigning for, 12–13
   Reagan's support for, xxix, 12–13, 122–123, 175, 181, 182
   succeeds Roosevelt as president, xxviii, 10
Truman Doctrine, xxxiv, 33, 42, 63
Turner, Stansfield, 52–53

Urban renewal, 130–131

Veterans' Day ceremony, Reagan's remarks
   on lessons learned from Vietnam, 234
   on living love, 234
   on remembrance, 234
   text (primary document), 233–235
Vietnam Syndrome, 179
Vietnam War
   class divide and, 43–44
   draft deferments, 24–25, 29
   drug addiction and, 43
   Goldwater on, 41–42
   Gulf of Tonkin Resolution, 23
   Johnson administration, xxxii, 18, 20–21, 23–25
   Selective Service draft, 24–25
   Selective Service lottery, xxxiii, 29
   Tet Offensive, xxxii, 25, 142
Volcker, Paul, 90–91
Voting Rights Act of 1965, xxxii, 22, 27, 113, 198

Walesa, Lech, xxxv, 59
Wallace, George, xxxiii, 29, 125
Wallace, Henry, xxix, 12, 39–41
Wanniski, Jude, xxxiv, 78–81, 102, 200
War and antiwar films, 144–145
Warner, Jack, 26
Warner Brothers, xxvii, 7, 140
Watts riot (Los Angeles), xxxii, 25, 196
Webb, James, 184, 190
Weinberger, Caspar, 55, 87

Wicker, Tom, 62
Will, George, 67–68
Woodward, Bob, 143
Wyman, Jane, xxviii, 8, 13–14, 16–17, 147, 158

Yorkin, Bud, 143–144, 162
Young, Andrew, 125
Young Americans for Freedom, 125, 216

Zionism, 55, 120, 195

About the Author

Kenneth J. Heineman is professor of history and global security studies at Angelo State University. He is the author of six previous books, including *The Rise of Contemporary Conservatism in the United States* and *God Is a Conservative: Religion, Politics, and Morality in Contemporary America*. He has received the Philip S. Klein Book Prize for history writing and serves on the editorial board of *Pennsylvania History*.

www.ingramcontent.com/pod-product-compliance
Lightning Source LLC
Chambersburg PA
CBHW060944230426
43665CB00015B/2056